COVERING
the COURT

A 50-Year Love Affair
with the Game of Tennis
by
AL LANEY

SIMON AND SCHUSTER   NEW YORK

FOREWORD

THE FIRST HOLE at the Oakmont Country Club, near Pittsburgh, slopes downward away from the clubhouse toward the deep cut through which the Pennsylvania Turnpike passes, and the second tee lies at the foot of the rising ground on the other side. In mid-morning of a June Saturday of 1953, the final day of the National Open Golf Championship, I was sitting on a shooting stick in the shade of a large tree behind the nearby fourth green, waiting for Ben Hogan, who had taken a great throng up the second fairway, to turn at the top of the hill and come back.

With me there, similarly occupied, were half a dozen golf reporters from widely separated places, come to cover Hogan's fourth and final victory in the Open. As we sat there discussing this and that, Charlie Bartlett, of the Chicago *Tribune*, a somewhat more peripatetic and less sedentary observer of the golfing scene, came by.

"Say," Charlie called to me, "did you see the morning papers? Bill Tilden died. You'll have to write something. The obits are terrible. You're the only one can do it properly."

These remarks started a lively discussion under the tree, and there was plenty of time during that last day of the 1953 Open to ponder the comments of my golf-writing colleagues. Hogan, who was mid-way through the finest year of his illustrious career, moved without stress or strain to his victory, never once appearing likely to be caught.

The lack of understanding among the golf writers who sat with me there of the backgrounds of the game of tennis and of Tilden, its greatest practitioner, astonished me. These men came from cities all over the country and some boasted by-lines known everywhere. All of them could go a long way back in golf. They had strong opinions of the game at which they were specialists, of its greatest players and its techniques. On the history of golf they could speak with knowledge and authority.

5

But about tennis they were plainly naïve. Their acceptance of me as an authority was flattering but a little touching. Not one had seen much tennis at the top level, and none had real knowledge of its backgrounds. And yet this was a game played by more millions than their game of golf, and its major competition, the Davis Cup, was participated in by teams of half a hundred nations annually right around the world. Tennis had, moreover, provided through the years some of the most exciting moments of the sports history of which these men were the chroniclers.

All through the long day, when I ought really to have been concerned with Hogan, who was making golf history, I brooded over tennis history. Tilden's long career, nearly the whole of which I had been directly concerned with, rolled out in retrospective tableau. I returned again and again to the subject to wonder how it had come about that I, almost alone among my sportswriting contemporaries, had acquired the knowledge and experience that would permit a proper survey of the whole tennis scene.

There emerged finally, I thought, a certain pattern of development in which destiny had played its unrevealed role. The intention to pass a whole adult lifetime writing about this particular game could hardly have been consciously present from the first, but since it is clear that many of our actions contain effects that are revealed only in the future, the karmic connections are recognizable in looking back.

These reflections led backward to the fateful summer of 1914, to a schoolboy on blessed, unexpected holiday where, with what seemed incredible good fortune, he came into the presence of probably the most glamorous and exciting figure of tennis history, Maurice McLoughlin, in his moment of glory at the moment when the game itself burst into bloom, so to speak, as a genuine spectator sport.

It seemed to me, musing on destiny's strange ways that day at Oakmont, that the fact that so much of my adult life had been devoted to watching and recording the playing of games, especially tennis, was directly traceable to that combination of circumstances which permitted me, a teen-age Florida schoolboy, to be present in New York that blistering August week when a famous Davis Cup Challenge Round was played at the new tennis club in Forest Hills with the guns of World War I already firing in Europe.

There was played on this occasion one of the celebrated contests of sports history, the match in which McLoughlin, American, defeated Norman Brookes, Australian. This match may be said to have been the first truly "big" tennis occasion in this country, the first tennis encounter that really caught the imagination of the whole nation, and it did for tennis something comparable to what the victory of Francis Ouimet over Harry Vardon and Ted Ray, the great British golfers, had done for golf exactly one year earlier at Brookline, Massachusetts. It put tennis on the front page, as we are fond of saying, and its effect on the destiny of a tennis reporter very likely was as decisive.

In those days before we had radio and movie newsreels, boys took their sports heroes more on faith as truly heroic figures. We depended entirely on the newspapers for information and I, already a practicing journalist in a small way, with a regular after-school job on the Pensacola *Journal*, was the chief source of the materials of hero worship.

I had access to a number of New York papers which came to the shop days late, and the old *Sun* of Charles A. Dana came into my home on subscription. Our sports gods were almost exclusively baseball players. We knew nothing of golf and very little of other sports, but we knew baseball better, I think, than do boys of the present, who have many opportunities to see it played at second hand on the screen and adopt as their own the endlessly repeated clichés of the announcers.

We were all romantics then, it seemed, adult and adolescent alike. Young men still were enamored of the flagrantly sentimental verses of *A Shropshire Lad*, and our older contemporaries were still pathetically optimistic about the idea of freedom.

Far removed as we were from the scenes of their action, our heroes were not quite mere mortals, but more or less types laid up in heaven. We had had direct contact, it is true, but for me it was with the wrong team. The Cleveland Indians, then called the Naps, had come to town for training one spring, causing much absenteeism in the schools for several weeks. It was a thrilling enough experience to speak with Joe Jackson and Napoleon Lajoie, but of course they were not the Giants. In those years Christy Mathewson was a shining knight, and if the Giants won, then were the gods just and life a lyric.

Into this dream world the dramatic figure of McLoughlin had

come storming out of the West with dynamic service and overhead smashes to electrify the small enclosed tennis world of the Eastern Seaboard and draw non-tennis crowds to a game theretofore largely ignored and faintly despised by the public. The whole circumstance of McLoughlin's unheralded arrival on the sports scene was immensely exciting, and he quickly became the chief hero to a group of boys who had dared to play tennis publicly when it still was considered by many people a sissy game.

I do not remember that we suffered any of the public taunts that other tennis addicts of the time have reported, but we were considered unusual if not actually queer. Otherwise we were entirely normal. We hid behind the barn or in its loft to smoke rabbit tobacco and corn silks; we read surreptitiously and swapped back and forth with the others the Merriwell books and the dime novels of Nick Carter and the Wild West. And we also, of course, read such parentally approved works as the stories of prep school life by Owen Johnson and the then popular historical novels of G. A. Henty.

But we also followed McLoughlin's career from afar with much devotion by means of the papers I consulted and shared with my tennis-playing companions. The California Comet, he was called, a name with a fine ring to it, suitable for a hero, and the pictures of him, though perhaps not good by later standards, were very satisfying to young hero worshipers. There was one splendid shot, in *Leslie's Weekly* I think it was, that showed the Comet leaping from the ground to make a "kill," and the caption referred to him as "flame thatched." This one adorned the walls of my room for years —after we had passed it back and forth until it was frayed, trying to figure out how he did it, with endless unsuccessful attempts dangerous to life and limb. We knew McLoughlin's record at Wimbledon, Newport, and elsewhere as we knew Ty Cobb's exact batting average and how many times that villainous Three Finger Brown of the Cubs had beaten our Giants.

We dreamed of being McLoughlin and longed to see him play. And then suddenly came the unbelievable good luck of a chance to be in New York that August week when the incredible Braves of 1914 were to be at the Polo Grounds and McLoughlin was to play at Forest Hills. For a teen-ager this was the stuff of dreams, and the fact that all during that wondrous week I favored tennis over baseball, even with Matty pitching, is most significant. I had fallen in love with tennis, and this book is the account of that love affair.

The impressions of that very first week were confused at the time and are not likely to be clearer after so many years. What remain are flashes of light and dark as in a train journey through mountainous country, but the bright scenes are very bright and those in which McLoughlin appeared are bathed in a glow that can never fade.

CHAPTER ONE

The Hotel Bretton Hall still stands at Broadway and 86th Street, but surely it can never have been so luxurious as it seemed on the steaming August night of my first frightening contact with New York. No hotel, whether on the Champs Élysées, Park Lane, at Deauville, Biarritz, the Lido, San Moritz, or on Nob Hill in San Francisco, has ever appeared so elegant as this quite ordinary hostelry to a frightened schoolboy far away from home for the first time.

New York was in one of its heat waves, and the air was already hot and damp at six o'clock that Tuesday morning when, because of excitement and the heat itself, I was unable to sleep. The lobby was deserted and the breakfast room would not open for another hour. The tennis matches were to be played Thursday, Friday, and Saturday, and I still had to decide how I should divide my days between Forest Hills and the Polo Grounds. A cruel decision for a boy to have to make and I decided to postpone it at least until I had read the morning papers.

Baseball exerted a strong pull because I could accompany a kind relative who had provided this wonderful opportunity, whereas I would have to go all alone to the tennis matches and have no one with whom to share the great adventure. The fear of being alone in the big city, which could rise to something like terror, is not easy to communicate, but I still can feel it a little so it must have been very strong at the time. I was very much afraid of losing my way in a place of such terrifying bigness. You could hardly get lost walking straight up the street and back so early in the morning, though, and it was a relief to be almost alone on a street from which last night's confusing bustle had departed.

At the 96th Street subway entrances men and boys were already selling papers, shouting the names in a confused chant that ran them all together. I bought the lot of them—*World*, *Times*, *Tribune*,

American, Herald, Sun—and brought them back to the lobby. There I sat, a small, forlorn figure probing into his future and not knowing it. The headlines, big and black, spoke of the violation of Belgian neutrality and said that British mobilization was complete. They meant nothing. The chain of tragic events set in motion by the shot fired at Sarajevo was beyond the understanding, beyond the interest even, of a schoolboy who was nonetheless to be caught up in them before attaining maturity.

I turned to the sports pages, and there for the first time was a small item that did make the war seem a little nearer. It said that the German Davis Cup team of Otto Froitzheim and Otto Kreuger, beaten by the Australians in Pittsburgh on the day England declared war on Germany, had been taken from a ship in mid-Atlantic by a British warship and would be interned.

The Tuesday papers already had long stories about the coming tennis matches, and after reading them I was so eager to get there I decided I could give up only one day to the Giants, although they were in first place and the "onrushing Braves," as they were dubbed, already were close. It was a beautiful Polo Grounds experience on this day as the Giants beat St. Louis 8–2, marred only by the fact that Jeff Tesreau pitched instead of Matty. But Matty was there and all the others too—Larry Doyle, Red Murray, Art Fletcher, and Fred Merkle. There would be still one chance to come back for more if rain didn't extend the tennis program beyond the scheduled days.

The night clerk at the hotel, who knew nothing about it, had told me that I could easily get in to see the teams practice on the days before the matches, and this misinformation was what decided me to desert the Giants on Wednesday on the mere chance of seeing Mc-Loughlin. I was impelled also by the necessity of making a trial run through that terra incognita of New York to where the matches were to be played so the way might be found easily when it would be so terribly important to be there in plenty of time.

With directions carefully memorized I set out into an already stifling day about eight o'clock, and my eventual arrival at Penn Station through those waves of frantic, inhuman rush-hour crowds, pushing into subway trains already too full, seemed a small miracle. I got somehow into the proper Long Island train and the relief was so great I did not mind the stifling heat so much. I had a new batch of papers to read and now I slipped under the seat all but the sports sections.

Play, they said, would begin at two o'clock on Thursday with Tony Wilding, the New Zealander who had been Wimbledon champion for four years, against R. Norris Williams, described as "a young college boy from Harvard," a phrase which puzzled me since, from where I sat, a Harvard man was no young boy. The big match, McLoughlin versus Brookes, the current Wimbledon champion, would follow and there would be doubles on Friday.

The experts were unanimous in the opinion that McLoughlin would have to beat both Brookes and Wilding if the United States, holder of the trophy, was to have any chance of retaining it. It seemed we had "only an outside chance" of winning the doubles, and so young Williams would have "to do his share by winning one of the singles."

I marveled at the assurance, the certainty with which these men wrote. How could they know? How could they be so sure? This week was to be my first encounter with the sports expert into whose ranks destiny was to lead me some years later; the first occasion on which I was able to read in the Metropolitan papers reports of things actually seen by me and written by reporters presumed to be first rate. During this whole week all the New York papers, and there were about fifteen of them, were read carefully and the sports sections torn out and kept to be studied for a long time after. This was the only course of journalism then available, and the idea of trying to become a sports reporter myself was born at this time.

My knowledge of geography was slight, and I was still fearful of having got on the wrong train, but the sight from the train window of the wooden stands that had been erected in front of the West Side Tennis Clubhouse was reassuring. The club was surrounded by a sort of meadowland on its side of the railway line, and there was a pleasant small-town atmosphere about the village. A few people got off the train, but it was hardly more than midmorning yet, and only one or two walked down the path toward the club. The whole place seemed deserted and the courts that could be seen from outside the grounds were empty.

A walk around the whole place revealed little. The clubhouse and wooden stands enclosed and concealed everything that had to do with the coming matches. I longed to go inside but dared not try,

13

even though there seemed to be no one guarding the entrance to the clubhouse. Fear of being spoken to sharply or asked my business by someone in uniform was a strong deterrent. I began to realize I had made a mistake.

Just to hang around outside all day seemed senseless, and I was considering trying to get back to the hotel in time to make the ball game when I saw through the wire fence at a corner of the grounds a couple of figures in white come out to one of the courts along the street and begin to hit a ball back and forth. In no time, then, the situation changed. The wait was not going to be futile after all. Here began the education of a tennis writer.

These players, whatever their proficiency at the game, were a revelation. This was not the game I and my companions had been playing, however much we admired one another's skill. This was the game I was to see at the top level tomorrow, for, looking back, I now believe these to have been very good players if not actually first-ten men. I had read about this game but had had no real conception of it. However ardent we had been back home, however faithfully we practiced to perfect strokes, we would never, I saw instantly, arrive at the game being played here. We were on the wrong road altogether. This kind of tennis was not known in our town in 1914.

The revelation was something of a shock. What now of those dreams of conquest? Never mind that, in the phrase of the day, ten years and a millionaire father were needed to acquire a ranking in the country's first ten. McLoughlin had no millionaire background and already, one thought, considerable progress had been made. Alas, for the dreams of youth and farewell to them. On the other hand, here, looking through the fence, fingers hooked into the wire netting, at players who were close to the heart of the game, began that close observation, that critical inspection of strokes that was to prove of value a decade or so later when my tennis reporting days finally arrived.

Here I saw a method of striking the ball very different from the strokes my boyhood opponents and I employed. This, I thought, must be the real thing, the way the great ones do it, and every single detail of it must be carefully observed and stored in memory to take home and put into practice.

I had not at this time read any tennis instruction books, which I rate a most fortunate circumstance, since I was able to observe without being misled by their fallacies and errors. Hour after hour I stood on tired legs outside the fence as groups of players came and went, trying to isolate the procedures which these men followed and which appeared to be fundamental, though the styles differed.

As the afternoon wore on, doubles players came, bringing still another revelation, other techniques to observe and remember, since a boy seldom has anything about his person on which to make notes, nor knows what notes to make if he does. It is the visual note that is most helpful in such matters, though, and very few have been really successful in reducing the techniques of games to words. This chance to see really good players from close up was valuable in preparing me for what was to come. During the big matches I was so wrapped up in the wonder of it all that little details could be observed and retained.

For some time, as I stood with fingers hooked into the wire of the fence, there had been signs of approaching rain, cooling the air. And the discomfort of standing so long was so great I decided to walk around a bit. I also was in great need of food, and thought there might be a place to buy a sandwich. An attendant barred the entrance to the clubhouse now, but I happened to arrive there simultaneously with a group of a dozen or more young men who promptly enveloped me. One of them announced that they were "from Columbia," and with an "all right, boys" they were passed in, I in their midst. It turned out presently that they were part of a contingent of Columbia University students who were to be ushers, and they were there to get their positions and instructions for next day and do a little rehearsing. I was still fearful of discovery but immensely pleased to be mistaken for a college man.

We all went through the clubhouse and out onto a terrace in some confusion, and while they stood about waiting for someone to come up and tell them what to do, I had enough presence of mind to slip off into the stands enclosing three sides of the court. A few dozen people were scattered about the stands, and there was some play going on below. I hardly dared look at the courts until I felt safe from discovery.

An expanse of green grass was enclosed by these towering wooden stands, and two courts were marked out with white lines. I did not at once notice that they were singles courts, so great was my surprise that the matches were going to be played on grass, showing how ill informed we were in the small towns in those days before radio. The courts that I had been watching from the street had been of clay, wonderful courts compared to ours at home, and it never had occurred to me that those inside would be different.

But it was beautiful, this perfect-looking green grass with the white lines upon it. It was just about the most beautiful sight I had ever seen. Two men were playing singles on one of the courts but obviously neither was the right one. I knew what my man looked like. These were lesser members of one of the teams, and it did not interest me much to know either which team or their names. Actually, I did learn many years later that one of them was Stanley Doust, an Australian player who became tennis correspondent for the London *Daily Mail* and a very good friend. But in August of 1914 if a tennis player was not Maurice McLoughlin he did not count for much.

After a while I got bold enough to get into conversation with a man sitting nearby. I wanted to ask if McLoughlin was going to practice and learned that all the principal actors in tomorrow's drama had finished and gone while I was outside watching lesser men through the fence. This friendly man seemed astonished to learn that I had come all the way from Florida to see the matches. He looked at me closely and said he knew a young man who had gone to Florida and never come back, giving the impression that it was rather a tremendous thing for a boy to do. Having established this, he then set me right on a budding misconception about court surfaces. I admired the wonderful-looking grass courts but remarked that they must be pretty slow compared with clay or other hard-surfaced courts. He said that was what most people thought who never had played on grass, and that was most people, I suppose. But grass was the fastest surface of all for playing tennis, he told me, except the indoor board court. I did not really believe this at the time, but I remembered it, and when a year or so later I had the chance to play on grass, I saw it was true. In that way I avoided the mistake of ever writing the opposite, a mistake which some quite authoritative commentators in the so-called Golden Age were unable to avoid.

The drizzle had become more wetting now and I was dreadfully tired and hungry. I tried to find my way out without going back through the clubhouse, where I was sure I would be spotted for an interloper, but the gates for the public were not yet open. There was nothing for it, so I tried to look as though I belonged. I got safely through and onto the path to the station without being accosted, but I have thought of that slinking passage through the rooms many times while going back and forth in later years.

When I finally got back to Penn Station it seemed strangely quiet compared to the morning's stampede, so it must have been quite a while past the evening rush. A new batch of papers informed me both that "Braves Checked O-O by Red Ames; at Polo Grounds tomorrow" and "First Great Battle Impending; Americans Fill West-Bound Liners."

The night of August 12–13, 1914, may be remembered by participants in and spectators of the Davis Cup Challenge Round of that year for other reasons, but for me, a subtropical visitor in New York, it stands out as the most uncomfortably hot night ever experienced. Unable to sleep, I indulged half a dozen times in the unaccustomed luxury of a shower, and was still a little groggy next morning when I set out, not later than nine o'clock, for Forest Hills and the great adventure.

This time I had missed most of the crush in the subway, although there still were plenty of them, and it was a wonderful feeling to know one's way about and not be so afraid. All of Long Island was already baking when I walked once more down the path from the station, drinking in the slow draft of anticipation. Near the entrance I stood in a spot of shade beside the railroad embankment for a long time contemplating the scene.

I saw again it had been a mistake to come too early. There was no sign of life about the place, and the gates were not to open until noon. I had thrown away all the war news in the morning papers, retaining only the sports sections carefully folded and stuffed into a back pants pocket opposite the two sandwiches which the kind waiter at the hotel had got for me. There still were two hours to wait, and I was thinking of hunting a cooler place when more players came out, as on the day before. I could not leave then. This time it was all doubles and even more rewarding since I knew better now what to look for.

This also was a demonstration of a concept of the game I had not known, and I accepted without question that it was the correct manner of playing doubles. I had never known that the proper alignment of partners was parallel, not one up and one back, and was surprised to see that each pair sought the net together at every opportunity. Also that one always stood near the net even while his partner was serving. I had never seen the server rush to the net behind his serve. The Pensacola system of double plays was for both to stand at the base line while one served.

A maneuver that delighted me no end was employed now and then. Just as the ball was served, the man at the net—and how dangerously close in, it seemed to me, he stood—would move quickly across the court still close to the net, and the server would run in to replace him. This apparently was done on signal, but look as closely as I could, I never did discover when it might come.

I thought this must be standard practice that was no doubt employed by everyone who played the doubles game properly. It added to my store of learning, and I determined to try it out along with the other new things learned as soon as I could tell my friends back home about it. It also added to my store of amusement when, forty years later, I read that this trick was "invented" by one of our Davis Cup captains who had not even managed to get himself born in 1914 and was introduced into a Challenge Round doubles match in Australia. It was cited in the account of the match cabled back as a stroke of genius, and the one thing that had insured an American victory.

By that time, though, a score or more of Challenge Rounds and nearly as many Wimbledons and National Championships were behind me, and I had long since become accustomed to the foolish things people say and write about this game. I also had learned that the most one ought to permit oneself should be mild amusement, since one of the valuable lessons of experience is that you can so easily be caught out yourself.

The players left the courts a little before noon and the gates were opened. There was an entrance just where the wooden stands did not quite meet the clubhouse terrace, and you walked across another hard court to get there. I stopped on the way to examine the court carefully underfoot and marveled at its firmness and smoothness. We had nothing like it back home in spite of pulling a heavy roller back and forth interminably.

A small wooden house very like one of those outdoor privies so common at home had been set up for a ticket booth, but I had mine already. I had perhaps a hundred times made certain it still was there in my pocket. It was for a seat high up on the rim of the stands and in a corner diagonally opposite where I had entered. It was a good spot from which to view the surrounding country and no doubt was a bit cooler than down below, but the courts seemed disappointingly far away. Two courts were lined on the grass now, one directly below me, the other over by the terrace of the clubhouse. They had no nets yet, but presently two men came out to put them up. This was an interesting procedure, for they tightened the net cord with a little wheel attached to the post. A much better way, I thought, than trying to draw the net tight enough by hand, as was our way. For us it always seemed to slip, no matter what kind of sailor's knot we tied, and had to be pulled and tied over again every few games.

It was getting on toward one o'clock now and I began to realize I was hungry. So out came the sandwiches, made of bologna, a substance new to me. They are worth mentioning only because the wonderful taste of them is more easily recalled and more vividly remembered than more important impressions from that confusing day. Nothing since ever has seemed quite so good except the taste of the cold beef and ginger beer of a lost vintage consumed so often in later years on the terrace of the clubhouse at the Queens Club in London after a morning of play on those not always perfect grass courts.

People had begun to come in at the entrances now, first a trickle and then a flood. The line began to extend back down the path toward the station, and off to the right there was another line of motorcars going somewhere to park and raising great clouds of dust from the unpaved road. There were more automobiles than I had ever seen in one place, and a morning paper had reported that "a space has been marked off beginning at the L.I. railroad station and extending in an easterly direction to the grounds and no automobile will be allowed west of that line. So persons walking from the station need have no fear of the hundreds of automobiles that will be going to Forest Hills."

In a short time the stands were nearly full, and a few had taken their seats on the terrace, where the tiers rose almost to the second-floor balcony. Just above the balcony on the roof there were flags, and someone said the one with the six large stars was the Australian flag. The sun was fierce and a number of sunshades in bright colors began to be raised, especially on the terrace. The same two men who had fixed the net came out carrying the umpire's high seat and placed it beside the near court, its back to my side of the arena. Then they placed chairs on the extensions of every line of the court. I had never seen a match with umpires and linesmen.

I overheard a neighbor high on the rim volunteer the information that Teddy Roosevelt was supposed to come and probably already was in the clubhouse. All I knew about him was that he had something called a Tennis Cabinet while President and had formed a Bull Moose party which had made possible the election of Woodrow Wilson, to the great joy of the owners of the Pensacola *Journal* and all good Democrats.

T. R. had reigned at a time when politics had not yet entered the consciousness of small boys, but only that morning on the way out I had read an interview in one of the papers. Curiously, I cannot remember if I ever did see him, but the substance of the interview remains. Someone had remarked that the war would be over by Christmas, to which T. R. had replied, "Which Christmas?" adding that many might come and go before it was done.

The stands were really packed now and there did not seem to be vacant space anywhere. An odd impression of the crowd that remains is of a solid sea of hard straw hats of the kind we called the straw kady. Looking down from the rim you could see nothing but the tops of those hats. Many of the women in the crowd wore larger versions with pins sticking out. A great many things have passed from the memory but the picture of this ocean of straw remains. Every head among the fourteen thousand seemed to have one, except for the occasional soft Panama, and so, too, for that matter did mine.

A few people were still trying to find their places, and I was standing up to watch the snakelike progress of the automobiles in the distance, when there was a burst of applause and two white-clad figures appeared at the top of the steps leading down from the terrace to the court. Williams and Wilding. Since these were two of the finest players of the game I was to write millions of words about, it would be nice if I could recall something about their match. But I can find little, certainly nothing of importance. I can hardly remember what they looked like then without getting pictures from the files.

Undoubtedly I grew excited, cheered along with the others, and must have followed the play closely, since this was really the first tennis match I had ever seen, but practically everything I recall today about it I learned later by looking it up and reading about it in books. This would be the only time ever of seeing Wilding, and many times I have regretted the lost opportunity. I know that they came and played before my eyes and that Wilding won in straight sets, but I recall only that the defeat of Williams put a great burden on my man, and I carried away a faint resentment of Williams on that account. But I was there to see McLoughlin, not really to see tennis, and strictly speaking, I did not see tennis, because when McLoughlin came onto the stage the action, now magnified, became larger than life, so that no really reliable report of the match with Brookes ever could be made by me.

Nevertheless, the drama of it, often agonizing, can still be lived through a little. In that thirty-two-game service-governed first set, I lived and died with McLoughlin, and I never in the years since have witnessed what seemed to me so grim a fight or an athletic contest of any kind the winning or losing of which meant so much to me. I can well remember how these two looked as they came down the steps and stood for their pictures to be taken. Brookes, long of face and solemn, wore long sleeves and had in his hand a cap which he would wear throughout the match. McLoughlin's shirt was open at the neck and the sleeves were cut off at the elbows. He really did have that mop of hair I had read about, and altogether he was a most satisfactory-looking hero.

I had complete confidence in him and I watched every move during the preliminary hitting of balls back and forth. They were playing on the far court by the terrace, but we could still see from our seats that McLoughlin smiled a lot. Brookes seemed very dour. My confidence was shaken many times before that terribly long first set was over. Brookes gave the impression he would never yield no matter how many thunderbolts our man might hurl at him, blows one never could have imagined possible with a tennis racket. Several times a line from that poem of schoolboy recitation, "Horatius at the Bridge," came into my mind: "Will not the villain drown?" I said it over and over, and once I must have said it aloud, since a man alongside turned and said, "I beg your pardon?"

About halfway through, and after what seemed an eternity, Brookes, who had served first and thus was forcing McLoughlin to battle for his life every time the American served, was love-40 against the service. You would have to be a teen-ager again, I suppose, to suffer as I suffered then. But at this crisis, McLoughlin served three balls that Brookes could not even touch with his queer-shaped racket.

Other crises came later, near the end we could not know was near. Brookes again was within a point of winning the set, and each time the answer was the same, an unreturnable service. Was ever boyhood hero more worthy of worship? I have read and reread everything about this famous match that I could lay my hands on, and visual memory is all mixed up with other people's observations and opinions. Where the emotions are so terribly involved some details are blurred, others enlarged out of all proportion.

One picture, though, must be my very own. It is of McLoughlin, all fire and dash, leaping from the ground to smash a lob and, as the ball bit into the turf and bounded impossibly away, of Brookes dropping his racket, raising both hands above his head in despair and calling on high heaven to witness his misfortune. This happened several times near the end of that tense set, and whenever in the years that have run into memory's reservoir I have thought of this first exciting encounter with tennis of the highest class, this one picture repeats itself as if it actually were being seen again.

With McLoughlin winning this match for the United States 17–15, 6–3, 6–3, the series was tied and now would go, the experts said, the way they had predicted: victory for Australia by three matches to two. And so it did. I do not remember about the doubles. I remember only McLoughlin in that match and the fact that Tom Bundy, his partner, wore a handkerchief around his head as though he had a splitting headache, but actually to keep the perspiration out of his eyes, a practice which I adopted myself a little later. Neither do I remember much of Brookes and Williams in the match that decided the issue, but of McLoughlin and Wilding there were things to note.

I was called upon to make a decision on a problem with the enormity of which no schoolboy should have to contend. I had to make up my mind whether I should go to Forest Hills on Saturday to see McLoughlin play again in a match the experts said would mean nothing after Brookes had beaten Williams, or go to the Polo Grounds to see the Giants play the Braves in the final game of their series. After wrestling with the problem overnight I returned to watch the tennis and so deprived myself of the right later to boast, and thereby acquire distinction in my set, that I had seen the fabulous Braves beat the immortal Matty.

McLoughlin versus Wilding, where I watched my hero rather than carefully observing the match at the time, acquired a certain pathos and significance in later years, and I went over it carefully in the papers I had saved. It was the last tennis match Wilding would play, and McLoughlin never won another important victory. Two weeks later McLoughlin was beaten by Williams in the final round of the National Championship at Newport, and before spring came round again Wilding was in a grave in Flanders Field, killed in action in the early months of the war.

Dame Mabel Brookes has written of the final meeting between Brookes and Wilding in her delightful book *Crowded Galleries*. They all left for England immediately after the Challenge Round, Wilding to join his regiment. They met for the last time in Boulogne, across the English Channel, in a small dockside hotel "that had that smell of new bread, tobacco, and lavatories that impregnates a certain type of French hostelry."

"Tony came," Dame Mabel recalled, "from nearby Belgium, where he was operating a trailer gun in the Westminster outfit. He was fit and full of energy. . . . he looked handsome in the fatigue cap and uniform that was something like an airman's. As usual, he was untidy, one button dangling by a thread. . . . He was leaving at dawn . . . and after a while bade a speechless, shoulder-holding farewell to him [Norman], for they were very close."

The account continues, "It was barely light when I threw back the shutters and the air came in sharp with a hint of autumn. . . . Tony strode out on the cobbled road, kicked his starter into action, contained, remote and lonely. He waved and wheeled out over the pavé to the bridge and, as he crossed and turned into the distance, he waved again. The smell of burning charcoal came up, mixed with the reek of exhaust from his bike, and drifted, ephemeral as the passing moment, leaving only memory. We never saw him again."

When I learned that Williams had beaten McLoughlin in the Nationals, I was back home working out a new forehand, studying the writing in the many sports sections I had saved, and dreaming of having a job on a New York paper. The shock of McLoughlin's defeat was great. I wondered at first if there could be some mistake. It was as if something had gone wrong with natural law, and it was difficult to forgive Williams when I knew it was true.

I could not, fortunately, foresee anything of this on those wonderful blistering days at Forest Hills, and there was nothing to mar the profound effect McLoughlin made on the individual as he had also caught and stirred the imagination of the millions. What remains to wonder at about that week of August is that I could have been so blissfully unaware and unconcerned about the war that was to change things so greatly in so short a time. The Challenge Round of 1914 was the last international tennis gathering for five years. For Tony Wilding, still in his twenties, it was the end of fun and games. For me, still in my teens, only the beginning.

CHAPTER TWO

THE post–high school, prewar way led indirectly to the Twin Cities of Minneapolis and St. Paul, where apprenticeship to journalism and to life had been slightly advanced when the time came to put on a uniform in the early summer of 1917. I was still possessed of the idea of writing about tennis as well as playing it, and although the Northwest did not at first appear a promising proving ground for either, I had during this period an opportunity to confirm and revise some of the impressions of 1914 and a chance to put into practice on the court some lessons learned.

Much more important, I became acquainted with two tennis personalities whose influence, in retrospect, appears of greater value for my life and for tennis reporting than could be understood at the time. I had joined the St. Paul Tennis Club, where I enjoyed a certain standing, not justified by talent, but because of having seen the famous McLoughlin-Brookes match. There I encountered Joseph Armstrong, a man toward whom I still feel grateful.

Joe Armstrong was the best player in the Northwest and one of the best in the country later when he earned ranking in the first ten after he moved to Philadelphia and played the tournament circuit. He was an understanding man and he took time to play with and talk to younger members and help them improve. Because of him I discovered early some things I might never have learned. In Joe Armstrong I learned to admire the man more than his strokes which, heavily sliced, were not beautiful although quite effective against most players. This type of stroke, I discovered, could be adequate for defensive purposes and could be used for attack at times, but could not take its owner to the very top in a game where McLoughlin, Billy Johnston, and Dick Williams were operating, and Tilden was moving up year by year.

Joe Armstrong's greatest contribution to the game of tennis may well have been that he gave that splendid sliced backhand to Tilden as a model for Big Bill's second best backhand, as Tilden was to confide years later. It also was during this period that I saw and studied such first-ten players as George Church and Dean Mathey and, knocked right off the court by a Minneapolis player named John Adams, learned that a big forehand can outweigh and smother a whole collection of merely pretty strokes. Church was the first real net rusher I saw at close range. His game was modeled after McLoughlin's.

With Mathey as partner, he came to Deephaven, the estate of Ward Burton on Lake Minnetonka, to play in the Northwestern Sectional Tournament. My first experience of grass courts was at Deephaven, where Mr. Burton would permit the mildly talented young to play whenever a court was free, and better players always were willing to give lesser ones a game.

It was a charming scene. The courts lay in tiny wooded valleys running down to the lake, where it was pleasant to sit or recline and watch the play. This beautiful picture of tennis in what I thought an ideal setting has remained bright through the years. Such youthful impressions do not lose in attractiveness by the passage of time, but I really do not think I ever have encountered on either side of the ocean a more delightful place in which to play tennis.

In those days the tournament always attracted first-ten players, especially Californians on their way to the Eastern grass court tournaments. The sectional had been won by McLoughlin earlier and would be won later by Johnston. The best players of the Midwest and Missouri Valley areas also came, and the standard of play was high. As a classroom for a student still hoping to graduate to tennis writing, it could hardly have been better. My first tentative efforts for a long since extinct paper called the Minneapolis *News* were considered acceptable, but I can still blush to recall them.

They had, however, the significant effect—I almost wrote purpose, for so it seems to me—of bringing me perhaps the most important of all my tennis friendships. Sam Hardy came upon this idyllic scene one summer and, having read my feeble effort to describe a doubles match in which he had played, came up and spoke to me. I try as I write to recall the doubles partner who came with him that year, but I cannot. It may have been Charles Garland, but I cannot be sure.

I can still remember the embarrassment of the moment well

enough, though, to experience it again. Sam Hardy was considered at that time an expert in the art of doubles with his brother, Dr. Sumner Hardy, and this early contact surely was one of the most fortunate things for me that could have happened. He was a kind and gentle man, and I was awed when he took the trouble to sit with an overeager young man during a match and speak, in his soft voice, of what to look for. I surprised myself and no doubt the gentle Sam by telling him of my faint hopes as a player and of my tennis writing ambitions. He pretended to take both as seriously as I did, but being a wise man, he discouraged the one while commending the other.

He said he did not think there were any specialists writing tennis in America and it might be a good thing to prepare for, since I could not be good enough to become a tournament player. Traveling from one tournament to another was a pleasant way of life, and he gave me an alluring picture of tennis meetings at places the very names of which sounded enchanting.

He spoke to me also about strokes, stirred my interest again and made me think of the boy who had stood with fingers hooked into the fence at Forest Hills, not knowing what to look for. In noting the importance of careful watching, Sam Hardy quoted Sherlock Holmes to me, and I have quoted him to myself thousands of times since: "You see very well, Watson, but you do not observe." He also spoke of various leading players of the day, especially of Williams, who would be champion a second time in this year of 1916, and of Billy Johnston, who won the year before, and of how very different were their methods.

A few weeks after he left, there came from this nice man a packet of books about the game, with a note advising that I read them but take some things said with a grain of salt, leaving me to find the fallacies without help. From this beginning I must, in my time, have read more tennis books of instruction than any man alive. I began here to learn that the writers of many such books are neighbor to the bore. Far too many tennis books, I was to learn with some pain, are ill written, lack flavor, are packed with noncommittal clichés, and are quite unreadable. Moreover, regarding the techniques of the game and the way strokes should be made, they too often contain misinformation.

I was to encounter Sam Hardy frequently along the tennis trail in the years ahead, when he was twice Davis Cup captain. He became a well-loved friend with whom I corresponded over the years, exchanging books and ideas. A dear, sweet man to whom I owe much and whose memory I revere.

This brief association with such a man meant a lot to me at a time when my education, and not only in tennis, was making some progress. I was completely enamored of the game by now, and my regard for my ability to play it had begun to increase rapidly. Sam Hardy had advised me that my ambitions might be furthered by going to New York to work, but that seemed still a far-off, unattainable goal.

Suddenly everything was changed before the 1917 season had got well under way; the war could have stopped everything forever but it actually was not for very long. The less important check in my physical development as a possible tournament player was permanent, but the opportunity for valuable observation suffered only a short break. Then there emerged the chance that was to have equal importance with Deephaven, perhaps even more so, in the winter of 1918–19.

The Army had arranged a big service tournament at Cannes, on the French Riviera, and since I was on post-Armistice sick leave in Nice at the time, I was able to attend daily. And here came another of those seemingly casual encounters that are more than that because they have a strong influence on the future.

The Riviera was overrun with uniforms that first winter of peace. It was holiday time for all Allied soldiers who could get leaves, and there were many things arranged for their entertainment. The tennis tournament was one of the things thought up to fill the long period of waiting between Armistice and transport home, and the Army had brought players from wherever in Europe they might be stationed.

There must have been a couple of hundred of them, and all but a handful were tournament players only by courtesy. Nonetheless some bore famous names, and it was these I wanted to see. Especially Williams. I had not seen him since that memorable week at Forest Hills, when I could hardly say I had seen him at all because McLoughlin stood between us, outshining everything. Partly for this reason he now had a special attraction for me, almost a fascination.

I had learned from Sam Hardy to think of him as Dick Williams, instead of Norris, and I looked upon him as the reigning champion, since he had won the title again in 1916 and had not competed since. Now, at the beginning of 1919, with the war behind, I thought of myself as thoroughly grown up, and I had long since forgiven Williams for beating McLoughlin so soon after the Forest Hills experience. I could recall the shock of the shattering of an idol, but I now looked upon it as a youthful weakness to have supposed McLoughlin invincible.

I knew now that Williams had been born in Switzerland and that he had survived the *Titanic* disaster in which his father was lost; that as a son of wealth and position he had gone to school abroad, lived much in Europe and now wore a captain's uniform. Cosmopolite was a word much in use at the time, and it seemed to me to fit Williams perfectly.

On the first day I went over to Cannes, where the tournament was being played, I picked up a ride with the driver of one of those old Packard trucks the Army operated in France by the thousands. He drove it right up to the entrance of the elegant Carlton Hotel to let me down, causing some slight disturbance to the dignity of the attendant in field marshal's uniform. The small Carlton Tennis Club, where the more important matches were held, was around behind the hotel in a side street.

This club was to be the scene of one of the most unusual matches of tennis history, the meeting of Suzanne Lenglen and Helen Wills, seven years later, but at the moment I never had heard of either of these remarkable girls.

On the way over I had tried to dredge up some impressions of Williams from 1914 but could find nothing. Where his figure should have existed, my memory was blank. But this whole week I saw him plainly and the picture still is perfectly clear. Such an effect as Williams made I have not experienced again, and I wonder if there ever has been anyone who played this game in such a joyful, carefree way as he did that week. A dashing, handsome, glamorous young man and a thrilling performer. How splendid to be Dick Williams! How could one ever forget the experience of standing beside these red rubble courts in the thin Mediterranean sunshine and watching him go gaily through round after round as though playing tennis were the greatest fun in the world.

The fact that the war was over and everybody soon would be back home and out of uniform made it a particularly joyous time, and that condition no doubt has a lot to do with one's memories. In those happy, innocent days of peace, we actually believed we had taken part in the war to end war, not just World War I, which we called the Great War, but all war. We took quite literally Woodrow Wilson's magnificent, but subsequently meaningless words about making the world safe for democracy, and we supposed everything would be settled amicably and justly when the nations would gather for the Peace Conference at Versailles in the months just ahead.

I have tried to recall Williams' opponents during this week but I cannot, until he met and defeated Captain Watson Washburn in the final. It mattered little who was on the other side of the net. I was concentrating on Williams, and he has ever since seemed to embody all the attractiveness with which I had invested the game of tennis in my youthful imagination. We were both young in 1919 and I was bold enough to go up and speak to him after he had finished a match. This brief first encounter did not disturb the picture at all. He made an even greater impression with his ease of manner and graciousness toward one of dozens of soldiers who felt they could bother a captain who also was a champion.

On the first day that I sought out the court where Williams played, there came and stood beside me a man in a British captain's uniform. We began to talk about Williams and tennis in general, and when the match was over we walked together to the terrace of a small café from which we could look out across the Croisette to the blue of the sea.

This became a daily practice with the two of us each late afternoon, and it distresses me that I cannot remember the man's name, because this chance encounter was as important to me as my meeting with Sam Hardy had been. His name never became fixed in my mind because we addressed one another always by our ranks. I never gave up hoping through the following years that I might encounter him again visiting the tournaments of England and the Continent, but I never did.

I learned much from my new friend. He felt a certain obligation to fill in my background after I told him, without shame, that I had been a fledgling tennis reporter just before the war; and one day when Williams was not playing, he insisted that I come see some doubles at courts some distance away from the Carlton. I had planned to take off for some sightseeing but luckily went along to where Colonel William Larned and Major Wrenn were playing. I have not forgotten the one remark with which the Captain induced me to go with him.

"You should see these men," he said. "They were champions before you were born, and no one ever again is going to win seven championships."

He was speaking of Larned and he was mistaken. Tilden, who had won no titles at that time, had also won seven within ten years of that day. I think my friend was wrong about which Wrenn it was, too, since it must have been the younger one, George, that we saw rather than Robert, who had been champion in 1893.

I was a little ashamed that an Englishman had to tell me about Larned and Wrenn. I did not know Larned had won seven titles or that Robert had been champion so long ago. These were for me just a couple of old guys dating back to the game's infancy, but having been there, I was led in later years to a not quite honest boasting that, oh yes, I had seen Larned play.

I did not need to have Colonel Dwight Davis explained to me. I knew him as the donor of the famous trophy, but I had never seen him and would not have known which player he was. With his partner, Davis was playing a match nearby, and a day or so later I saw them defeat Larned and Wrenn, probably a doubles semifinal, since Davis and his unremembered partner were beaten by Williams and Washburn in the final.

I was advised by my friend to notice especially the "American" service of the left-handed Davis. He had learned this "twist," I was told from Holcombe Ward, another new name to me, and it had been sensational when they first brought it to England. I didn't know this either. Nor did I realize until long afterward how fortunate I was to have seen these men even when they were long past their best tennis days, and certainly were not in very good practice after a couple of years in uniform. They belonged to another sort of golden age, that period of the first decade of the century, which may well have been as luminous in its way as the later one we think of as the real golden age of sport, which had not yet quite begun at this holiday time in the South of France.

I cannot pretend that I remember much about either the personalities or the individual strokes of these men. They stir a faint mauvelike dust in the memory and it is more just the fact of having

31

seen them at all that is still important to me. In any event it would be impossible to separate what I retained from observation from what my friend told me in a last long, fine tennis talk before we parted.

I remember nothing about Wrenn except that he wore one of those dreadful ill-fitting homemade, sleeveless sweaters somebody was always knitting and sending to the boys overseas. The picture of Larned that I retain is of a man with black hair flecked with gray, parted exactly in the middle and slicked down, and I have a faint memory that he had a certain flair and was rather exciting to watch. I remember the hair because of remarking to myself that it was old-fashioned. Such small things. It is not much but it pleases me that I remember even this.

Williams defeated Washburn quickly in the final. That I recall well. It was no more than midafternoon on this final day when the Captain and I took our seats at the café and began one of the pleasantest and, on the whole, most rewarding tennis conversations of a lifetime. The Captain had played all over the Continent before the war and particularly had been a Riviera regular. But he would never play again because a piece of shrapnel had torn a hole in his right shoulder.

Now, as we sat there, he revived sweet, happy memories of tennis-playing days, and evoked a medley of Riviera images of a time when Cannes was the mecca not only of Continental tennis, but the focal point of the so-called prewar high life—Russian grand dukes and other titled personages, royalty, demi-mondaines, famous Continental beauties, yachts at anchor, bejeweled women with piles of plaques in front, and all the stuff of an E. Phillips Oppenheim novel.

The Captain spoke of the war as the end of an era, which it certainly was for him, but it seemed to me on that day more the beginning of something. Actually, the greater development of that glamorous strip of French coast line known as the Côte d'Azur was still ahead. We did not know this, though, as we sat and talked of what had been.

The Captain had "come out," as the British say, at a time when the twentieth century was still young and the Great War was only a dim cloud on a distant horizon, and he had not missed a winter until that of 1914–15. The Riviera seemed an enchanted place for him, both because he was young then, and because the time had now passed.

Many of the world's best players came regularly to the Azure Coast, but the Riviera was mostly British until after the war. The Doherty brothers, Hugh and Reggie, had come every winter during the early years, but in those years just before the war which had meant so much to the Captain, Tony Wilding had dominated the tournaments. And in that last wonderful winter season of 1913–14, Brookes also had come to begin preparation for that quest of the Davis Cup whose climax I had seen at Forest Hills.

Everybody paid his own way then. The personal tennis expense account had not been heard of except for Davis Cup team play, and the resort hotels had not yet learned the full value of exploitation through sport. You played where and when you wanted to, or could afford to, and there was a regular round of tournaments, Cannes, Nice, Beaulieu, Menton, and the climax of the winter season at Monte Carlo.

The Captain told me of the first time he had seen Dick Williams, and I remember how he spoke of the experience, which I could well understand at the end of this week. He had been playing a friendly game, he said, at a club in Switzerland—Montreux, I think it was— and, at the end of it, was walking back to the clubhouse when he saw this young boy "having a knock," as the English call a practice session, with A. R. F. Kingscote, a first-class British player I never saw at his best, and the only person I have ever known with the first name of Algernon.

Just as so many were to be later, the Captain was enthralled by what he saw. The schoolboy was making the most astonishing shots, and during the time my friend watched, so fine and experienced a player as Kingscote frequently was helpless. I knew exactly the feeling the Captain had at that moment. For several years after that he had encountered Williams here and there about the Continent but had not seen him for six or seven years. It was to see what the astonishing schoolboy had become as champion that the Captain came and stood beside me that first day, a circumstance that turned out so pleasantly and so profitably for me.

Probably what had made us companions for a week was the supposed bond of having come out of the war unable to play tennis. There was a very big difference to be sure. For the Captain it was permanent, the absolute end of playing days and he had been a player of an altogether higher level of skill. All tournament players, of even the lowest class, are in a class well above the mere club player. There is no doubt that I let the Captain get the impression that I had been much better than the "rabbits," as we used to call them, for there are ways of denying skill at games that implies that you were, even so, pretty darn good. I can justify the deception in retrospect by believing that we never would have had our fine talks if we had not discovered immediately this supposed thing in common.

The Captain, who was not much beyond thirty, was experiencing the pain of a deep regret. He was glad to talk to someone who had not known him in the old days but would understand, and I was thrilled to listen. He was speaking of a time of the tennis romantics that would never return for him, but I was on the threshold of my own romantic tennis world.

He had grown up gay and carefree in the golden twilight of that Victorian peace which appeared permanent and secure, a world that was innocent and happy and hopeless. For him the period had become now a stagnant pool into which the dead leaves of past summers dropped mournfully. He spoke of Rupert Brooke, whom he had known at Oxford, and of Siegfried Sassoon, who wrote of "that unreturning army which is youth." The verses of Brooke had strong appeal to young romantics, and both of us could quote extensively from them.

The Captain spoke particularly of that last radiant summer of peace, when his generation, doomed but unaware, played tennis right up to the edge of the abyss, so to speak. "The old world in its sunset was fair to see," wrote Winston Churchill of the Europe of 1914.

I heard at length of the last tournament the Captain ever would play. It was the tournament then called the World Hard Court Championship at the beautiful tennis ground beside the forest of St. Cloud just outside Paris, which ended only a little while before the fateful shots at Sarajevo. He talked so warmly of that last prewar tennis meeting and described the scene so exactly that I felt as if I had been there before when I actually did go years later.

"I can never be happier in my life than when I joined up," he said. These radiant young figures on whom everything life had to offer seemed to have been showered had gone in starry-eyed and full of high spirits, for they could not know that the sacrifice would not achieve the purpose for which it was made. And the Captain spoke of last farewells at the long bar of the Trocadero, just off Piccadilly Circus, as young men dashed off for Victoria Station and a muddy death in Flanders, where Tony Wilding lay.

And it was here on the terrace of this small café, with the incredible blue of the Mediterranean in the distance and the saucers piled high on the table, that I first heard, during the glowing description of St. Cloud, the name of Suzanne Lenglen. The Captain had seen a lot of her when she came as a child to play the Riviera tournaments and had been her opponent at Beaulieu when she played with Wilding as partner. She was then just a little girl with hair caught in one large curl down her back, but already she was quite sensational. She had, he said, even as a child the most extraordinary accuracy of stroke and mobility that permitted her to make incredible leaps about the court with never a loss of balance.

I heard the story of the delicate small child in Picardy working endlessly under the tutelage of her father, Charles Lenglen, to perfect her technique. In prewar days, the Captain said, Suzanne was a charming and very clever little girl with whom it was great fun to play. And she still was a prodigy when, just short of her fifteenth birthday in 1914, she won that last tournament at St. Cloud. Although that was his own last tournament of all, my friend seemed to remember Suzanne's matches as vividly as his own, possibly, he thought, because of the ecstatic reaction of the French public to her every victory.

Now, in 1919, although championship tennis had been abandoned for nearly five years, he felt sure that Suzanne had become the finest player of her sex there ever had been. As soon as the tournaments were resumed this next season, she would be so proclaimed. It would be a pity not to see her, and there would be a chance. She was to play in the tournament at the Beau Site courts beginning the next day.

I had no intention of returning to Cannes. With only a couple of days leave left I had not even seen Monte Carlo. But I did go back and I have never regretted it. The memory of my first glimpse of Lenglen, and it was only a glimpse because I did not see her play a tournament match, is all entwined with the unexpected beauty of the gardens of the Beau Site Hotel. The courts were set in the midst of orange trees and sweet-scented shrubs, and through the tortured branches of the tamaracks there were wide glimpses of the dazzling ultramarine beyond the wide sun-bleached arc of the shore, looking more Mediterranean than a picture postcard of it. The most glamorous people were wandering about flower-decked pathways, and one could imagine the most exciting things about them.

The first glimpse of Suzanne was disappointing after the buildup the Captain had given her. She was seated on a bench at the side of a court alongside a rather fat woman with prominent eyes. I learned later that this was her mother, and wherever you saw Suzanne you would also see her. As likely as not she would have a small dog under her arm, as she did on this occasion.

Suzanne seemed a plain girl with dull, almost sallow colorless skin and strong irregular teeth. She had large hands and feet for so slim a person, and her face in repose had a strong melancholy cast. But when the man with whom she was waiting to practice came up she was at once all animation and vivacity. How sudden the change and how immediate the effect.

Lenglen had not at this time adopted the costume that she would soon make famous. She wore a plain dress with quarter sleeves and of modest length, and a white felt hat with brim turned up all around. She presented a very different picture from what I had expected and from the one I was to see a year or so later.

As soon as she began to play, all the people who had been wandering came and stood or sat by the court, neglecting tournament play to see Lenglen practice. This was a foreshadowing of what was to come, of the saying that became well known at Wimbledon— namely, that while Lenglen was not the only player who could fill the center court, she was the only one who could empty it by playing outside.

She and the man player, possibly a professional, maybe Darsonval, the leading French pro at the time, played a series of games in which score was kept. It was a revelation. I had not at this time seen any top-class women's tennis at all, and here was a girl with as much skill as, and a greater variety of strokes and greater ease of execution than, any man I had encountered. And with it a natural grace of movement I had never seen equaled on a tennis court, and still have not. Later there came two other men to make up a doubles game, and here too Suzanne held up her end. She was the equal of the men in everything but severity, and their superior in mobility and accuracy.

At this time Lenglen was nineteen and most of her conquests lay ahead. A few months later she was to ascend the throne of Wimbledon in a challenge match with Mrs. Lambert Chambers, a seven-times champion, that those who saw declare to have been the finest women's match ever played. And this was, in fact, the beginning of the rise of French tennis, although some years were to pass before the name Musketeers would be applied to the men who would bring the Davis Cup to that country. It was Suzanne who showed the way and provided the inspiration.

CHAPTER THREE

THE first postwar Championship in late summer of 1919 occupies a special place in my memory and, I think, in tennis history. I had arrived back at Yaphank on Long Island to await discharge (or demobilization, as it was called then) and, with no particular duties, was able to go to Forest Hills each day.

I could see no great change in the place from five years earlier, but I felt large changes in myself. Though still learning, I now knew more and, more important, knew better what to look for. I knew definitely also that I would try for a sportswriting job in New York as soon as possible, with special emphasis on tennis.

Because this tournament always has seemed a special and significant occasion, I remember it in better detail than some which are decades closer in time. This particular tennis meeting represented a special connecting period between what had been and what was to come, and as play progressed from day to day I began to feel a stronger connection with the past while having a faint glimpse ahead. I was to see McLoughlin, representing a big part of that past, for the last time, and Tilden and Billy Johnston, about to ride the crest of the wave of the future, for the first time. Each of these encounters involved me strongly and emotionally.

Many of the leading players from the tennis era that had come to an end in August 1914 were at this 1919 tournament, and those who were to play leading roles in the first postwar decade, that which we call the Golden Age of sport, also were present.

The end of war brought a return of all the big tournaments that year and players came back to them with enthusiasm, expecting that things would pick up where they had left off. That, of course, was not possible. Things were not any longer as they had been. That wave of the future, which the French already were calling the *nouvelle vague*, had begun to roll at Wimbledon in June, when the two main titles were won by players who never had appeared there before, Lenglen and Gerald Patterson, the beefy young Australian.

The famous old playground of the Dohertys, Renshaws, Brookes, and Wilding in the Worple Road was doomed by the great overflow crowds of that first postwar meeting, but neither the spacious stands of the new Wimbledon nor the great concrete stadium at Forest Hills was yet contemplated. And that other and more beautiful tennis ground, the Stade Roland Garros that was to rise on the edge of the Bois de Boulogne in Paris, was only a distant dream.

To Forest Hills that September came all the old top players of international tennis who had survived the war and could make it, and all the promising young ones who had escaped it. Chief among the former, besides Brookes and Williams, were Lindley Murray, the wartime champion; Dean Mathey; Randolph Lycett, the great British doubles player of the prewar decade; T. R. Pell, Fred Alexander, Charles Garland, Clarence Griffin, Karl Behr, N. W. Niles, and Craig Biddle.

Not understanding completely why at the time, I sought out these older players continually during the tournament because they were from that more leisurely and charming tennis age which I had touched briefly in 1914 just before the game was to change over, and even more faintly in the glimpses of Dwight Davis and Larned at Cannes.

Brookes played four matches before being beaten by Tilden in the quarterfinal, and they were so spaced that I could see them all. I did not learn until years later that his first-round opponent was Walter Pate, an outstanding tennis personality with whom I was to have much pleasant contact in the later years when, as Davis Cup captain, he twice brought the trophy back home, from England in 1937 and from Australia after World War II. Brookes beat Garland on the same day that Tilden beat the Japanese Kumagae, and the Brookes match was so long drawn out I was not able to see much of this new Japanese who was to take a prominent place in Golden Age tennis. As I watched Garland lose to the aging Australian artist, he did not seem a very familiar figure, and I decided I probably had not seen him with Sam Hardy at Deephaven after all.

I first became conscious of the mingling of past and future in the present of this 1919 meeting when I saw Williams come down the clubhouse steps on the second day with Vincent Richards, a slim blond boy of sixteen who had shown me the day before, in a lively three-set match with a long forgotten opponent, the finest volleying touch I ever was to see, although I did not then recognize it as such.

I trailed them to an outside court, where Williams won 7–5, 6–1, 6–2, and spoke to them after they had finished, walking a little way along. I did not remind Williams that we had met at Cannes and I don't think he was conscious of it, but he was as always kind and gracious. Richards chatted away in his youthful manner, and this was the first of many pleasant encounters as our destinies became lightly entwined through the subsequent years.

I had strange mixed feelings as I watched McLoughlin through a series of early matches, one of them on the same court where he had been so luminous a few years earlier. He was the same dashing figure and I could see nothing outwardly different. There was the same dynamic service and overhead play with which he had thrilled Forest Hills in 1914. The relentless years had not stood still for him, though, for I had heard everywhere that the old California Comet had declined and had read that he probably would retire after this season.

Strangely, this knowledge did not disturb me as I thought it should. I had seen him in his glory, but what had been concealed from the schoolboy's eye was now revealed. Now I realized, as I watched the old Comet play on the same court, that both Brookes and Wilding could have beaten him on tennis alone, but could not withstand the inspired outbursts that made him godlike, with the light of heaven flashing from his racket. I recalled quite easily the intensity of feeling at the news of his defeat by Williams so soon after, but alas, how sadly time dilutes shock!

I had still a warm feeling for my boyhood hero, but I felt that I had grown beyond hero worship, and I realized that I did not greatly care that he would not win the tournament. He belonged to the past now and I was looking eagerly ahead. So I had no strong feeling of regret when Williams defeated him in the quarterfinals. I felt I ought to care more but I took it as a sign of maturity that I did not. Just the same, my reaction puzzled and disturbed me a little. I searched for these feelings of 1914 and found only the memory of them. Because they had been so intense, they could be called forth, but although I remembered them I was not to experience them again. Actually, McLoughlin still was a young man. He was only twenty-nine on the day he played his last championship match, only three years older than Tilden, whose whole wonderful prolonged career lay still ahead.

The fact was that I had been more eager to see Tilden in these days, I realized afterward, because I had heard and read so much about him. The papers were full of him, and I had resumed my practice of studying the sportswriting in them. Already past twenty-six in 1919, a year older than Johnston, who had been champion in 1915, Tilden had not yet reached full development. He had, however, become a subject of rather bitter partisan comment, a situation that was to follow him throughout his career. Some of the comment I read was scurrilous. Big Bill, who was not yet called that, was freely criticized and his personality apparently cordially disliked.

Tilden had not played in the Nationals at all until he was twenty-three, in 1916, the year of Williams' second victory, and was beaten in the first round by Harold Throckmorton, a player who never ranked among the country's first ten. In 1917, the year of the so-called National Patriotic Tournament that replaced the Nationals, Tilden was beaten by Lindley Murray, also in an early round, but in 1918 he reached the final. The first time he reached the plateau of the first ten, therefore, he was ranked second to the champion, Murray. Now in 1919 the feeling of the public, and among players too it was said, seemed to be "beat Tilden at any cost."

Five minutes after encountering him for the first time I shared this feeling, although antagonism soon was mingled with a fascination with this strange man. The encounter occurred a day before tournament play began, on a practice court far removed from the clubhouse, with two photographers taking action pictures.

Tilden was in charge, telling them exactly how they should do their work. He was not to be champion for another year but already was acting the part and a little more, and doing it in a particularly offensive way. He seemed all flanneled legs and shoulders with the waistline just under the armpits. These legs had covered a hundred yards in ten seconds and were to give Tilden the quickest start in tennis for the next six or seven years.

The lantern jaw and wide straight mouth above the long neck were familiar from pictures. They suggested great determination and it was a face on which no expression of humility seemed possible. It was lit with enthusiasm when I first saw it, and there seemed to be a conscious feeling of superiority.

I thought as I watched, though, that I never had seen such arrogance and such distasteful mannerisms. This was not in the tennis tradition I had pictured to myself. It definitely was not in keeping with the past. I walked away with a feeling close to disgust and an unreasonable antagonism toward the man soon to be the greatest player of all. This feeling, unfortunately, remained with me for too long a time, retarding my recognition of Tilden's surpassing ability as player and showman and of the fact that he was one of the most intelligent of all champions.

All these things occurred before my first glimpse of Billy Johnston, and had the order been reversed my emotions might have been even more marked. Because I fell in love with Little Bill instantly, completely and without reservation. I had worshiped McLoughlin from afar, knowing all about him long before I first saw him. Little Bill burst upon me all unexpected, although of course I knew he had been champion.

It is strange that he did not project anything toward me and catch my interest before I had seen him play. This was not hero worship in the McLoughlin sense. It was love, and once I had fallen, little else seemed to matter so much as seeing him again and seeing him win. Many had this same experience, and the younger they were the more they were smitten.

It was easy to see why people loved Little Bill, a tiny David slaying Goliaths. Actually, he was not so small as all that, being above five feet eight, but he never weighed much more than 120 pounds and he gave an impression of frailty. I was fascinated, as were others, to see so frail a body producing such force, and I was determined to see how that forehand which hurled projectiles was executed. I had not encountered the so-called Western grip, and the result was so extraordinary I decided this must be the ultimate.

I had never heard of Little Bill's early opponents and do not recall any of them until he reached Gerald Patterson in the fourth round, although I had seen every stroke of every match. I also had seen Patterson beat Watson Washburn, and since the Australian was newly crowned Wimbledon champion, I feared for Little Bill. Patterson's service was the biggest I had seen, and I am not sure it isn't still. A real thunderbolt. He had what has been described as a "battle-axe" type of game, a real banger of the ball on service and volley. He seemed awesome to me then, and I was not to observe until much later how really vulnerable he was with his weak backhand and insecure forehand.

The match with Johnston went on a long time. Little Bill won only in the twelfth game of a fifth set, the scores being 6–2, 3–6, 6–4, 4–6, 7–5, and I had many anxious moments. It did not seem possible Johnston could win against such service power. When he had done so I tried to figure why the big man with the tremendous service could not dominate a comparatively tiny and frail player. Some years were required to learn the lesson that the specialist, however brilliant, is handicapped in dealing with the complete player.

I almost missed the start of the Williams-McLoughlin quarterfinal because Johnston and Murray were playing outside the enclosure at about the same time, but if I was not disturbed when Williams beat the old hero, I was terribly upset when Tilden, having beaten Norman Brookes on an adjoining court, then defeated Williams next day in the semifinal.

Everyone was upset. No one expected this, and I had gone to the match confidently expecting to see Tilden knocked out of the tournament. People appeared to be horrified at this result, and there was a certain resentment against Williams that he had permitted himself to be beaten by such a fellow. But we did not lose confidence that Johnston would take care of the matter.

And so he did. On the last day, I and many others had the great pleasure of seeing Tilden beaten, and very well beaten, in straight sets. It was beautiful and the cheering was thunderous. A most satisfying experience, for there never was any doubt at all of the result. So there never was a moment of anxiety.

Johnston seemed to me the perfect tennis player. He hurled his projectiles into Tilden's court, pounding the backhand to a pulp, and he served, smashed, and volleyed decisively, controlling the game at will. Tilden, whose repertoire of strokes was to become the finest ever seen, revealed no outstanding shot at all in this match aside from his fast first service, not yet called the cannonball.

In losing to Johnston, Tilden still sliced the ball most of the time on both wings, and his forehand did not seem to me anywhere near the equal of Little Bill's mighty blast. Neither did Tilden show any such decisive overhead smash as Johnston owned, and his volley was not only inferior to Johnston's but below that of the schoolboy, Richards.

I had a low opinion of Tilden's stroke technique when I left Forest Hills in the calm belief that Little Bill had put this upstart in his place and disposed of him for good. Alas! I never was to see it again and no one else ever was to see it either. For a couple of years I could hardly stand it when Tilden won. Each time I was certain beforehand that Johnston would win and be champion again, until finally the reluctant realization was forced upon me that Big Bill was without doubt the master, not only of Little Bill but of all other tennis players anywhere.

Because of dislike of Tilden and something stronger, I overlooked the chance to observe this player in the final stages of development of that marvelous game. In later years I came to know Tilden about as well probably as it was possible to know so strange a personality, and had the opportunity of discussing this with him. I learned that he looked upon the 1919 tournament as, one might say, the completion of his graduate studies. During this week of play, and especially in the final with Johnston, Tilden said he had learned exactly what he needed to do to make himself a complete tennis player.

During the months which now intervened before I was to see first-class tennis again, I tried to sort out the impressions of this first postwar tournament. There remained a gap between perception and understanding. The perception of a thing is experienced directly. The explanations for the experience are thought up afterward. One of the things that puzzled me was that the most vivid pictures that remained were not of Johnston but of Williams. I kept on loving Johnson but seeing Williams. Finally, I arrived at a reason for this, or at least at an explanation that satisfied me.

Williams, I decided, had become for me a bridge over which I could pass backward to an understanding of that earlier tennis age I had not known. Williams would, of course, remain active for many years, giving immense pleasure at times with his brilliant flashes, and he would twice be doubles champion with Richards. But his days as singles champion belonged to that earlier time when men played the game loving it and loving the beauty they spread about the court. Even the biggest tennis events then had something of a garden party atmosphere that could never be revived; men played more for fun.

And Dick Williams, as I remembered him from Cannes and from Forest Hills in the same year, came to be, along with that tournament itself, a real link with the older time. The game, like many other things, was approaching a change in that early postwar period. It was on its way to becoming more a popular public spectacle and the actors who would play the leading roles on the world stage during the coming age already were waiting in the wings.

Tennis would never again be quite the same as it had been in that time of which the Captain spoke on the terrace at Cannes, and of which I had no direct experience but felt now that I could understand a little. I had seen there at Forest Hills a bit of the new and a good deal of the old in a tournament that was neither completely the one or the other, but a suspension hanging between them.

CHAPTER FOUR

I ARRIVED back in New York soon after the return of the Davis Cup, which I had seen lost to Australia, or rather Australasia, in 1914. The United States had held out of the world tournament the first year it was renewed in 1919, but Tilden and Johnston, with Sam Hardy as captain, had won through to challenge the holders without the loss of a match in 1920. Then they won all five matches against Brookes and Patterson, again representing Australasia, in the Challenge Round played at Auckland, New Zealand, December 30 and 31 and January 1, 1921. They came back bearing the Cup a month later.

I had come to New York with no plan or prospects but confident of finding a job on a newspaper, since there were fifteen or sixteen of them published daily in the city. It was at the beginning of that exciting period which Westbrook Pegler taught us to call the Era of Wonderful Nonsense, the time of the speakeasy, roof gardens, and cabarets such as Shanleys in the old Putnam Building, where the prizefight managers had their offices, and where the Paramount Theater stood for three decades; of Jack's Restaurant on Sixth Avenue and vaudeville at the Palace; a period when knees came in and breasts went out, and there was a widespread belief that gin made in a bathbub was fit to drink. It also was the beginning of what in sports we call the Golden Age, in recalling which we should keep in mind that golden ages may possibly seem dull to those who come after.

Into this New York a young man with a bit of newspaper experience could come and be reasonably sure of landing a job before his money would run out. I was less confident of getting into sportswriting, but still hopeful, and the connection I made with the old *Evening Mail* after a few weeks was fortunate for that. The *Mail* had a small sports staff housed in a back corner of the city room down on

City Hall Place, off Park Row, and they sometimes called on willing hands across the border of the city side for help.

It did not take many months on the street in the fierce competition of New York newspaper reporting of that day to convince me that a really successful reporter must have a professional ruthlessness that I lacked. I shrank from intruding on people's privacy, and this was a weakness no reporter on the streets of New York at that time dared permit himself. With so many papers competing for circulation, the competition among reporters was correspondingly keen. I had come with large reportorial ambitions distilled from highly colored stories about the exploits of the great ones. I gave these up quickly and willingly but a little sadly just the same, when it became clear that I was better equipped for writing news than for chasing it about the city. The young afternoon-paper reporter did not, in any event, get much chance to use a typewriter. He used the telephone a great deal, and after a while I was able to wangle a rewrite job that put me on the writing end of the phone in the office. From then on I cast longing glances toward the sports department.

The giants of sportswriting were working in the city at that time —W. O. McGeehan, Heywood Broun, Grantland Rice, Damon Runyan, Hugh Fullerton, occasionally Irvin Cobb and Gene Fowler, Ring Lardner, Westbrook Pegler, Bob Edgren, Bill Hanna, Charley Van Loan, Charley Dryden, Harry Cross. The list is long. I admired them greatly and studied them diligently, but hindsight suggests that some may not have been quite so colossal as they then seemed.

The more I studied these men and their world of tiny giants and giant dwarfs it seemed to me that the chronicler of sports events had, on the whole, been provided with one of the most agreeable jobs any subdivision of literature could offer. It did not escape my notice either that quite important people sought the acquaintance of sports reporters and were flattered to be seen in their company.

Warren Brown, one of the adornments of our craft, who later adorned Chicago papers, was sports editor of the *Mail*, and he was sympathetic toward my hopes. He explained that there were no tennis writing specialists, strictly speaking, on any of the New York papers, and he thought it might be worthwhile to aim for such a job. The sport was getting more popular and the personalities in it more interesting. There might be enough soon to keep a man fairly busy on a morning paper, but the afternoon papers had neither big enough staffs nor enough space to cover the less important events. They just picked someone from the regular staff when the big ones came near New York, and he would be glad to pick me sometime if it became possible. Make a study of Tilden, he advised, and maybe the *Mail* could use some stuff, for which he could pay space rates.

There was a lot of tennis to be seen around New York in those early years of the 1920s with no more than a subway ride or short train trip. Hardly any of the tournaments were covered day by day by the afternoon papers, but they would accept what were called "overnights," or feature pieces about play from staff members. The papers were keen for overnight features at that time, often with accompanying sketches by a staff artist. Among overnights I remember doing in those years was the first marathon dance at the Roseland Academy, then on Broadway, and what I remember best about it is being made to look dreadfully amateurish by the piece Frank Sullivan did on the same day for the *Morning World*.

Usually it was Ed Sullivan, the now famous TV man, who did tennis and golf for the *Mail* then, but he went only to important tournaments and the Davis Cup Challenge Round matches, which were played at Forest Hills each September until 1924. The National Singles Tournament was in Philadelphia during these years, but it still was possible to see a lot of the play. It was Sullivan, I suppose, who wrote the pieces appearing in the paper under the by-line of Vincent Richards, who had become national doubles champion with Tilden as partner and was known as the Boy Wonder. Young Vinnie was in the office frequently; our acquaintance soon became a friendship, and I would go whenever I could to wherever he was playing.

Another outside source of tennis information at this time was Sigmund Spaeth, the Tune Detective of radio, whose wife, Katherine, was the *Mail's* music critic. Spaeth would come to the shop from time to time, and he was a most thoughtful tennis enthusiast with all sorts of theories about which he loved to talk. He was fascinated by Tilden, and some of the things set down in this account may well have come out of these talks.

There were tournaments on the turf courts of the North Meadow in Central Park; at the Crescent Athletic Club in Bay Ridge, Brooklyn; at the New York Tennis Club on St. Nicholas Avenue; at the Amackassen Club in Yonkers; and at several nearby places in New

Jersey. It was at the Amackassen Club that I first saw Zenzo Shimizu, the other Japanese player who, along with Kumagae, was in the process of winning through to the Challenge Round that summer of 1921. I remember seeing Richards, still the national junior champion, beat Kumagae there and again on the grass at Bay Ridge, and the notes I wrote down then indicate that I was much more impressed with Shimizu's phenomenal steadiness and accuracy than with Kumagae's more celebrated left-handed top-spin forehand.

There were accounts of these tournaments unsigned in the *Times* and under the by-line of a girl named Lenihan in the *Morning World,* and my clipping file for comparing and criticizing began to grow. Then suddenly, in August of that year, all the papers turned loose full blast on that remarkable affair of Suzanne Lenglen and Molla Mallory, and my file, if not my cup, ran over. The women's championship, held as a separate event then, was brought to New York for the first time that year, and none before or since has attracted the attention this one got.

In looking back over a few pleasant decades of attending sports activities on both sides of the Atlantic, there are discovered few games played by women that seem worth recalling in detail. There have been high spots and exciting moments, but the dears are, on the whole, comparatively dull performers in sport, and nearly always it is clashing personalities rather than skill or outstanding performance that make the occasion memorable. Unless something other than actual tennis has intervened to grace the occasion you will search long through the history of the game to find matches suitable for embalming in the hackneyed superlatives of the sportswriter.

I was to be involved in several such occasions eminently worthy of attention, however, and the first was this extravagant affair which came soon after the dawn of the Era of Wonderful Nonsense. It provided me with an excellent exercise in tennis reporting by comparing my own observations with what appeared in all the papers. I found considerable disagreement between my own view and that of my new colleagues. Memory is notoriously faulty, especially where the emotions may be involved or prejudice present, but I really think I am secure here.

What is difficult to recall about the affair is the furor and sensation of it. A whole nation, seemingly, became exercised over what really was a small thing, making of it an international incident. Sport was to turn up a number of these sensational incidents before the Jazz Age was done. I was also puzzled that there was so little agreement among reporters assigned to the match as to what had occurred in the highly charged atmosphere of the meeting of these two girls. The match had suddenly become important to papers on which tennis had been more or less ignored, and some of the commentators who spoke with great authority had never covered a tennis tournament before.

Women's tennis was not at the time very exciting. Molla—first as Miss Bjurstedt, a Norwegian, and then as Mrs. Franklin Mallory, an American—had won five of the last six U.S. titles and seemed likely to go on winning. The girls' tournament needed something to give it interest, and when it was learned that the great Lenglen would come for it, the papers began to whoop it up. Suzanne, as we have seen, had become something of a celebrity in 1914 when, still a child, she had won at St. Cloud. Her name, if not her figure, had become known in all the tennis-playing countries before the war, and she still was under twenty when the tournaments were resumed in 1919. Her first visit to Wimbledon for this renewal of that most famous of all tennis meetings had been sensational, and Suzanne quickly became a world-famous personality.

During the next two years she probably did more for women's tennis than any girl who ever played it. She broke down barriers and created a vogue, reforming tennis dress, substituting acrobatics and something of the art of the ballet where decorum had been the rule. In England and on the Continent this slim, not very pretty but fascinating French maiden was the most popular performer in sport or out of it on the postwar scene. From Biarritz to Monte Carlo, from Deauville to St. Moritz and Baden, she became the rage, almost a cult. Businessmen canceled appointments and internationally famous hostesses postponed parties that conflicted with Suzanne's appearances because they knew no one would attend. Even royalty gave her its favor and she partnered King Gustav of Sweden in the mixed doubles more than once.

She became almost an obsession, attracting adoring crowds wherever she went, for she was more than a tennis player. She was acrobat, dancer, a spectacular artiste, actress and compelling personality. Just to see her crush some unfortunate girl 6–0, 6–0 was an event.

She created fashions in dress followed by thousands of girls who could not hit a ball over the net, and her famous bandeaux were worn all over the world by women who never saw her.

Wherever Suzanne played she took the attention away from the men, and men treated her as a queen. She made the game popular in quarters where it hardly had been noticed, and she was compared to Pavlova and Bernhardt. Newspapers and magazines everywhere were forever full of her pictures in beautiful action, for the photographers and picture editors could resist her no more than the public.

Very few performers in any field have enjoyed such adulation. Everything she did on the court and off it, what she ate and what she wore, was important news. And together with all this, she brought to the courts a technique that was near perfection and a style of play that was the most wonderfully exciting the world had seen.

It was out of this splendid background that Lenglen made her first unhappy visit to the United States. In June she had won Wimbledon for the third time. She had not lost a set or come close to losing one anywhere for years, and in these last two years she had played and beaten every girl in the world of any class, including, of course, Molla Mallory.

Suzanne's visit was in a way as an official representative of her country. She was invited to come to the United States to play in the championship and then to play a series of exhibitions to help raise money for the relief of the regions in France devastated by the war. A fund was being raised and it was under the auspices of the committee headed by Miss Anne Morgan, together with the United States Lawn Tennis Association, that the tour had been arranged. For this reason also the event created much interest. Most Americans still were involved then in a love affair with the French, and you could hear repeated often the saying that every American had two countries, his own and France.

Lenglen was also, in a sense, returning the visit of Tilden and Mrs. Mallory, the two United States champions who had gone to Paris in the early summer before playing at Wimbledon. So the papers made a great deal of this coming event, and the approach of the Maid Marvel of France, as she was called, was heralded flamboyantly in keeping with the time.

But gradually the friendly visit began to be changed over in some of the papers to a sort of foreign invasion. Our girls were called upon to rise and repel the invader. There was even some talk of calling our old ones, such as May Sutton Bundy, the Wimbledon champion of 1905, out of retirement to help, and altogether the home forces got pretty well stirred up.

Unfortunately for the buildup, Suzanne did not arrive on schedule. The arranging of the trip had taken some doing, and Lenglen père, a poor sailor, refused to board a ship after agreeing most reluctantly that Suzanne could go. Monsieur Lenglen warned that the trip without him was not for the best. Suzanne took a later ship than at first planned, and it was delayed a little by storms. She landed in New York only a few days before she was scheduled to play her first match in the tournament.

When the draw had been made, with the French girl still at sea, it was seen that the big match to which everyone looked forward, the one against Molla, would come in the second round. The idea of a seeded draw, with the leading players arbitrarily placed so as to prevent such a meeting before the later rounds, had not yet been introduced.

Suzanne had been drawn in the first round against Eleanor Goss, a quite good American player whom she would have to play without having an opportunity to accustom herself to the strange new conditions, a decided handicap for a girl just off a ship. Even Tilden had found it impossible to play his game immediately after his arrival in France that summer. Suzanne was thought to be so wonderful that she would adjust more quickly to the faster balls and unfamiliar turf. She would not need practice, it was felt, and the match with Miss Goss would be quite enough to put her in top form for Molla.

Then Miss Goss defaulted, and Suzanne was required to go into court for her big test on the second day without benefit of a preliminary match. A lot was made of this default. It was announced that Miss Goss had withdrawn because of illness, but in some papers it was described as a clever bit of strategy by the "defenders." It was said that Miss Goss had been "persuaded" to withdraw so that the "invader" would be forced to come into the arena thus further handicapped. I am ashamed to say that I took some stock in this proposition for just a little while.

I am afraid I still believed it premeditated when I arrived at Forest Hills, but before the extraordinary climax, I had begun to resent the implications of it. I now doubt that it had any truth in it at all, even though I subscribed briefly. I had gone out early on this day, and since there were a number of matches being played, I wandered. On the path beyond the wooden stands, which already had been set up for the Challenge Round matches to follow in a few days, I saw coming toward me the familiar figure of Sam Hardy.

I wondered if he would remember me after four years, but of course it was silly to think such a man would not. I was so delighted to see him again I think I must have acted very youthful in my enthusiasm, but he made me feel that he was genuinely glad to see me too and had to know all about the war and what had happened to me since.

Sam was in tennis clothes with a couple of rackets under his arm, and he said he had been practicing back there with Lenglen and that she had not seemed very keen for the match. I am quite certain he said nothing about illness, even though I cannot remember what he actually did say. If he had mentioned illness I certainly would have remembered in view of what was going to happen soon after.

Meeting up with this dear man again put me in a pleasant glow, which I carried to my seat. When I had got settled and looked around I saw Suzanne as I had first seen her at the Beau Site. She was sitting quietly in a box with her mother beside her waiting her turn. In these two years she had changed into a world celebrity and outwardly she had changed greatly too. Gone was the long linen dress for a short sleeveless, pleated one more like a ballet skirt, and the funny little soft hat had been replaced by the now famous bandeau of many colors, a different one for each appearance.

Suzanne and Molla were preceded in the enclosure by two girls whose names have long since escaped me, but whose performance I have seen repeated over and over these many years on courts fast and slow, grass, clay, and cement in many countries. They played an interminable match, three long sets, and as I watched I learned for the first time that tennis can be boring. There was something prophetic in this, for it was to be my lot for many years to watch and write about this sort of thing, the purposeless hitting up and down the court by two girls, neither able to win when the chance comes, both forced to go on and on until one or the other finally loses.

By the time they were off the court and the preliminaries completed it was getting on late afternoon. All this time Lenglen had been sitting there watching the match while the rest of us watched her. This surely was not good preparation. Molla had been more sensible. She rested somewhere out of sight.

Finally Molla came out of the clubhouse and Suzanne rose to meet her at the top of the steps leading down to the court level, onto which they came together with all sorts of French and American officials in their wake and photographers walking backward in front of them. This was the moment for which we had all waited—about ten thousand were there, the papers said. There was a burst of applause and some cheers.

Lenglen was dressed in the costume with which we had all become so familiar through pictures in the rotogravure sections, which most Sunday papers still carried as supplements. I do not remember the color of the bandeau that enclosed the dark shining hair, but I noted that the white stockings now were rolled just above the knees. Molla also wore a band around her hair but what a difference! The defending champion wore a serious, even a severe expression and her costume was, by comparison, plain. She had pulled on a long thin dark sweater and the white of her dress shone through. The sweater was caught and held tight at the waist by a narrow leather belt, and it had a sort of skirt falling down over the dress, which was inches longer than Suzanne's. This also was her usual costume, long familiar, and there is no doubt that she looked a little drab in it beside her glittering, volatile companion. But she also looked very menacing with her dark, swarthy Indian-like features.

Memory says that Suzanne came in like a queen to her ordeal, but that may be only the result of seeing her do so in the years that followed. Since she was to show in a very few minutes that she was not herself and to declare that she was in fact ill, there may have been unnoticed signs of it from the first. But try as I will I cannot remember any such indication which preceded the play.

However, when the match began with Mrs. Mallory serving, Suzanne did little more than tap the ball back over the net gently. We thought that she would take a little time to get started, so we were not disturbed as they changed courts for the first time. But the second game which Suzanne served, went the same way to Molla, who hit the ball with great determination to the corners of the court, drawing feeble replies as Lenglen ran from corner to corner.

This gave the crowd a vague feeling of uneasiness. It was Suzanne's opponents who were supposed to run from corner to corner.

We had been looking forward to acrobatics and pirouettes. At 40–love to Molla in the third game, Suzanne began to show the first signs of distress. She began to cough. She seemed to get hold of herself quickly, though, and suddenly she began to hit out. With drives shrewdly directed she won five straight points. She had won Molla's service and the crisis seemed to have passed. The coughing stopped.

But when they had changed sides again, Molla attacked with real viciousness. The champion hit deep and hard. There was a relentless air about her, and Suzanne's efforts at defense were again weak. When Molla rushed ahead to 4–1 the coughing began again. Suzanne stopped under the umpire's chair at the change-over after the fifth game. She shrugged a little helplessly and had a more violent fit of coughing.

As she took her place the coughing continued. There was a nervous quality about it, and now Suzanne looked appealingly toward her mother. We were all a little dazed and puzzled too. This dazzling girl might not be able to hold the American champion in check, but surely she was better than this.

Molla took the two games she needed quickly and the first set 6–2. Her dour expression relaxed and she smiled. This was the first set she or anyone else had won from Lenglen on any court in two years and more. Suzanne, of course, was conscious of it too, and it could hardly have made her feel better. Sitting there all disappointed, I remember thinking that now anyhow the match would have to go three sets. I still could not imagine that the great Lenglen would lose in two.

I was sure of it for half a moment at the start of the second when Suzanne began in the way we had all expected her to play. Now she would play her game, it seemed. The very first point produced a long exchange during which there came a stream of fine shots from the French girl's racket. But Molla finally won the point and the game at love. And then came the disappointing end, suddenly.

Suzanne was serving the second game of the set and the score had gone to love–30 against her. Here she served a double fault, a thing she never did. Apparently it was a signal to her. She walked unsteadily to the umpire's chair, looked up, shook her head, and said something. Molla came up too, said something to Suzanne and then to the official. In the stands we could not hear, but we saw Suzanne shake her head again, and we guessed what was going on. Suzanne was saying that she was ill and could not continue.

We saw Molla put her face close to Suzanne, speak some words, and then run across to the clubhouse and disappear. Then we knew. No announcement was necessary. There was a mild burst for the American victory, but it subsided quickly as Suzanne sat there in the netcord judge's chair, a forlorn figure as the photographers rushed up to snap her in her misery. She got up after a bit and, with officials and photographers swirling about her, walked across the court and also disappeared into the clubhouse.

A faint but distinct hissing sound came from the stands as she crossed the terrace and passed from sight. It was a polite sort of hissing, but she certainly could not have failed to hear it or know its meaning. The crowd was branding her with that horrid American word "quitter."

In America we cannot abide a quitter. Our code is the die-for-dear-old-Rutgers code. We did not know then that in Europe they adopt the more sensible attitude that it is foolhardy to continue when ill. To retire from any athletic contest because of indisposition was the accepted thing, taken for granted. On this occasion, though, quite sensible people said unkind and untrue things, and some of the papers were especially caustic. For a little while after that day "to cough and quit" was a phrase heard often.

I left Forest Hills with a strong feeling of having been cheated, of not having seen the show that was advertised, and my resentment was great. I suppose everyone felt that way. I thought of the French girl with disfavor, but I really do not think now that I ever did accept the ugly word. I think I accepted the fact that she was not completely well, but I felt she could at least have gone on and made a match of it.

But when I joined the crowds at the station, and in the train on the way back to town, I heard people saying the nastiest things. Soon I began to swing over to Suzanne's side and found myself trying to make excuses for her. Then when I read all the scornful things in the papers the following days, I came to the quite erroneous conclusion that she probably would have won the match anyhow if she had decided to stick with it for a while longer. I did feel that she had not been feigning illness, as was said, and my opinion of the whole affair was reinforced by what happened months afterward.

Although she was said to have recovered quickly, Suzanne did not go through with her schedule of charity appearances. She did play an exhibition mixed doubles at Forest Hills, and she was reported in the papers to have played with the old verve, but I did not see it. Her chance to restore the balance came the following June when Mrs. Mallory went to Wimbledon again and reached the final. Against Suzanne in that match one newspaper report said that Molla "played shrewdly, courageously and probably as well as she ever played." But Suzanne required a scant twenty-six minutes to win 6–2, 6–0. Molla took only two games in two sets.

This result should always be placed alongside the one at Forest Hills, for it is a better gauge of the relative tennis merits of these two. Unfortunately, Lenglen is remembered in the United States far more for the former than for the latter. It was her destiny, it seemed, to be remembered more for the clouds under which she left the two great tennis grounds of the world, Forest Hills in 1921 and Wimbledon a few years later, than for the bright sunshine in which she basked most of her tennis life.

Suzanne was to return to America in 1926 to join Vincent Richards and Mary Browne in the first of a long series of exhibition tours under the banner of that fabulous figure of the Lawless Decade, Cash and Carry Pyle, of Bunion Derby fame. She was not much happier in this financially profitable venture, and earlier in the same year she figured in two more highly dramatic incidents before her dazzling amateur career was done. The first was a match that attracted even more attention, the famous meeting with Helen Wills at Cannes. The other was the last, sad incident of her amateur days at Wimbledon, when they said she insulted Queen Mary.

CHAPTER FIVE

I T WAS in the days following this tournament, when Molla moved firmly to her sixth of eight titles by beating Mary Browne 4–6, 6–4, 6–2 in the final, that I first heard of Helen Wills. Sam Hardy had remarked that there was a fifteen-year-old girl coming East next year who might be better than either Molla or Suzanne one day. This enthusiasm for a fellow Californian by a man for whose sound judgment I had such regard made me eager to see her play. So I went to Seabright one summer's day in 1922, by boat to Atlantic Highlands and then by train down the Jersey coast.

I was quite disappointed at first. Compared to Lenglen, Helen seemed dreadfully slow about the court. But she was so demure, so young and fresh, and she whacked the ball so lustily that she made a strong appeal nevertheless. I suppose it would be all right to say that her potentiality was revealed to me immediately, since there is nobody to deny it, but I think really it was only when I saw her beat Molla a year later to become champion at seventeen that I was actually conscious of it. By that time it was known to all the tennis world.

This was just two years after Suzanne's unfortunate visit, and the clamor for a meeting of Helen with the French girl already was beginning to be heard. The new stadium at Forest Hills had been begun by this time with the understanding, I think, that the West Side Club would have either the Championships or the Davis Cup Challenge Round for a period of years. The Cup matches had been held there for three years after the return of the trophy, with the United States defeating Japan, Australia, and Australia again with the loss of only two of fifteen matches. Only one of these matches remains especially vivid, the meeting of Tilden with Zenzo Shimizu of Japan in 1921, about which I am again in disagreement with most tennis authorities.

Tilden was by now acknowledged everywhere as the world's finest player. He had won at Wimbledon in 1920 and 1921, and in their second final in the American Nationals, Johnston had failed to solve the problem of Tilden's new backhand in five exciting sets. That was the day when two aviators crashed to their death within sight of the Forest Hills grounds while the match was in progress.

As the climax of the 1921 season approached, Tilden was unbeaten in any important match for two seasons, but he still was thought to be surpassed in individual strokes by other players. His forehand was thought to have neither the pace nor the accuracy of Johnston's, his slices no better than Wallace Johnson's, his volley inferior to Richards', his overhead less decisive than McLoughlin's, and the famous cannonball service not noticeably faster than Patterson's.

As an all-court tactician Tilden was not rated with Brookes. He had not the wonderful touch, rhythm, and economy of movement of Williams, it was said, and Shimizu made far fewer errors while being a much better retriever.

The Tilden-Shimizu meeting on the first day of the Challenge Round, was a famous tennis match played only a few weeks after that other celebrated affair of 1921, the Lenglen-Mallory match, and on the same turf. Shimizu won the first two sets 7–5, 6–4 and was within two points of beating Tilden in the third. But Tilden pulled out the third set 7–5 and then, after the rest period, won the fourth and fifth sets 6–2, 6–1.

There is something strange about the accounts of this match and of the memory of it when people talked about it and wrote about it in later years. It has been made a memorable tennis occasion, but other people's memories of it do not coincide with mine.

It usually is depicted as an occasion when Tilden, deliberately placing himself in a position that appeared hopeless, letting himself go, in fact, to the brink of defeat so as to display his unsurpassed ability to pull out of it, almost got caught. And the accounts, more often than not, intimated that it would have served the silly fellow right if he had got caught.

Tilden did have this reputation, and when you consider the number of times he pulled out a match within a point or so of defeat, it is not surprising. He had done it only a few months earlier against Brian Norton, the South African challenger at Wimbledon. Johnston had won the first two sets in their 1920 final, and others had forced Tilden to the edge of defeat only to go over themselves in the end.

Tilden scored more important victories after seeming to be beaten than any other champion. He won these matches with super tennis, but I do not think it compatible with Tilden's greatness to hold, as many did, that he deliberately toyed with an opponent for the pleasure of snatching victory from his grasp.

Against outclassed opponents he did not always use the full force of his game, since there was no need to, but I decline to believe that he let up against first-class players to tantalize and finally crush them. The fact that this occurred so often probably was part of the peculiar genius of the man. It may have been part of his feeling for showmanship, his real desire to give the crowd a full value and put on a proper show.

There was, for instance, an occasion somewhat later when, with H. Levan Richards, probably the best tennis umpire we have had, in the chair, Tilden was playing someone who was normally a pretty good player but was now hopelessly outclassed. Seeing how easily and quickly he was going to win, Tilden began to offer up shots his opponent could make best, so as to produce longer exchanges.

Big Bill also began a show of petulance and temperament that soon put the crowd in a hostile uproar. Tilden glared at linesmen after decisions that everyone could see were correct, stormed about the court, and called on heaven to witness the injustice of it all. At one point he stopped in mid-court, placed hands on hips, and shouted at the chair for all to hear, "For heaven's sake, Lev! Are you blind?"

This brought boos from the stands, just as it was calculated to do, and there were shouts of "Play the game, Tilden" and "Play ball."

But when the last point was played and Tilden had won as inevitably he must with the greatest ease, though he had made the other man look quite good, he went to the chair and, extending his hand, said to Richards, "I'm sorry, Lev. I apologize. But they really deserved a show, don't you think?"

So Tilden was capable of such antics, but in the case of Shimizu I am certain the popular view is wrong. Tilden would never have taken such a chance with a player of Shimizu's known class, and the evidence, in any event as I remember it, is conclusive.

Tilden had been quite ill during Wimbledon and had got out of bed to win the Challenge Round match from Norton, who had won what was then called the All Comers Tournament. Fortunately for

Tilden the champion was not required to play through, but stood out until a "challenger" was found. This method was abandoned the following year.

Tilden began this match with Shimizu with a ripe carbuncle, or boil, on his right foot, at the instep I think. He was in much pain all through the first three sets, especially when he attempted to come forward. That is why Big Bill appeared so unaggressive. During the intermission after the third set, he got relief when a doctor came to the locker room, lanced the boil, and removed the pus. Tilden came back to the court with the wound tightly bandaged.

I am indebted for these details to Vinnie Richards, who had just recently won the national doubles title for the first time as Tilden's partner. Richards was writing pieces for the *Mail* at this time, or at any rate signing them. As mentioned, they may have been written by Ed Sullivan, who was covering tennis for the paper then. Vinnie was in the office frequently. I remember very well speaking with him about the match. He was present when the foot was lanced, and since Tilden himself confirmed it in later years I do not think there can be any doubt.

People simply forget such details, and since Tilden was not popular it was perhaps the more easily forgotten. So some still to this day speak about and write about the match the other way, and that other way has become almost a historical fact. They also refer to it as a critical Davis Cup match, but as a matter of fact it had no bearing on the result, since the United States team won the series from Japan by five matches to none.

One reason for the misconception is that Tilden never spoke of the handicap under which he played and never wrote about it in any of his books. He said many years later, after he had become a professional, that he never spoke of it because it would have been unfair to Shimizu, who played magnificently.

Tilden was a generous man where his opponents were concerned. Too generous. I thought he always seemed to give them a little too much the best of it. He refers to this match in his book *My Story*, published in 1948, as a "freak match." He says there that the situation might not have arisen "if I had fully recovered from the illness which almost cost me my Wimbledon title."

"I was far from well," he continued. "I knew how Shimizu

should be played, but he met my attack with a lobbing defense that ran me miles. I had reached 5–3 in the first set when suddenly the heat got me."

I never saw Tilden after he wrote this book and he had not, in fact too long to live. I puzzled over why, so long after the event, he should omit all reference to the boil on the foot. Had he also forgotten? The book is full of errors of fact and examples of faulty memory. I wrote Tilden asking about this but never received a reply. Only a few days before Tilden was found dead in his furnished room in California, Richards, then vice-president of Dunlop Tire and Rubber Company, showed me a letter he had received from Big Bill asking, "Vinnie, could you please send me a couple of dozen balls and a racket or two? If I had them I think I could get some lessons to give. I need the money badly."

But the greatest tennis player the world has seen was dead when the packet arrived. He had less than five dollars in his pocket and there was no one to care.

CHAPTER SIX

URING the early years of the 1920s Tilden and Johnston had met each September in the National Singles Championship and Tilden had won each time. I had not seen the first victory in 1920 but had gone down to Philadelphia for the others. I had also seen many other matches at Germantown involving Richards and other ranking players.

One of the things which puzzled me was that Tilden continued to have trouble beating the schoolboy Richards, while Johnston was handled more easily as time passed. Moreover, Richards seemed to have no chance against Little Bill, but appeared to have a good chance to beat Big Bill each time they met. It may have been that Tilden, who had twice won the doubles title with Richards as partner, continued to look upon Vinnie as a small boy with a small boy's game and, in fact, underestimated him.

There had been a final at Germantown in 1921 that caused a lot of talk and for other reasons offered me considerable grounds for thought. It was before the day of seeded draw, in which leading players are placed so that they cannot meet before the later rounds. So Johnston had beaten Richards in an early round and had been beaten by Big Bill a day or two before the final, to which Wallace Johnson had survived to play Tilden.

Johnson used the chop stroke exclusively off the ground, and he may have been the finest exponent of this not very pretty stroke ever seen. I recall this final round match here for two reasons. The first is that it adds something to the picture I am trying to build of Tilden, the complete lawn tennis player. The second is to show how faulty memory can be, especially mine.

For many years I spoke of this match as though I had seen every stroke of it, and I honesty believed that I had. I would tell, and sometimes write, how Tilden, playing the one-stroke specialist, the greatest exponent of the chop, at his own game, beat him by executing that stroke better.

I could be positive about how Big Bill chopped away throughout the match, returning chop for chop and showing clearly that his own version of the stroke was the superior. It was, I related, a dull match for this reason. I thought of it for years as the only dull match I had ever seen Tilden play, but one that did as much as anything else to convince me that, in Tilden, we had to do with the complete master. How different the real story was!

When I went to the record books to check the score in this match that I thought had bored me, I found to my astonishment that I had not seen it at all and that Tilden had chopped hardly once in the course of it. It all came back to me once I had taken the trouble to check the facts. The final was scheduled for a Saturday in September, the nineteenth. As I rode down to North Philadelphia in the morning a light but steady rain beat against the train windows, and it still was falling when I arrived at Germantown.

I was met on the platform at North Philly by a former soldier friend who assured me there would be no play that day. There should not have been really, but they began on a wet and treacherous court that had not been covered during the hours of rain. The rain had ceased but seemed very likely to start again at any minute. The leaden sky pressed down close overhead like the dirty glass of the roofed-in train shed at the old Broad Street Station.

Johnson could cover the court well with his speed of foot, and he began the match by slicing the ball from one sideline to the other with astonishing accuracy. These were tricky shots and it seemed that they had Tilden worried. One could see that. Bill served wonderfully, winning his games easily, and then used Johnson's service games as practice sessions to master the chop himself on the heavy surface, from which the spin-invested ball would not rise very far. They went along thus winning alternate games until about 6–all, by which time Tilden had become the better chopper of the two in the poor conditions.

That I had pictured this to myself and others as a dull process for so many years amazes me. Even in retrospect it is fascinating to follow the process by which Tilden got on top. It seemed more than a little likely that Tilden would win the set, since he grew more confident, and so more bold, but just as Johnson saved his service game with great difficulty for 7–all, it began to rain again. And as 8–all was called, it came down in buckets.

Everybody scrambled from the stands and ran for cover in the clubhouse. I was drenched, and now that I have gone through the process of recalling the whole thing, I can even feel the soggy shirt on my back. On the following Monday they threw out the sixteen games of that moisture-laden set and started all over again. Conditions were ideal, sunshine and a dry court. Ideal for Tilden. Big Bill won 6–1, 6–3, 6–1, hitting out and smothering the chop-stroke artist under a stream of drives. The chopped ball now came off the floor higher and hung there long enough for Tilden to swing on it and rake Johnson's court, leaving him helpless.

I did not see any of this and the knowledge of how wrong, how greatly mistaken I was about my being there on this tennis occasion makes me wonder how often in the intervening years I have deceived myself and therefore others.

Not so faulty as this, I'm reasonably sure, is the memory of the first championship at Forest Hills after the stadium was completed in 1924. That one remains especially clear for me because I have returned to it so many times in retrospect. First of all, it is described in an old clipping preserved from the period as "the greatest field in the history of tennis and featured a series of upsets unparalleled in the game," and even if both these statements may now be questioned, they contained truth at the time.

All the best players of the world seem to have been there, and there was the added fact that the Frenchmen, who were to take charge of tennis before long, could be seen and studied at some length. It developed later that I did not take full advantage of the opportunity to know the men who already were being called the Musketeers, but I did see Borotra and Lacoste in several matches. Borotra was beaten in the third round by John Hennessy, according to the record book, and Lacoste by Johnston in the quarterfinal.

I remember the Johnston-Lacoste match well for it was a fine one which Johnston won because he could get to the net behind his booming forehand drives and volley decisively. In later years Lacoste spoke of this match as one which especially convinced him that, if he and his companions were to overtake Johnston and Tilden, he must perfect his own volley, which Johnston revealed to him on this occasion as not yet decisive enough.

These are not, however, the things I think of particularly when I recall the Forest Hills of 1924. More meaningful for me later was the day when Gerald Patterson and his opponent were moving from the clubhouse toward the court for their match in about the third round. Sam Hardy, with whom I was strolling, stopped them and asked the man, who seemed small beside the bulky Australian, to shake hands with me. This was Alain Gerbault, a Frenchman who was already known as the lone mariner because of his solitary voyages in a small sailboat.

Gerbault was not known to me, but I never forgot him afterward, and he was to figure dramatically in the Davis Cup story a few years later. The strange Frenchman was a good friend of Hardy's, and they kept up a warm correspondence until Gerbault's death somewhere in the South Pacific. I watched his match with Patterson and saw Gerbault beaten quickly, but I believe he was a better player than he appeared that day.

Even more important to me and my story, I think, were the last three matches of this championship of 1924. Johnston, having beaten Lacoste, was to play Patterson in one semifinal, and Tilden and Richards had come through in the other side of the draw. Three Americans and an Australian, with all the Frenchmen eliminated. I did not begin to see the handwriting that undoubtedly already was on the wall. But who among us did?

Early memories of tennis in New York and especially of Forest Hills seem to be associated an awful lot with awful heat. This 1924 tournament was held at the end of August, and by the day of the semifinals had run over into September. The papers said that New York had never experienced such September heat, or hardly ever. It was well in the nineties with the humidity high. Many people had brought parasols for protection in the uncovered seats, and it must have been hotter down in the court.

Johnston played Patterson first, and Little Bill won so quickly and so decisively, while Tilden was so near defeat by Richards, that hope rose that Johnston would become champion again next day. Little Bill was devastating. He needed little more than half an hour to win three sets from Patterson, forty minutes my notes said, and I could scarcely believe the further information contained in them that Johnston had taken sixteen games in succession, including two love sets. From 2-all in the first set the Australian never won another game.

Patterson had been twice Wimbledon champion, the second time only two years before, and he owned one of the hardest services ever seen. He was big and strong. Johnston was small and frail-looking. Probably Little Bill did not weigh more than 120 pounds that day, since he usually wound up the season under that figure. And yet, I think I never since have seen a first-class player so completely dominated, and the picture of Johnston's whiplash forehand hitting that big service for outright winners remains clear. I thought back to their five-set match in the 1919 tournament, when I had been almost overcome by fear that Patterson would beat Little Bill.

This demonstration provided still another early tennis lesson which was to be repeated and confirmed often in later years, that a big service, however hard it is hit, cannot prevail against the best players when not supported by all-round excellence. I do not suppose many have served a tennis ball as hard as Patterson's thunderbolts, and yet he had no more chance against Little Bill that day than an ordinary club player with no service at all.

The play of Johnston in this match was, I thought, the most wonderful thing I had seen in tennis. Perhaps it was, but I was to see even more wonderful things next day. By the time Tilden came out to play Richards, though, I had persuaded myself, out of love of Little Bill, that the evidence of the last four years was faulty. Tomorrow, I now was convinced, Johnston was going to be champion again after five years.

This was merely wishful thinking but it became conviction during the other semifinal. This one continued for more than two hours in broiling sun, and Tilden was more than once in jeopardy. I longed for Richards to win, partly because I had seen Little Bill handle Vinnie so easily now and then, and I felt that he could do it again in the final.

The details of this match have faded to dimness and cannot be called back by my scanty notes. I know that Tilden was saved from defeat because in spite of heat and fatigue he could summon the old cannonball serve to his aid in the crises of the fifth set. My notes do say that Richards, leading 2–1 in this fifth set, was within a point of winning Tilden's service for 3–1 but that he never got his racket on the service that came over the net. Also it is written down that Tilden scored outright with aces six times in his last two service games. I do not really remember these details, and I am indebted to Richards himself for some of them. I do remember Tilden pausing to pour ice water over his head as he passed the umpire's chair.

I also recall that many of Tilden's fierce drives hit the net or went out of court, giving me hope, and I can see Richards' astonishingly accurate deep volleys off some of Tilden's hardest-hit attempts to pass. I was greatly encouraged by Tilden's many driving errors, for he certainly would not hold Johnston if he did not drive accurately.

All these things made the final a seemingly happy occasion in prospect. After that first meeting of the two, Tilden had seemed to win a little more easily each year, or at least to be a little more certain of winning however long the match might go. But now in 1924, on the day of the match, the odds had suddenly been reduced to even money because of what had happened in the semifinals. What a surprise, what a shock, some of us received, and I am not sure Little Bill was not the most surprised and shocked of all.

Tilden dominated the play from the start and won the first set 6–1. In the fourth game he won Johnston's service at love with four drives, two from each side, that were absolutely unreturnable. These drives, two forehand, two backhand, were not completely out of reach. They traveled so rapidly, coming off the racket with the crack of small explosions, and dug in so near the base line that I do not believe the player ever lived who could have handled them. Then Tilden followed with three service aces and another unanswerable backhand in the fifth game. This was just the sort of devastating attack to which Johnston had treated Patterson, and under it Little Bill's game broke just as Patterson's had.

Johnston won the first game of the second set with his service, but Tilden led 3–2 by breaking through in the third game. Little Bill seemed to have got over the first shock now, though, and for the remainder of the second set the play was of a brilliance only these two in all the world at that time could produce. Johnston got back even at 4–all by capturing Tilden's service with a series of lightning drives that put Big Bill out of position in a corner and let Johnston end the game with a volley far out of reach. Little Bill, his confidence restored, was at his brilliant best and held his serve to go to 5–4.

Three cannonballs brought Tilden back to 5–all, and they went on to 7–all, Tilden winning his service games easily, Johnston with more effort, using the service as the first blow in a winning series of blows. But here Tilden broke through again, and the way he won Johnston's service is important. Little Bill was serving and driving as well as he had at any time through the level stretch from 4–all, but now he was forced to come forward to try the point-winning volley after driving a ball on which Tilden had put spin.

Such a ball had to be hit with special care to produce a proper forcing shot, and this gave the defender a fraction more time for the encircling reply. On three of the four points Tilden won in this fifteenth game Johnston had to make a second volley. Tilden twice passed him off the second and, on the final point of the game, off the third volley. The significant thing here is that Tilden's replies increased in speed with each reply. It was a method he often used from that time on to cheat the entrenched volleyer, making him move and stretch a little more for each drive. It was for this reason, I think, that Borotra, one of the finest of volleyers, never was able to beat Tilden on any outdoor court even after Big Bill had declined far below his best.

When Tilden had served out at 9–7 for a two-set-to-love lead, he had played entirely from the base line, leaving it only to take a short ball and then returning. With his service, the devastating speed of his drives from both forehand and backhand, he could command the court. When Johnston came to the net, Big Bill had ready the angled or straight passing shot or, if the way was blocked, he could offer the volleyer a spinning ball that made almost certain a defensive volley that could be picked up and fired back a second time. In these moments I realized for the first time what a marvelous variety of strokes Tilden had from which to choose in thwarting the attacker.

In the third set Johnston showed the results of continuous pressure. His driving, which had been wonderful too for a time, deteriorated. Still playing from the back of the court, Tilden raced through at 6–2, just beating a thunderstorm which arrived as they left the court but leaving me and thousands of others to take a soaking. I wondered at the time if Tilden had not shortened the last few games just so he could beat the storm. He certainly was able to win as he pleased by that time.

I thought a great deal about this match in the days and weeks that followed and probably for that reason can recall its details better than other significant ones about which I was to write later. It has remained vivid for me because it was a jolting tennis experience at about the time when I had youthful confidence in my ability to judge tennis values accurately. This match put the final stamp of greatness on Tilden's game for me only one day after I thought I had, after all, misjudged things again. I suppose that such experiences of wavering judgment and fluctuations of sympathy are necessary to bring one to a position where values can be considered calmly.

At any rate here was where I bade a sad farewell, so to speak, to Little Bill, whom I loved, and swung over completely to Big Bill, whom I did not yet esteem as I was to later, but whom I now recognized beyond possible doubt as the greatest, the king of them all. Between the final I had seen at Germantown in 1923, when Johnston, fresh from winning at Wimbledon, had lost to Tilden in three sets also, and the Forest Hills of 1924, all of Tilden's ground strokes had increased in speed to the point where they were superior to Johnston's to a degree fully measurable by the eye.

This was especially true of the backhand, which Tilden then hit as nearly "flat" as it is possible to strike a tennis ball, and about as far as Johnston's hurricane forehand. This statement Little Bill's admirers will not accept, but for me it is true, although I loved Little Bill as ardently as anyone could.

It is a considered statement. I was reluctant to admit it to myself at the time, but reflection on the evidence forced me to do so. Tilden's backhand drive seemed to me to travel at a pace equal to that of Johnston's famous forehand and to be more accurate. And Big Bill always had in reserve that marvelous sliced backhand with which it seemed he could hit any given spot in the court almost endlessly.

The acquisition of this flat backhand had changed everything. It was the shot that made it impossible to keep Tilden on the defensive for long or break down that defense. It was the one stroke that put him above the class of his contemporaries, and there is some ground for believing it the finest single stroke ever developed in tennis. Tilden was to remain invincible so long as this stroke remained as it was that day at Forest Hills. The subsequent chase of the Frenchmen after him could succeed only when it had become less certain, as Big Bill moved through the fourth decade of his life, when he was forced to fall back on the old slice.

Johnston's forehand was justly famous, also a superlative stroke in its way. Taken shoulder high on a rising ball, with a grip that made it almost a reverse smash, it came across the net carrying spin and with such pace that few players of the day could handle it successfully. The backhand, slightly undercut, steady and accurate and often struck quite hard, could be a weapon of offense, but was chiefly defensive. Like the backhand of Patterson and of certain other Californians of the time, Little Bill's was, strictly speaking, technically incorrect, being hit with the same face of the racket as the forehand, which limited the swing.

Johnston was a wonderful volleyer from about the middle of the court, a position which he was forced to take up because of his short stature, but he could kill from there and was extraordinarily hard to pass.

Tilden's backhand was absolutely free and flexible. He could give it as much speed as he wanted from almost any position in the court, swinging it across court or down the line with undiminished pace as he pleased. In an exchange of backhands with this stroke, Johnston was cruelly handicapped, as were all other players of the day.

It was the realization of this increase in controlled pace on both sides, I think, that broke Johnston's confidence, which had been high before the match. At this time Tilden had been absolute monarch of the courts for four years. During this period, until the semifinal against Richards, he had not been seriously challenged when he was healthy in any championship match anywhere in the world. It is possible that Tilden did not realize how fine a player Richards had become, although Vinnie had won the Olympic title in Paris only a few weeks earlier. He may have taken Richards too lightly, or he may have been conserving his ammunition for the final.

The great game we were to see next day did not appear until Richards had Tilden fighting for his life in the fifth set. Tilden came out of this crisis with the same fierce and accurate driving, a brief flash to carry him to where the service could win for him. And the service produced seven clean aces in Tilden's last three games at the end of a long, tiring match on a brutally hot day.

But if Tilden underestimated Richards he never underestimated Johnston. He knew what was there. In the final he went all out all the time, taking no chances with Little Bill's well-known ability to scale the heights on occasion. At the critical points, Tilden's concentration was absolute and visible. Even when within sight of the end and in virtually complete control, he did not relax. In the last three games of the match Johnston scored only three points.

In practically a lifetime of observing and writing of tennis of the top class, I have never seen such hitting and such astonishing control from both sides as Tilden displayed on this occasion, and I am prepared to believe that no such exhibition had previously been given on any court at any time anywhere in the world. Johnston, twice United States champion as well as Wimbledon champion, surely was one of the finest players the game has known. Little Bill, I think, must be placed on anybody's list of greatest players, and in 1924 he was in full possession of his wonderful powers.

Yet Tilden overwhelmed him without coming to the net at all, and I do not believe any player, past or present could have survived against such stuff. That was Tilden at his absolute peak, and I have not since seen the like of it.

I took this new picture of Tilden with me aboard the old *Rochambeau* of the French Line not long after the 1924 tournament ended, and it remained clear for so long a time I suffered from an illusion as to the continuance of Tilden's invincibility. Obscured by his masterful performance in this final, which continued to burn in memory with all the glowing heat and brilliance of the actual experience, the point at which something went from Tilden's game in the year or so just ahead came and passed unobserved.

I had also taken aboard with me a bag full of clippings from papers and magazines and a mass of notes with the idea of sorting out a lot of thoughts and impressions on the week-long voyage. Some of the clippings were interviews with Tilden, and they gave the impression that a champion may be the last man to consult about how he does it. There was among them, however, one particular piece about Tilden that fascinated me. It had been written by Stanley K. Wilson for the old *Sunday World*, and it pointed out a misconception the discovery of which sent me on an interesting line of thought about temperamental tennis players. It also led to modest remuneration for pieces inspired by his ideas, if not actually lifted from his article. I never knew Mr. Wilson in tennis or any other connection, but I offer him belated thanks for uncredited use of his thoughts, even though these may well be posthumous some forty-odd years later.

Most people who wrote or spoke about Tilden, the most controversial figure the game has known, said that he reached the heights by conquering his temperament. I also accepted this view until Wilson suggested that the only trouble with this explanation of Tilden's greatness was that it was not true. Tilden did no such thing, it was suggested. He did not conquer his temperament. On the contrary he used it and made it serve him in achieving his triumphs.

This view, though it upset conventional belief, was immensely interesting, but I had put it aside for future consideration. Now in the leisurely days at sea I took it up again, pursuing it to a point where it could reveal something previously obscured. I had been repelled though fascinated by Tilden's personality, but having had this now obvious fact revealed, he had become an object for closer observation and study. In the light of what I had seen and was to see later, I believe the observation to have been correct, and I note that Tilden remained to the end of his long career just as mercurial, irascible, and easily upset and sent into rages as he had been in the years of his rise to world supremacy.

He seemed to have learned early that when he tried to curb his temperament, to rein it in, he lost matches; that when he gave it unleashed play, he won. The time required to learn and apply this lesson may account for the fact that Tilden did not reach the top until after his twenty-seventh birthday. Wilson said that "one must play around with the word genius to estimate justly this wizard of the courts," and there is justification for the feeling that for Tilden, temperamental release and free flow did amount to a special genius.

"The grand, almost regal manner with which Tilden is wont to destroy his opponents," Wilson wrote, "the insouciance with which in September he reverses a July setback; the overwhelming drama and color his personality and methods infuse into his game, make him quite the most magnificent champion of tennis history."

The many times Tilden pulled out a match after being within a point or so of defeat were cited to support this rather extravagant appraisal, and it was contended that "this unconscionable relish of his for the prolonged battle and deferred rush to victory, is not volitional but belongs to the temperament and the peculiar genius of the man."

Tilden, in short, became the greatest of champions because he could turn creative artistry into unparalleled performance. His game was technically and tactically of a supremely high order, but the real reason for his greatness palpably lay outside technique and tactics. Only one other player who came under my observation over a period of years exemplified in this way the supreme value of unharnessed temperament. That was Williams, but what a difference! McLoughlin, I think, may have been very like Tilden in this one respect of whipping up rather than restraining temperament, knowing well, as Big Bill was to discover, the power of untethered exuberance. But McLoughlin was a subject of worship rather than study, and his one great moment, when he blew Brookes off the field with torrid blasts of temperament, was missed for what it really was.

They tell of a match in the National Championships at Newport in which Wallace Johnson, with crafty precision, chopped and sliced McLoughlin to shreds for two sets and part of a third. The champion staggered about the court vainly trying to dig up Johnson's wicked shots and, with the score 2–6, 2–6, 2–4 against him, faced almost certain defeat. At this crisis he had nothing but temperament to call upon, so in the desperate situation he let it blaze, throwing caution overboard. He pulled out the match.

His record shows McLoughlin's kinship with Tilden, but his inspired moments were not united with adequate technical ability, and so he could not produce consistent success. On the other hand, Williams at his best could stand, technically speaking, with any man who ever played the game, and he too owed his greatest moments to the free release of temperament. Where he differed from Tilden, and no doubt from McLoughlin also, was that he waited for the spirit to move him.

When the spirit was lazy, Williams appeared nonchalant, not seeming to care particularly, a quality that often brought a delightful feeling of joy into his play. And then suddenly it seemed that the incomparable and easy control could come to invest him with invincibility. In these moments Williams was greater than any other, and those who were present saw tennis that touched heights to which it has not again been taken. If the spirit did not descend readily, however, Williams appeared to accept even defeat fatalistically, without concern, enjoying the game while waiting for the next time.

Tilden could never accept defeat. If on occasion he lacked the natural spark to ignite his game, he crowded on the temperament. He could tap a vein of something like divine frenzy by pulling out all the stops in that often deplorable but priceless temperament. Tilden could play superlative tennis while boiling with anger against an opponent.

Billy Johnston, a model of style, would sacrifice comfort, looks, and dignity to win a crucial point if it happened to mean victory or defeat. Richards also had this ability to scramble, but Williams was not willing to scramble to force the spirit to descend. For this reason he often touched but failed to maintain the heights to which his irresistible game could have carried him.

CHAPTER SEVEN

I AM delighted, enchanted, amazed, and interested and I think I never saw anything more beautiful and gay than Paris."

So Queen Victoria wrote home during her state visit to Napoleon III in 1850. So might Victoria's great-great-granddaughter have written on her own state visit more than a hundred years later, and so might Victoria's son and great-grandson, the two Edwards, for both were enamored of Paris. And so might and did all who went in the 1920s.

The Jet Age, in which you can encounter nightly in Toots Shor's restaurant in New York someone who has lunched in London, has shrunk the world to tiny proportions, but it still was a large place in 1924 and going to Paris was still an adventure. A lot of nonsense has been written about Paris in the twenties, when that formless con-glomeration of nationalities called the Lost Generation made the cafés of Montparnasse hideous with their noisy talk and so many splendid liberties now thought to be old-fashioned were being taken with the English language. It was nevertheless an exciting time.

Efforts are still made to evoke its flavor. Paris, the hub of intellec-tual culture and all that sort of thing; Hemingway meeting with Gide, Valéry, Joyce, and Gertrude Stein; the little magazines; Pi-casso painting portraits with blocks of wood for heads as a just com-mentary on the times; Fitzgerald writing his own tragedy and living it; the Latin Quarter, Boul' Mich' and the Atelier; cognac and Pernod for the cultivation of the higher conversation; the breath of summer nights that are past, the scent of flowers that are dust.

It leaves one wistful and a little sad until one recalls that there were more than eight thousand cafés in Paris and only three or four of them at the confluence of the Boulevards Montparnasse and Ras-pail. It is easy to forget how little notice was taken of the noisy Left Bank activity, how little aware of it were French men and women, and how most of us alive and young at the time never knew at all that we were living in the Fabulous 1920s.

France was still a peasant society ruled from the countryside. The new world was stirring, but the old social forces were still alive as both France and England clung for a while to the lost cause of Empire. The French had many things to worry about and not many to make them happy, but one thing that would bring them joy for a time was slowly developing. Just these very mid-years of peace were to be the setting for perhaps the most exciting period of tennis history, and France's hour of glory lay only a little way ahead.

A new star of the first magnitude was rising in the tennis heavens, and it would soon burst into supercelestial brilliance. The adventure that going to Europe still was, turned out to be, partly at least, a tennis adventure to match the times. The appearance of the so-called Musketeers of France on the international scene as a very young and very talented, but as yet undeveloped, group of players coincided almost exactly with the rise of Tilden as world champion and of the United States to world supremacy in Davis Cup play.

On a day when the sixteen-year-old René Lacoste had his first revealing glimpse of Tilden at St. Cloud in the 1921 World Hard Court Championships, Henri Cochet was still six months short of his twentieth birthday and a year short of winning his first important title, the same one that Tilden won the day Lacoste was there. Just a year later, excitement about the future of French tennis began to rise when Lacoste, now barely seventeen, defeatd the veteran Herbert Roper-Barrett, one of England's finest and most famous players, in the Belgian Championships at Brussels.

Borotra was twenty-three and had just about completed the transfer of those highly individual strokes of his from his native Basque game of pelota to the tennis court. From this point the collective skill of these three ripened rapidly, and the chase across the 1920s after Tilden and Johnston took on the elements of a crusade.

Probably there never has been in international sport so determined a drive, pursued with such zeal through many setbacks and disappointments, as these young Frenchmen waged with patriotic fervor and spirit. Very likely there never has been a national sports group with such devotion to the common purpose, nor teammates presenting such striking contrasts in background, personality, and methods.

Borotra was talented in many directions, a graduate engineer already beginning to be highly successful in business; clever linguist, of a calculating mind but a brilliant dissembler; a master at masking his intentions both on the court and off. Borotra's temperament was reflected in his game, for he was an extremely clever opportunist, playing by ear, grasping every chance instantly, questionable or not, using the crowd to his purpose.

Cochet, of no profound cultural background, more like a street gamin who had learned to take care of himself in any situation, had the touch of genius. Simple and natural but lazy of mind, and unwilling to work hard to achieve his ends, he nonetheless was extremely confident and capable of periods of brilliance matched by very few who have played this game. This little man had a truly astonishing aptitude for the game and, it seemed at times, the luck of the devil.

Cochet gave the impression of a charmingly naughty child who refused to study his lessons, or even to attend school at all at times, but who could confound his professors by outdoing them when he wanted to. Henri's charm of manner was absolutely genuine and untutored, as opposed to Borotra's calculated pleasantries.

Lacoste was as different from both as could well be. Never robust, as were these other natural athletes, he had to work hard for everything he achieved on a tennis court. He came from a cultured and wealthy home where his burning desire to become a tennis champion was indulged. He was sent to England as a child to learn both the language and the game. No champion ever worked harder. René seemed to be of the most profoundly melancholy temperament, but he was profound, too, in his understanding and his intelligence. He never played by ear, for his preparation had been complete, and he could carry out a well-conceived campaign to its successful concluson, or adjust quickly to new situations.

Jacques Brugnon was the oldest of the Musketeers, the least conspicuous and the least ambitious. He was, in fact, lacking in ambition altogether, it seemed at times; but he was one of the finest doubles players ever seen, and his presence on the team made certain that France could have at least three first-class combinations, giving a wide choice of selection. Brugnon was so retiring it was hard to think of him as a Frenchman at all, but he was an important member of the group.

Lacoste, the youngest member, seemed dull beside Borotra's flashing personality, and his method appeared dull beside Cochet's brilliance. But René was the leader of the group, the one whose sound judgment directed the campaign, and in the end he ranks above the other two as a player as well. His purpose and theirs was to bring the Davis Cup, symbol of supremacy in at least one thing, to France. And theirs was a crusade in which all France seemed to take part until its successful conclusion re-established, for a brief span of years, some of the national self-respect that had begun to slip away during the uneasy armistice between the wars.

By the time the French Championships of 1925 came around, no telescope was needed to pick out this rising tennis threat. The comparison with the Musketeers of Dumas fils although contrived, was quite a natural thing and, one might say, inevitable. As early as this summer of 1925, before France had yet got near to the Challenge Round, the one-for-all-and-all-for-France motif was present, almost audible and visible. Frenchmen everywhere were looking to these young men to recapture national honor, and Borotra, Lacoste, Cochet, and Brugnon already were conscious of the role they were expected to play.

In America the champion of champions came to the throne in the face of hostility which took the form of abuse, insults, and misunderstanding from public, press, and officials. It was thought that Tilden was merely "showing off" most of the time. In France the rise to tennis power was accompanied by loyal support from press and public, to whom the Mousquetaires were great men even when they were not winning.

Borotra had won the Wimbledon title in 1924, defeating Richards on the way, and Lacoste had beaten Dick Williams. That was the first step, and there were to be no finalists other than Frenchmen at Wimbledon for the next five years. On the perfect lawns of the All-England Club, which offered the finest playing surfaces in the world, the Frenchmen refined their art, but the winning of individual titles, however satisfying personally, was not their principal goal.

That was the winning of the Cup, and they considered Tilden, who had last been at Wimbledon in 1921, their main enemy and their principal target. Tilden did not visit Europe at all from 1921 to 1927, and if he would not come to them, then they would seek him out at home, challenge him, and try to find out how he could be beaten. They recognized very early that so long as Tilden remained unbeaten, France would remain a secondary tennis nation. In 1925 they still were working to improve and still learning. The real invasion would begin the following year.

The 1925 tournament at St. Cloud was made worthwhile also by the opportunity to see Lenglen again. I had got a good look at her for the first time since Forest Hills on the Riviera a few months earlier while resting up from too long a contemplation of Romanesque architecture. I had even spoken a few words with her, to which she responded in the manner of queen to a subject, which was fairly close to our relationship at that.

I had stopped off to see the South of France Championships at the Nice Tennis Club, which was then in the center of town at the Place Mozart. Suzanne played and won there every winter. Her father, Charles Lenglen, had some sort of connection with the club as secretary or manager, and it was Riviera headquarters for Suzanne. She practiced there every day, and always with men players.

I was brought into the presence and presented by Charley Aeschliman, with whom Suzanne also won the mixed doubles that year. Aeschliman was Swiss, the husband of Leslie Bancroft, a charming left-handed American girl who had been ranked number two in the United States in 1922, even above Helen Wills, who was not yet seventeen then. Suzanne was waiting to play her final round match against Elizabeth Ryan when I had my little visit with her. I had watched carefully every stroke of four earlier matches she had played in the tournament and, fascinated by her astonishing accuracy, had kept note of her outs and nets. Seeking to impress the "Queen" with my close attention to her play, I asked if she realized she had hit the net only four times in four matches. Suzanne looked at me with much condescension and replied, as though speaking to a small child, "But, of course, my little one. Once with Mademoiselle Bouman in the first round, twice with Mrs. Satterthwaite on Wednesday, and once with Mademoiselle Vlasto yesterday. I have been very careless this week, *n'est-ce pas?*"

What impressed me most about this reply was not that she missed so little but that she knew, at the end of a tournament, exactly when and where she had missed. I took it for granted she also had made note of all the balls she had driven beyond the lines during the week, and it was not until much later, when Suzanne had been a professional for ten years or so and was conducting a tennis school in Paris, that I learned different.

She said then, when the incident which she had naturally not remembered was recalled, that of course she hadn't kept track of all her errors, only the net, the reason being that "clear the net" had been drummed into her as a child by her father, and hitting it had been made to seem almost a crime. That, she said, was proper, since to hit the net was silly. The moment you did that the point was presented to your opponent with no effort on his part, whereas if you hit the ball too far there still might be a chance you could win the point. The ball might be hit by your opponent before going out, the wind might check it, or a sleepy lineman might make a mistake in your favor. None of these things could happen if you put the ball into the net. I seem to remember Suzanne's saying that Mary Browne, three times U. S. Champion, with whom she toured as a professional, was the only other woman player who really understood this. But then, of course, she added, Mary was always, perforce, hitting the net when she played Suzanne.

"I never did hit the net," she said, adding what was almost the exact truth: "Nobody could hurry me enough for that. Well, except Helen Wills a little, *un tout petit peu.*"

This digression for a short stop off along the Riviera that winter also reminds me that it was there, though not in the same tournament, that I first saw Lili de Alvarez, the Spanish girl, and was completely captivated. It was at a tournament called the Championships of the Côte d'Azur, and the señorita won the singles. I do not remember any of her opponents because I paid no attention to them. They were just foils, and I have never since been so surprised and delighted as at the dashing way this girl played tennis. She was to take part later in the finest tennis match I have ever seen played by two women in all the years I have watched, her opponent being Helen Wills; and on the whole, the dashing señorita has provided me with as much tennis pleasure as any other girl, although she did not win any big titles.

The French National Championships had not yet become, in 1925, one of the big four along with Wimbledon, Forest Hills, and Australia, but they were somewhat more important than previously. When the International Federation of Tennis Associations was formed in

Paris in 1912, it authorized World Hard Court and World Grass Court Championships and awarded them to Paris and Wimbledon. These had been held, except for the war years, until they were abandoned in 1923.

Both Tilden and Johnston had won these grandiose titles, but for two years now the French Championships had been strictly national, or closed tournaments restricted to French players. In 1925 they were opened again to players of whatever nationality and there were many foreigners at St. Cloud.

I found the ground of the Stade Français, in what was called the Parc de la Faisanderie, beside the forest across the Seine from the Bois de Boulogne, about as the Captain had described them to me back on the café terrace in Cannes six years earlier. I thought often of my old friend on that first day, half expecting to encounter him here or there about the place and hoping I might.

There was an air of informality, an atmosphere almost of improvisation about the tournament that I was to learn later was typical of French tennis. The wooden stands around the center court, expanded somewhat this year in anticipation of bigger things to come, were roofless and not very sturdily constructed. They seemed cramped when full, but around the other courts there was ample room for movement, and the grounds were spacious in a delightful setting of many acres of parkland.

From the main court you walked several hundred yards through glades to reach the clubhouse, or pavilion, as the English call such buildings, where refreshments were to be had. The English among the spectators and players could take their tea at tables under the trees, complaining rather loudly about the quality of the brew.

It is quite impossible for the British, a well-disposed race normally, to understand how any nation could be so barbarous and ungodly as to suppose that tea could be made by dousing a muslin bag into tepid water. Like the comment, one thought, of the lady after a disappointing survey of the pyramids. "The shape," she said severely, "is very un-English."

This little bag holding a pinch of powdered leaves could be had in France at most establishments catering to British and American trade, and especially those providing ingredients for "le five o'clock," meaning afternoon tea. It was called *un teaball de thé*, a designation comparable to *un biftek de porc* and the label on a can of powdered cinnamon, which described the contents as *le cinnamon toast,* pronounced *seena-mun tust.*

All this made St. Cloud possibly the world's quaintest and pleasantest tennis ground and there are no doubt many of us old-timers who think it more attractive than it really was, now that we have not seen it for so many years and never will again. Its courts were rock-like baked sand of a color somewhere between yellow and brown, and they gave off a strong glare in the sun.

There were not really many matches that I recall from this tournament, but it was important to me for two things other than those mentioned. I was able to see, and for the only time I can remember, André Gobert, who had been France's finest player before the appearance of the Musketeers and was thought by many to have been the finest player ever on an indoor board surface. Gobert certainly was well past his best days, but he still had flashes of the decisive volley, the service of magnificent length and the fine cross drives that had made him a terror before the war. I was fortunate to see some of these strokes in a long match in which Gobert defeated Dr. P. D. B. Spence, one of South Africa's leading players.

Of the other players I saw on that first visit to St. Cloud, I was most interested in Cochet because I had seen less of him, and I must say the little Lyonese was a disappointment. He played listlessly against Jean Washer and was beaten rather easily, so that I did not at all properly appraise or appreciate his genius for the game. Cochet was twenty-four then and already fully developed, but the defeat by a man who was quickly and soundly beaten by Borotra next day left me underestimating him badly. Lacoste was entirely satisfactory in defeating Borotra in the final, however, and I had a new respect for both. Lenglen moved majestically and calmly through the tournament. In the semifinal she defeated Evelyn Colyer, a healthy, acrobatic English girl with a good serve, good volley, a chopped forehand, and no backhand at all other than a push with nothing on the ball. For the final with Kitty McKane a crowd of five thousand tried to get into the center court stands built for a thousand fewer. Suzanne won, losing only a game or two, making her subjects once more delirious with joy. It still was Lenglen who drew the crowds. All of France was stirring to the Davis Cup possibilities of the future, but the time was not yet.

The Davis Cup tie between France and Italy was played in Paris only a week or so after St. Cloud, and it was poorly attended. I was glad of still another opportunity to study the Musketeers, but I was further misled by the exclusion of Cochet from the team. France won all five matches, with Lacoste and Borotra playing the first two singles, and then a player obviously inferior to Cochet, Paul Feret, was substituted for Lacoste on the third day. I am afraid I let this influence me a little too much with regard to downgrading Cochet, who was just about ready to embark on some of his most sensational exploits.

CHAPTER EIGHT

T HE golden sun of the Era of Wonderful Nonsense was somewhat beyond the meridian at the beginning of 1926, but the art of ballyhoo was at the peak. In sports, as in other areas of life, sensational occurrences took place more or less year long, rising to a summit with the defeat of Jack Dempsey by Gene Tunney in another Battle of the Century in September. In tennis the year also was on the flamboyant side, beginning in February, when the Musketeers put the handwriting plainly on the wall (for all to ignore) by sweeping the U. S. National Indoor Championships at the Seventh Regiment Armory in New York. With Tilden and Richards in the field, Lacoste and Borotra reached the final, and Lacoste became champion of the United States.

I was not in New York for the indoor tournament but the tennis parade began for me even earlier, and for France, three thousand miles from the Armory. This was the meeting of two girls, one French, the other American, in an otherwise unimportant tournament on the French Riviera. Only a girls' tennis match, but it was blown up into a titanic struggle such as the world had never seen before. This was to be the only meeting of those transatlantic rivals, Suzanne Lenglen and Helen Wills, and it came on February 16 in the final round of an ordinary resort tournament at the small Carlton Club in Cannes, of which I had such pleasant memories.

By the time it came off it was of worldwide interest, and never again in the history of sport was such an event allowed to go under such ridiculous and fantastic conditions. It probably could have filled Yankee Stadium the way it was built up, but it was played at a not very attractive club of six or so courts, with almost no facilities for dressing and with stands still being hurriedly knocked together when the crowds stormed the place the day of the match.

The thing had been growing for three years or more, ever since the California schoolgirl had begun to demonstrate that she was the best our country ever produced and might be the very best in the world. The only way to find out about that was for her to meet the world champion, and people everywhere, even those who never attended tennis tournaments, were looking forward to that meeting. Miss Wills also seemed to want it, and it was she who came seeking it.

On her first trip to Wimbledon in 1924, Helen would have encountered Suzanne had not the French girl been forced to retire from the tournament after being near collapse at the end of a match with Elizabeth Ryan. The winter before, Suzanne had contracted a slight first touch of hepatitis, the disease of which she died in 1938. Helen went to the final, where she was beaten by Kitty McKane, and since she did not go to Europe at all in 1925, this winter of 1926 was the earliest time a meeting with Suzanne was possible.

So, immediately it was announced from California early in January that Helen, accompanied by her mother, would soon leave for France "to study and play a little tennis," the loud bazoo began to sound. From that moment on, volumes of nonsense were written, and some of the best brains of the writing profession were applied to the matter. The minute details of the past lives of the two young women were published, and Miss Wills, who was barely twenty, was pictured as something of a girlish knight going out to slay the dragon.

It is a little hard to credit, but that was only one of many minor events of that third decade of the century that was blown up to unlikely proportions. It could hardly have occurred, though, in just the same way anywhere else than exactly where it did. The revival of the Riviera as a playground, both actual and in the imagination, had been rapid after the war, and tennis generally experienced a remarkably swift growth in France following the Armistice. Already popularized by Gobert and others, the game was now looked upon as a major international sport at which Frenchmen could excel.

In the early 1920s clubs were springing up in every sizable community, and soon the yellow-red courts stretched completely around the coast of France from Menton, on the Italian border, to Boulogne. the far Channel port. Every resort along the way, Le Touquet, Deauville, Biarritz, and the others, scheduled tournaments during their "seasons" and offered inducements to the international name players to come.

The young boys and girls the Captain had mentioned as taking up the game before the war had grown up, and among them were the Musketeers themselves. The enthusiasm Lenglen had generated and the boost she had given to the French collective ego can hardly be calculated, but it was enormous. This feeling was all tied up with the feeling of France about the war debts owed the United States and with a growing anti-American attitude everywhere. The Uncle Shylock image, fostered by politicians and the press, had grown ever larger as the French currency declined. To overcome an American, even if only in a game of tennis, became important to the individual Frenchman, who blamed Washington for everything, especially the disappearance of his life's savings.

By mid-decade the delightful winter-season life along the pleasure stations of the Côte d'Azur had reached the high plateau on which it would remain for a few more pre-Depression years. There had been a great influx of wealthy North American, English, and South American visitors; and refugees from the Russian Revolution who had come through that upheaval with quantities of gold were spending almost as liberally as the grand dukes of old. Every nationality and every type was present—crooks, pimps, great ladies, and prostitutes by the hundreds, famous persons from stage and Hollywood, titled gentlemen from every European country where titles remained intact.

In this world Suzanne Lenglen ruled as the champion of champions, the queen of queens. Never beaten in her own country, she was a truly national figure, and a visit to the Riviera without seeing Suzanne play was like a visit to Rome without seeing St. Peter's. Every club between Cannes and Monte Carlo competed for her favors, and every function felt it had scored a triumph if Suzanne appeared. Her mere presence made any affair a success. For six years she had reigned unchallenged anywhere, but especially along the Azure Coast from December to March. She played tennis where she pleased, bestowing her favors where she could be induced in one way or another to bestow them, and very often she danced away the night at some brilliant social gathering, where she outshone all the ladies present, of whatever rank or stature.

This short glittering coastline belonged to Suzanne in a certain sense, and the plan of the young girl from California to come and play the tournaments was looked upon as an "invasion" of Suzanne's territory. Mademoiselle Lenglen was reported to have said she thought it "cheeky," although I do not know what the French word for cheeky might be.

Whatever she may have thought about Miss Wills personally, Suzanne certainly did resent the shift of attention from herself to Helen as soon as the American girl arrived in Cannes toward the end of January. For a while then, Miss Wills was the main show, and Lenglen never before had played any but the star's role.

And what a contrast they presented! Between them lay a gap far larger than the distance between the homeland of Miss Wills on the shores of the Pacific and Suzanne's sunny Mediterranean playground. Lenglen, a Latin and an actress to her fingertips, was slender, almost thin, with nothing about her figure suggesting the athlete, but supple, marvelously graceful, and full of accompanying acrobatics calculated to bring cheers from the crowd. An artist with a true sense of the dramatic.

She was far from beautiful. In fact, her face was homely in repose, with a long crooked nose, irregular teeth, sallow complexion, and eyes that were so neutral that their color could hardly be determined. It was a face on which hardly anything was right. And yet, in a drawing room, this homely girl could dominate everything, taking the attention away from dozens of women far prettier or even notorious for one reason or another. She could, in an extraordinary way, make quite fashionable women appear just a little dull, if not actually dowdy, beside her. For an ugly girl she had more charm and vivacity than a hundred pretty girls you might meet. And Suzanne had suitors. Plenty of them.

Miss Wills, on the other hand, presented a picture of a typical young American girl, sturdy, well built, and healthy-looking, with a strong suggestion of girlish simplicity. The picture of her as some sort of avenger was wholly false. The affair with Molla at Forest Hills was dragged up, and it was said that Suzanne had "cheated" an American girl of a proper victory, forgetting that Molla really was a Norwegian girl.

Miss Wills had done nothing more than announce from her home in Berkeley that she would go to France, when immediately the nonsense began to appear in the papers; and a meeting, or series of meetings, with Lenglen was taken for granted, although even one match was not certain for quite a while. It is amusing, almost embarrassing, to read some of the old clippings, especially from the more popular

London papers. Such experts on tennis as Blasco-Ibáñez, the popular Spanish novelist, were hired to comment beforehand and to "cover" the matches, and it was reported that some of them were receiving "fabulous" compensation.

The commotion in the press, already great, increased as Miss Wills approached the Continent, and when she arrived in Paris she was met by a delegation of the French Association and an army of newspapermen and photographers. Then a real storm broke over the Riviera when she put up with her mother at the Hotel Gallia in Cannes, from which she was to motor back and forth to the tournaments she played. Later, they would move to the more fashionable Carlton, and the fact that they were given the suite recently occupied by Aristide Briand during the Cannes Conference is indicative of their importance. Of course, the Willses had not known the gradations in fashionableness among Riviera hotels before arriving.

There now began a chase after news of Miss Wills by dozens of reporters, and she made efforts to keep all but those representing the International News Service from getting any. Miss Wills had signed a contract to provide this agency with exclusive articles, and she tried conscientiously to live up to the "exclusive" part of it.

My own arrival from Paris was practically simultaneous with that of Miss Wills's entourage, but since I had to find a place to stay I had to neglect her for a day. I could not afford to put up at any of the big hotels along the Croisette where the sports and political reporters for the big London papers now assigned to the tennis story were staying. What I needed was a small, cheap, and inelegant hotel, of which fortunately there were many hidden away up and down the coast, although at this moment there were not many vacant rooms anywhere. I found one, though, at the Jeanne d'Arc on the Avenue de la Palmeraie, which really was in the village of Golfe Jean, a few miles from the center of Cannes on the way to Nice. It had about a dozen rooms and a large garden where dinner was served under the trees in good weather.

Cannes was overrun with reporters by now, and the whole Riviera focused its attention on tennis. The coming match and its possibilities were the chief, sometimes the only, topic of conversation everywhere, and people who had heretofore taken little or no interest in the game now discussed it with great authority. All the big press associations had one or two reporters on the job, and there were men from papers in Scandinavia and South America as well as from all over the continent of Europe.

I was pretty nervous about my ability to get hold of the information I needed. There was no other piece of news running to compare with this story, and the competition for something original to write was great. Many of these men knew little of tennis but were competent rough-and-tumble reporters, and anyhow tennis played little part in the prematch reporting. Some of those who hadn't information made it up, but I was not well equipped for that.

There was not any special newspaper gathering place in Cannes where one could get acquainted and exchange ideas if not information. Some of these reporters assigned temporarily to the great event later became friends of mine, but then I hardly knew any of them. For this reason I had then and still have a special feeling about the fact that John Tunis, who had begun to make it big as a magazine writer and tennis reporter, took kindly notice of me. He had a wide acquaintance along the Riviera and had played doubles in some of the tournaments with some pretty good partners. So he knew more about tennis than the big shots and could, for that matter, write rings around most of them on practically any subject. I was flattered when Tunis treated me as an equal, as practically no one else did during these confusing weeks.

Even after Helen began to play in tournaments there still was no assurance that she and Suzanne would meet on the court. While Helen dodged reporters, Suzanne seemed to be dodging Helen. Lenglen had been playing the tournaments for a month or so, mostly in doubles and mixed doubles, but with the American girl actually on the scene she confined her activity to practicing by day and dancing by night at the Ambassadeurs. She was the one who had everything to lose and she would choose the conditions that suited her. It appeared that she was merely keeping the thing alive and suspenseful so that the Riviera could reap the full benefit. She had no intention of avoiding the challenge, and in plenty of time to get full value from the announcement she sent in her entry for the Carlton tournament.

Meanwhile, Miss Wills, very busy indeed, had captured the Riviera set by the refreshing simplicity and charm of her manner. "*Une petite fille de province*," the *Éclairer de Nice*, the South of France's biggest paper, called her, and she certainly did give an impression of a simple, rather pretty girl from the suburbs. She had appointments almost daily with Paris dress houses eager to clothe her, and she drove nearly every day to a tournament somewhere, adjusting quickly to the new playing conditions.

After playing at the Gallia tournament at her own hotel, she played the Métropole, also in Cannes, and then, the week before Carlton, she motored to Nice for her matches in the South of France Championships. This was at Lenglen's own home club, and by now everyone, including Suzanne, had seen that here was a real menace. Interest was intense.

Miss Wills's agreement with the International News Service was that she would not pose for cameramen or give interviews to representatives of other services or newspapers, and from the moment she arrived she was engaged in an incessant battle to outwit those excluded from her favor. She employed, or at any rate she had in her service, a staff of young American volunteers whose duty it was to see that the coast was clear of nuisances before she would come out of hiding. We called these young men the Wills Boy Scout Troop.

They were not altogether successful, for we did get through to her, and as a result Miss Wills was forever stalling the rest of us in the interests of her employer. Having accepted pay from INS Miss Wills appeared to feel she must not even say hello to other reporters, and this attitude, during a time when whatever she said or did, even what she ate and what time she went to bed and got up, was most important news, developed in me a slight feeling of resentment against Miss Wills that I retained to a certain extent throughout her tennis career.

I came out of these small personal encounters with tiny scars which, I am afraid, caused me to avoid further contact during the next dozen years or so when Miss Wills, in her turn, became the great lady of the courts and I a faithful chronicler of her triumphs. I realized well enough later that Miss Wills's rudeness was not part of her nature at all but only part of the whole crazy affair, but I could never quite wipe it out of my mind.

By the time the Nice tournament began we all knew that the Carlton would be the big one, so we pressed forward, storming the ramparts of the Gallia, so to speak. Now Miss Wills's new clothes were about ready, so she took a day off from the tournament and we had the experience of standing around outside the Cannes branch of a famous Paris couturier while Helen had her final fittings. She had got us there before the place opened for the day, but our long wait was rewarded when she finally appeared.

We had all been giving the Little Miss Poker Face theme a pretty good workout, because even when Miss Wills must have been quite nervous she presented a calm unruffled front. This name had been given her by Arthur Guiterman, a poet who wrote some light verse about her soon after she became champion, and everybody had picked it up, not knowing or caring where it came from.

It was a different girl who came out of the dress shop. This was an eager schoolgirl in a new frock, and for the first time we saw that Miss Wills was really beautiful. I don't think any of us had realized it before. We didn't see much of the schoolgirl after that, but from time to time we saw some of the new creations, which were especially designed to accentuate Miss Wills's fine features. They were said to have cost a total of 25,000 francs, and the one I remember best was a rose coat trimmed in fur. Miss Wills looked very fetching in it, I must say. The news accounts from the Riviera now began to refer to Miss Wills as statuesque, beautiful in the mold of a statue in the classic style.

I do not remember much about the early rounds of the Carlton tournament. In fact, nothing. I remember the mounting excitement as day by day the ladies came closer together and that the atmosphere of a heavyweight championship fight had somehow developed around this amateur tennis match between two nice girls. Only a few of the biggest fights have generated this kind of on-the-scene tension and turmoil.

Afterward, I learned a lot more about the Carlton Club and the conduct of the tournament than I knew that day. The club was run by two Irish professionals, Albert and Edmund Burke, sons of old Tom Burke, who had moved to the Riviera many years before and may have been the first tennis professional in France. Tom, junior, a younger brother who was still at the club after World War II, was born in Cannes. I never did know Tom, but during the preliminaries I renewed a slight acquaintance with Albert and later got to know him very well. We spoke often of this day, and some of the things I now relate come from later conversations.

It would have been hard to choose a more unlikely ground for an event of such worldwide interest. The six courts of the club were squeezed into a small plot on a narrow, dirty street behind the Carlton Hotel a few hundred yards back from the Croisette, and a narrow alley ran down one side. Normally there was a "center" court with small wooden stands along one side with seats for perhaps a thousand or so. Behind this was a one-story building, a garage, I think. Outside the grounds on the other side was a small factory of some sort from which came the wasplike buzz of machinery. Beyond and to one side of this were two or three small villas with orange tiles for roofs and with eucalyptus trees in front. High above were the towers of the Carlton Hotel.

Such arrangements as were found here were perfectly adequate at most times and were, in fact, more commodious than at most clubs west of Monte Carlo. The Riviera tournaments usually drew a few hundred spectators, but a couple of thousand when Lenglen played. Some clubs had no stands at all, only benches and chairs, and nearly all the tournaments were played at hotels with no real tennis club in operation. On special occasions collapsible circus seats were used.

The Burkes had plenty of warning but were astonished like all the rest of us when people began clamoring to force into their hands three hundred francs each for seats. This was an enormous price for a Frenchman, with the franc at about twenty-five to the dollar. The promoters, eager to reap all the grain that was possible, decided to enlarge the stands and add other seats, but they decided very late. The sound of carpenters' hammers could be heard almost up to the start of the famous match.

It was customary on the Riviera to schedule important matches early in the afternoon so as to be done with play before the sun was low, when a chill came quickly into the Mediterranean air. This one, however, was set for eleven o'clock in the morning. Many wondered at the odd time, but those of us who had played on the Carlton courts suspected why. The six courts were so badly laid out with regard to the sun that just before and just after midday was the only time when the center court was certain to be just right from both ends, although, of course, it was playable in the afternoon.

Anticipating some difficulty about press accommodations and being generally quite nervous about the whole thing, I was up early and at the club before nine o'clock. Already there was a long line waiting for the gates to open. The line stretched four or five abreast down the street beside the club toward the Croisette. I watched it grow until it reached that elegant promenade and was turned by policemen to extend under the palm trees alongside. They said the first people had appeared soon after dawn, and a quick estimate at nine-thirty indicated that already there were more in this line than could possibly get inside if the advance sale announced by Albert Burke was accurate. The crowd was orderly for a long time, but the French have not the Englishman's willingness to wait long and placidly in line. There were to be mob scenes in the narrow way where the club had the bad luck to have placed the main gate to the grounds, and there were premonitions of it when I decided a little before ten that I'd better try to get inside myself while I could.

I could not get near the gate I was supposed to enter. The crowd seeking to buy tickets had abandoned its orderly line and was milling about near the gate and shouting imprecations at the ticket sellers. There seemed to be no ticket booths at all and officials were trying to let in ticket holders at the same time as they sold tickets. With many others who had tickets in hand I was being pushed about and could get nowhere near the gate. Several photographers and others with press passes were crowded against a wall near me opposite the gate, and we all decided to work our way around to the other side of the club, where there was supposed to be a clubhouse gate. Someone said Albert Burke had shouted from inside that our tickets would get us in there, and it was obvious we were not going to make it on this side.

There was a gate on the other side, right enough, but another mob was storming it in the narrow confines of the alley. One of the Burkes and a couple of cops were trying unsuccessfully to control them. It must have been close to ten-thirty when several photographers, their cameras held high above their heads, formed a flying wedge to get us through in their wake. We made it all right, more easily in the end than I would have thought possible. Probably the voluble crowd knew by now they were not to get in at all, short of knocking the gate down, and had given up.

Once inside another few minutes were consumed trying to find out where I was supposed to sit. I never did. As they used to say at Ebbets Field in the dear dead days, it was everyone for theirself. I couldn't see anything that remotely resembled a press section, but here and there some of the best newspaper brains were wrestling with the problem of using knees for typewriter benches.

From the ground I saw Tom Topping of the Associated Press a few rows up, holding a large writing pad in his lap. He called to me to come on up and give him a hand. That was where I was supposed to be. A man of much experience in European reporting, he had foreseen that he wouldn't be able to use a typewriter. I found a seat directly behind him, and as he wrote he passed the sheets back to me with a request to read, correct, put a clip on, and throw to a man standing in the runway below the seats. Morning paper men had plenty of time, and I wouldn't have to write my story until hours after the match was over.

All around me were great men of the profession and the book-writing trade. From the top of the stand Tunis called cheerily down to me, and I wished I could be as certain of writing a good piece as he seemed to be. I tried to assume that air of assurance that the insecure and unsure so often wear. Stanley Doust, whom I had seen as a member of the 1914 Australian Davis Cup team, was there for the London *Daily Mail;* Bruce Harris, of the *Standard,* who was to become an especially good friend later; S. Powell Blackmore, of the *Daily Express,* I think it was then, who could always tell you by consulting his pocket notebook in what week the lady tennis players were certain to be ill; Edward Sampson, of the *Manchester Guardian,* who was to be my closest English journalistic friend; and among others I was to know well later but did not know now, McDonald of the *News.* Wallis Myers, of the *Daily Telegraph,* the best-known of all tennis writers, was somewhere, and Sparrow Robertson, my colleague from the Paris *Herald,* was somewhere else. James Thurber was there, too, to do a special piece for the Paris edition of the Chicago *Tribune,* but I did not see him. Of course, I did not know then that he was going to turn out to be James Thurber, or I would have made certain of knowing him. Tunis thought Thurber's was the finest piece to come out of Cannes that day, and although I don't remember ever seeing it, I'm sure he is right.

Topping, a fat, blasphemous, and explosive man with a surprising command of idiomatic French, especially the more vulgar and obscene parts, was writing away the whole time, and each time I'd throw down a sheet he'd send the little man on his way with a volley of French oaths and indecencies, listing also what would happen if the messenger failed to get the copy to the right place or didn't return immediately to his post. I think the AP had a phone line open to Paris somewhere near, for the messenger got out and back quickly.

I suggested that Topping was being slightly frantic, with the match not yet even begun. His reply, cleaned up, was, "You know where this wench comes from? Berkeley, California. You know what time it is in Berkeley, California? Three o'clock in the morning. Some of the A.M.'s are holding for this, and the guy gets there first gets his stuff in the paper." I looked around and all the other wire service men were just as busy, battling one another for those extra few seconds. I was glad I didn't have to keep up with the story that way.

As the time for the match to start drew nearer the crowd outside became noisier. We could not see them, but they were there and some still were trying to crash the gate. When it became certain that the majority would not get inside, they began to seek other places. Soon the trees overlooking the place held the more athletic of the frustrated, and the windows of a house nearby were filled. Presently the red tiles on its roof, removed from within, began to disappear and faces to pop through the holes. The roof of the garage was jammed, and people brought ladders to lean against its wall, behind the seats on one side. On every rung halfway to the top someone stood, hands on the shoulders of the one on the rung below. Every roof from which a part of the court could be seen had as many people as it would bear sitting or standing upon it, and every tree limb that would give a precarious perch was occupied. The police, who had gone up the trees with the apparent intention of routing the occupants, took the vacated places and remained to look. It seemed that there must have been a thousand people looking down on the court in these ways, almost as many seeing the match, or some portion of it, from outside as from inside.

The arrival of Suzanne at the clubhouse entrance in her chauffeur-driven car from Nice was hailed by an outburst of cheering outside and the calling of her name. This was followed by a great roar when, someone said, she blew them kisses. Helen had to come only from the nearby Carlton, whose tower windows also were full of people watching. Probably she had preceded Suzanne, who always made certain of her "entrance."

Meanwhile the part of the crowd to which I belonged had made note of the great number of celebrities, including royalty in the person of ex-King Manuel, of Portugal, the Grand Duke Michael, Prince George, and a number of maharajas and titled persons whose names escape me.

The suspense had begun to mount sharply even before the two girls entered together, making a nice picture for the battalion of photographers that immediately engulfed them. Suzanne came like a great actress making an entrance that stopped the show, with flashing smile, bowing, posing, blowing kisses, full of grace and ever gracious. Helen, walking beside the Queen and, as befits a lady in waiting, just a little to the rear, came in calm, impassive, and unruffled, looking nowhere but in front. She seemed sturdy and placidly unemotional, although she must surely have been nervous. I noted for the first time that Miss Wills had large, capable-looking hands, and I wondered if she really was the talented painter of pictures she was supposed to be. I don't suppose she took either literature or art very seriously at this time.

Suzanne wore a pure white coat with white fur collar over a short white dress and her famous bandeau was of salmon pink. Helen wore her usual tennis costume, middy blouse and pleated white skirt, and she had a dark coat over the arm not full of rackets. When the photographers were induced to retire, and the girls were about to take the court, Helen removed her sweater. Suzanne wore hers all through the match, although the sun now was hot. When the flashing entrance smile had been turned off, it was seen that Suzanne had a somewhat strained, pinched look. There were dark lines and the eyes seemed drawn. She did not look well.

The officials came out to their places while the balls were being hit back and forth in the preliminary warmup, and it was noted that nearly all were English, chosen no doubt for their neutrality. One lineman was Cyril Tolley, the golf champion and others were Lord Charles Hope, Sir Francis Towle, and Roman Najauch, professional at another Riviera tennis club. In the umpire's chair was Commander George Whiteside Hillyard, of the Royal Navy, who called the score throughout in English, never once using a French word or tennis term. English probably was the language of most of us, at that.

All during this time the crowd remained quite noisy both inside and out and the officials made several unsuccessful attempts to quiet it. A man seated with a group on benches behind the umpire's chair stood up and addressed the spectators, first in French and then in

English. At the time I knew who this man was, but now I have forgotten. I have not forgotten that he got the old raspberry for his efforts and a decent order never was achieved at any time. People continued to shout and make loud remarks, some merely rude, many vulgar, right to the end. These latter were all in French, and it was seen that many of the Frenchmen looking on had not had much previous experience of the game of tennis. They knew about Suzanne and she was on this day, if not on others, the greatest French personality, a compatriot who had brought great honor to La Patrie.

When the workmen with their hammers had been shooed out and the girls were ready to begin, I noted with surprise that it was only a little beyond the scheduled time. I had thought there must have been a long delay. Part of the excitement of this encounter came from the fact that Miss Wills, by her play in other tournaments, had convinced many people that she was now good enough to challenge the invincible Suzanne as the champion had not been challenged since 1919. Many qualified observers and practically all the Americans present thought Helen would win.

Up to this point I have been calling on perhaps faulty memory, my own and that of others, but once play began I wrote things down and I still have full confidence in what I now write. The notes are not altogether clear as to calligraphy, and some are not meaningful any more, but they tell a story and this is it.

The match lasted exactly one hour. Lenglen opened with a love game on her service, but Helen then began to hit her own faster drives deep, and controlled the back court exchanges just well enough to win the next two games for a 2–1 lead. She had won the champion's service, and when that service game was lost to a scoring shot from Helen's backhand off a fine Lenglen shot, you could sense the realization coming to Suzanne that she was in for a fight. No other girl ever had scored off such a shot. It must have been an unpleasant awakening. She knew now what she was facing. None could know it better. Here was an opponent her equal in controlled driving, and definitely more forceful. Helen's game was based on speed of stroke perfectly controlled, with drives more forceful than any woman and many men. Helen was not, however, Suzanne's equal in resourcefulness.

Helen had hit every backhand shot in these early games across court to the backhand line, often right into the backhand corner.

These were shots of high quality, immaculate in their purity of execution, but they were sent to Lenglen's backhand, one of the most accurate and precisely controlled strokes and altogether one of the finest shots ever seen in the game of tennis.

It might be noted here that Miss Wills, throughout her brilliant career, continued to prefer the backhand cross-court shot to the one down the opponent's forehand line. I saw the latter shot so seldom from her that I suspected more than once in later years that either she could not make this more difficult stroke well or had no real confidence in it, which amounts to the same thing. Against all her later opponents it made little difference, none at all really, since she was so good and so powerful elsewhere, but I believed that day in Cannes, and still believe, that it was this lack, this one chink in an otherwise complete armor, that removed the chance Miss Wills might have had to defeat Lenglen in their only encounter. I think it likely also that Miss Wills would have perfected this stroke if she and Suzanne had continued to meet, for she then would have had need of it.

At any rate Lenglen was quick to see the advantage it gave her. After losing the second and third games, she began with great confidence to take those booming backhand drives pitching close to her own backhand corner, certainly the hardest and deepest she ever had encountered from another girl. Initially they had surprised her, but she was not now hurried by them and it seemed she even invited them by playing her own shots to Miss Wills's left side. Suzanne took the ball cleanly in the exact center of her racket and with her slightly undercut stroke placed her return to the spot her eye had picked out, very short down each of Miss Wills's sidelines.

This often brought Helen forward, and each time she came she lost the point. These coups were much easier for Suzanne to bring off than would have been similar shots hit deep to her forehand corner, but Miss Wills never attacked that sector with her backhand. She seemed to think at this time that the Lenglen backhand was the wing to attack, and attack it she did with great strength.

In spite of it, though, Suzanne won ten straight points from 2–1 in Miss Wills's favor. She won them with unyielding defense against the hardest thrusts Helen could manage and from which she herself could counterattack with perfectly timed shots. These, placing Miss Wills in a losing position, were designed to draw errors. This was the game of women's tennis such as we would expect these two to play. Miss Wills was playing very well indeed and she was losing, but it took nearly perfect stroking and a well-conceived plan to check her. We expected that Miss Wills, with her equipment, would find the way to alter the course of the play, and she did.

Having lost her service twice and now behind 2–4, she came to the net to volley for the first time in the seventh game and won it with a not very neat but effective push out of reach. Suzanne seemed now to have decided upon her plan of action, however, and to have regained her confidence, which had been disturbed by the unexpectedly strong resistance of the American girl. Helen could win only two points in the next two games as Suzanne captured the first set 6–3 to a great burst of cheering.

This seemed a convincing enough margin, but the set had been played under considerable stress, nevertheless, and Suzanne went to the chair to sip brandy before taking her place for the start of the second. She seemed already tired and nervous. The disturbing noises from the crowd annoyed her much more than they bothered Helen, and several times Suzanne had looked with an appealing gesture toward the spot where a vehicle of some kind had been drawn up alongside the fence with a shouting group sitting on top of it. She had first ordered them to be silent and then, being ignored, had pleaded with them, with the same effect.

Helen began the second set as Suzanne had begun the first, by serving a love game. This was the first time the strong and well-placed American service itself had been a decisive factor, and its sudden increase in power seemed to surprise Lenglen. All Miss Wills's shots, in fact, appeared now to carry more pace, or what the English call "devil" and, choosing well the proper ball on which to hit out, she placed Suzanne altogether on the defensive for a time. The greater speed of stroke of the American girl now was quite noticeable.

Helen went to a lead of 3–1, and she was serving so well it seemed to us unlikely she would lose a service game at all. If she did not, she would win the second set by 6–3, even without breaking the French girl's service again. At one point in the fourth game she had passed Suzanne cleanly at the net with a sharply angled forehand across the body. Suzanne stopped at the chair again for another sip of brandy before returning to her position. This seemed an ominous sign, and we thought that Suzanne never would survive a third set. But it gave her time to consider her position, which was, as a matter of fact, critical. With Miss Wills serving with a 4–1 lead in sight, Suzanne knew well that the capture of the American's service was imperative at this point. She dare not fall behind 1–4.

And then I think Miss Wills made the tactical mistake that may well have cost her the victory, although it is difficult to be sure in the light of what came later. Anyhow, serving for this commanding lead, Miss Wills appeared deliberately to reduce the pace of the game. Instead of pressing her advantage she began to exchange deep and well-placed but slower drives with Suzanne.

Now, Miss Wills was not equipped to play this kind of game so well as Suzanne. Indeed, no girl that ever lived could do this. No matter where the ball was hit Suzanne could reach it with her marvelously fluid footwork and, given time for the stroke, she was again in control of the play. In such exchanges hers would be the last shot of each rally if it didn't end with an opponent's error. The shots that Helen missed now were those for which she was made to run and strain. Suzanne, for the second time, had a run of two games in which she lost only two points, both well earned by Helen. The score was now 3–3 and now surely the crisis was passed for Suzanne.

How wrong we were!

Now came the longest game of the match. With Helen serving, Suzanne was within a stroke of winning the game at 15–40 for a 4–3 lead and her own service to follow. Ten more points were to be played, however, and then Miss Wills won the game to give her that lead. Helen had brought out her very best game at this crisis, and we saw then the wonderful driving that only she in all the world could command and sustain over the next ten years or so.

The effect on Suzanne of losing this game from a winning position, and against play that indicated she might have met her match at last, was profound and visible. She was clearly surprised at such very strong resistance. She took more brandy and before taking up the balls to serve the eighth game, she appealed again to part of the crowd, now in a highly excited state, please to keep quiet.

As the play continued she appeared to falter, although actually she made no mistake in stroking at all. It was the way she looked. She seemed much more nervous, but at 30–all she received a small break that appeared to restore her a little while it depressed her opponent.

Suzanne drove to Miss Wills's forehand line a ball that could not have been returned but appeared to have pitched just outside. Cyril Tolley, who was judging the line, gave no sign and then, when Miss Wills looked an inquiry at him, indicated that the ball had been good. If he had given it the other way, as Miss Wills clearly thought he should, she would have been one point away from a 5–3 lead and in Lenglen's present state that might have been decisive.

Miss Wills lost the next point weakly, perhaps, while contemplating what might have been, but she then served very well to reach 5–4. And now for the second time at a critical moment Miss Wills became tentative. And once more Lenglen's great skill at maneuvering an opponent lacking in aggression came to the fore. Again she drew Helen to a forward position where the American girl, unable to find room for her full-blooded drives, hit out or into the net. Suzanne thus won at love a game whose loss would have carried with it the loss of the second set and, very likely, the third also. This was, if partly the result of Miss Wills's strange quietude, even more the true champion's response to danger. It was characteristic, and a few minutes later we were to see an even more impressive demonstration of it.

Having survived these several dangers brilliantly, Suzanne now appeared to be moving straight to victory. She won Miss Wills's service surely, if not easily, from 30–all in the eleventh game and then in the twelfth, serving perfectly to prevent a forcing reply, went straight to match point at 40–15. And then, one stroke away from a two-set victory for Lenglen, there was a long exchange of deep drives at the end of which Miss Wills, finding at last a ball she could flog, sent a screaming forehand toward Lenglen's forehand corner. It had the look of a winning stroke, but the call of "Out" was heard and both players thought the match over.

Suzanne threw into the air the ball she had held in her hand throughout the rally and ran to the net to receive the traditional winner's handshake across the barrier. Before she could reach Helen, the court was full of people, a regular mob scene. They came from all directions, carrying huge baskets of flowers and the photographers swarmed everywhere.

Through this throng of people and flowers, Lord Charles Hope, the lineman, pushed his way to the umpire's chair. Commander Hillyard leaned down to hear what was said amid the bedlam. Sir

Charles explained that the ball had been emphatically good, not out. It was not he who had called but some volunteer official, of whom there were hundreds in the stands. Hillyard immediately changed the decision, made the score 40–30, and began an effort that at first seemed futile to clear the court so the match could be resumed. In those pre-loudspeaker days it took some doing. Many minutes passed before the facts could be communicated to the crowd, all of whom were standing and most of whom were shouting. But justice must be done and it was finally accomplished.

Confusion still reigned for a while but in time all got back to their places. I could not see Lenglen's face when she first realized the situation. It must have been a study in dejection for she had a sorrowful cast of feature even when in repose and this for her was a tragic development. The highly charged emotional atmosphere had taken its toll of her nervous strength, but she had overcome all, including the strongest game she ever had faced, and come through successfully still queen and still champion at what cost only she probably knew. And now, exhausted from physical effort and nervous strain, she must go back and do it again under even worse strain. All was still uncertain and had to be played for.

And now Mademoiselle Lenglen confirmed and underscored her position as Queen of the Courts and one of the great champions of sports history. She had shown many petty traits of annoyance over trivial things and had acted in a haughty and arrogant manner many times in her years of triumph. Now, in her hour of trial, as the saying goes, she showed herself to be a real champion. Without a word or any outward sign, she walked steadily back to her place, picked up the discarded balls and served. Her face was drawn but even when Miss Wills won the next point, also a match point, and then eventually the game, to draw even again at 6–all, there still was no sign.

When Miss Wills stood within one point of winning the following game, the thirteenth, a point that would have given her the lead at 7–6, there was at last a nervous gesture from Suzanne which seemed to indicate she might now be near collapse. But she steadied herself, recovered her concentration and won the game against the American's service, which was at its biting best now.

And so, serving once more for the match a good quarter-hour after she had thought she had it won, Suzanne came at last to her third match point. It had not been easy to arrive there, for Miss Wills resisted beautifully and with calm judgment. Suzanne had played with nearly perfect strokes, which, under the circumstances, showed a hardihood we none of us suspected in so highly emotional a creature. Then, in sight of the end once more, she reacted. Suzanne served a double fault, so rare a thing with her as to make one wonder if she were not really at the end of her resources.

But once again the champion gathered her remaining strength. This remarkable woman now played with a certainty and restraint, with unshaken nerve and fortitude, that were difficult to believe in the supercharged atmosphere after all that had gone before. Having served the double fault at match point, she then needed two more points to get out from deuce. For the first she fenced with Miss Wills until she drew an error. For the last one of all, her fourth match point, she carefully drew a weak reply from Helen and then she won in the champion's way by hitting a winner. It was, in a word, magnificent.

This time Suzanne did not run to the net. She stood almost in a trance, it seemed, in mid-court, and was there engulfed again by the rush of partisans, photographers, and the baskets of flowers which returned for a monster horticultural display. I doubted she ever would reach the net, where Miss Wills waited to do the honors for the second time, if the photographers had not insisted upon it so they could take a thousand pictures of the kind photographers the world over must have.

Suzanne received an ovation beyond anything even she had previously experienced. Finally they sat her down on a bench at the side of the court and surrounded her with a wall of flowers until only her turbaned head showed above. She was surrounded also by a wall of hundreds of people, including lords and ladies, all pushing forward to congratulate and be near her. And directly behind where Suzanne sat, Helen stood for a few minutes, unnoticed, forgotten, and alone in the midst of the thing. I watched as Miss Wills, with hardly room to extend her arms, pulled on her sweater. Then, still alone, she turned and began quietly to push her way back through the indifferent crowd toward the gate. She disappeared among them and no one seemed to care that she was gone.

I had plenty of time so I watched the scene for a while and then went out and found a seat along the Croisette, where I could sit in the sun and think about the strange match. I have been thinking about it in sunshine and shadow ever since and the conclusion I reached while sitting in the bench in sight of the Mediterranean remain the same today.

I was to see Miss Wills many times afterward winning all her eight Wimbledon titles, all those in Paris and many of those at Forest Hills, besides her yearly Wightman Cup encounters. Suzanne was seen afterward only through the French Championships, which followed in Paris three months later in May, and at her last Wimbledon that June.

My feeling about the Cannes match was then, and is now, that if it had been played under normal conditions Lenglen would have won more easily and more decisively. I think also that if she and Miss Wills had met later that same year, which seemed likely then but turned out not to be, Lenglen also would have won but probably less easily. If they had continued both to play the tournaments through the next years, however, I am certain that Miss Wills would have overtaken Suzanne and passed her.

This does not mean that I place Miss Wills at her peak above Lenglen at hers, for I believe the opposite. But Helen showed at Cannes that she already was close and still improving and Lenglen, never very robust, already probably was declining a little in a tennis sense. She had been queen of Wimbledon for seven years in 1926. Miss Wills first became champion there in 1927 after Suzanne's departure. If we add seven years to that date, we will see Miss Wills in 1934 also seriously challenged by players of lesser talent than her own.

These two wonderful performers were really of different tennis generations, and had they met more they must inevitably have come level and one passed the other, the one going up, the other down. It is ever the fate of even the greatest of champions to be superseded and, since in this case one great one followed immediately after another, we probably were denied a series of superlative women's tennis matches by Lenglen's retirement from amateur tennis that same year. They might have been matches such as we enjoyed during that period of two or three years when the rising Musketeers were catching up to and passing Tilden. They were, in fact, the very same years, and the finest of them were just ahead.

CHAPTER NINE

BOTH girls remained on the Riviera playing tennis for many weeks but never entered the same tournament again, so that their next prospective meeting was to be in the French National Championships in Paris at the end of May. The tennis reporters and regular correspondents did not stay down for the lesser tournaments, leaving Miss Wills to the so-called string correspondents every paper and news service hired to keep track of the strange behavior of the famous, the notorious, and the fashionable characters who frequented the resort areas of Europe.

Miss Wills was still news and she was besieged by a mixed group of these stringers, fashion and society writers, moving picture people, dressmakers, milliners, shoe manufacturers, perfume dealers, automobile agents, and makers of this or that product, most of them offering their wares free. In spite of all this Miss Wills was reported to be enjoying herself much more now. Before the match she had no time to plunge into what the papers referred to as "the cosmopolitan life that characterizes the South of France," but she was now quoted a couple of times as saying she was enjoying herself as never before.

Moreover, romance had entered her life. She was escorted everywhere by a young man named Moody from San Francisco, who seemed all of a sudden to be omnipresent, whether it be just strolling about or at some elegant affair attended by the King of Sweden and the former King of Portugal. Miss Wills was in great demand to attend parties and functions, and young Mr. Moody seemed to be her only cavalier. None of us had been conscious of young Mr. Moody up to the time of the great match although he may well have been a member of the "Boy Scouts." Afterward his name kept cropping up in the dispatches from the Riviera as Miss Wills moved from one tournament to another.

She won the Monte Carlo Cup at the end of February and also won the ladies doubles there with Miss Contostavlos, a Greek girl who played all the tournaments and had sometimes partnered Lenglen. Miss Wills also won the Côte d'Azur title at Cannes and there she played mixed doubles with Cochet as partner, winning that title too. She took a little time off from tennis now and then, but even when she played, it was in the mornings so that nearly every day she and young Mr. Moody could go dancing at teatime. All in all Miss Wills seemed to be having a merry time of it in a quiet way, and I have often wondered if she did not look back upon these weeks along the enchanting Azure Coast, following the great Cannes match, when life was at the morning, as among the most enjoyable of her life.

Lenglen, meanwhile, played mostly in doubles and won the Beaumont Cup at Monte Carlo with Didi Vlasto, her usual doubles partner when she did not team up with Elizabeth Ryan. Suzanne and Helen encountered one another many times of course around tournament grounds and became well acquainted but never got near to another match. Suzanne played singles at the second winter tournament at the Nice Tennis Club, winning it of course. By this time it was April and the separate paths began to converge once more toward a crossing in the Bois de Boulogne, where the French Championships were scheduled at the grounds of an organization called the Racing Club de France. There was plenty of evidence to indicate that Miss Wills was looking forward to this second encounter with great eagerness and Suzanne with complete confidence.

The buildup was not quite so tremendous this time, although exciting enough. The two girls were not to be the whole show, merely the star turn. The international cast for the tournament was an impressive one, making a splendid background for the girls' match, but there were other good things to be anticipated in Paris. Vinnie Richards was competing, and since he had won the Olympic title in Paris a year or two earlier, most of us felt he would win the French title also unless he should have the bad luck to play all three Musketeers, an unlikely possibility unless the draw was rigged. It turned out he had to play only one of them.

Mary Browne, a former United States champion, also was in the singles and was going to play doubles with Miss Wills. A Franco-American final in that event between these two and the Lenglen-Vlasto team was a good possibility and an enticing one.

By the time she arrived in Paris and was settled with her mother at the Hotel Cecile, not far from the Étoile, Miss Wills had shifted her literary allegiance from International News Service to the United Press and was to do a daily piece for her new firm during the two weeks of the tournament. This made the tournament very important indeed for UP and the head of the Paris Bureau, a nice man named Bradford, hired me to supplement the staff covering the event.

As I recall, UP had sold Miss Wills's literary work to a number of papers in Great Britain and was very anxious to get its reports of the play from Paris into London ahead of its rivals on the theory that first come, first printed. My job was to file what were called "running" accounts in brief of all the Wills and Lenglen matches through the early rounds to New York by cable for immediate relay back under the Atlantic to London. This was a very expensive way of handling the stuff, but it beat the others who filed direct by French telegraph or by telephone, and nobody seemed to mind being extravagant in the mid-twenties.

We got through to London incredibly fast, though, for that day, and both Mr. Bradford and his New York office seemed happy with the arrangement. It was, in fact, much easier to reach New York by cable from the club than to reach Paris by phone, and that fact led to a strange effect before the tournament was half done.

The Racing Club was nearer Paris than the Stade Français in St. Cloud and the setting also was charming. The Bois enclosed the well wooded grounds, and the familiar red courts were set right among the trees, which put some of them in shadow most of the day. The principal courts were all right, though.

The tournament opened quietly on a Monday with none of the leading players in action. Some of the courts among the trees were occupied by club members on these early days, adding to the air of informality, and it was often hard to tell which were tournament matches. There was a large entry in the five events—men's and women's singles and doubles and mixed doubles—and some of the lesser tournament players were hardly better than those having a friendly game on neighboring courts.

Nothing much was happening on the first day, and I might just as well have gone out later since, with neither Lenglen nor Wills to worry about, I had nothing to do for UP until Tuesday. I had a chance to play often at the Racing Club later but at this time I had not even seen the club and I was eager to do so. I had arranged to have a ride out with somebody from UP who had a car, and I was to be picked up in front of a café a little way below the Place de la Madeleine just after the car, coming down the Boulevard des Italiens from the UP office beyond the Opéra, would turn left into the Rue Royale.

The terrace of this café, about whose name I am now vague, was on the same side of the Rue Royale as Maxim's, now frequented by even merrier widows and still haunted by ghosts of the nineties and the great days of the grand dukes. There were many such sitting places and in certain ways all were alike. On this day I sat about an hour before the car came, because I had purposely got there early. Whiling away an hour on a café terrace had become a fairly regular habit. Café sitting is one of the pleasantest and commonest things people do in Paris, and I mention this particular whiling away on this particular terrace in the light spring air, as the Parisian crowds went blithely about their business, for a particular reason.

It was the time of year when Paris begins to wear that garment of unreality that shows in so many paintings of city scenes. I had been in Europe nearly two years now and considered myself an old Paris hand. I had been moved to tears countless times in music hall, night club, and café concert by a hundred sad, husky tuneless songs declaiming that nothing ever changes, that Paree remains the same toujours. All of a sudden, sitting there that morning, it seemed that it would be a nice thing to go back to New York, for a short visit of course, in the late summer to see the Frenchmen play Tilden and Johnston and to see also what the Fabulous Twenties were getting to be like on home soil.

When the tiny Citroen car, looking no bigger than something to dangle from a charm bracelet, made the turn, I was pretty well decided to go if it could be arranged. I had settled for all my saucers in anticipation of a quick getaway and I had also settled that other matter when I hopped into the car at the curb.

The way to the Racing Club lay through the Place de la Concorde at the bottom of the Rue Royale, straight up the Champs Élysées, around the Square of the Star, and on out either the Avenue de Bois de Boulogne (later changed to the Avenue Foch) to the Porte Dauphine, or the Avenue de la Grande Armée to the Porte Maillot into the broad Allé de Longchamp. This certainly is a nice way to approach a tennis tournament and, although we didn't know it at the time, it was the last championship to be held on this ground, although not the last in or near the Bois.

The memory of these French Championships of 1926 will, for most people, center on an occurrence toward the end of the first week with everything else fading out. Miss Wills had appeared in two early matches, one a doubles, and had won both easily, although she had not seemed to be in such good form as on the Riviera. The reason for this was revealed when she was taken to the American Hospital in Neuilly one afternoon for an emergency operation to remove her appendix.

This naturally ended her tennis activities, ending also incidentally my extra job for the UP, and it was sensational news. And the United Press, because of its business arrangement with Miss Wills, was handed, on a silver platter so to speak, what we called a scoop, one of the best European news beats of that innocent time when the appearance of two girls on a tennis court was rated a world-historical event more important than international conferences to preserve the peace. UP had the story hours ahead of its rivals and this is how it came about.

At the tournament all we knew was that Mrs. Wills had asked that Helen's match with Kea Bouman, a Dutch girl, be postponed twenty-four hours, since Helen was not quite up to her best that day. Such postponements were common in the early rounds, especially with girls, and none of us gave it much importance. We all cabled the news to New York, I sending it to UP along with the others, and then we all went about our business.

That's all there was to it as far as anyone at the club knew, including the officials, but unknown to us Mrs. Wills had phoned the United Press office in Paris to tell them that Helen would not be able to write her article that day and to apologize. Miss Wills insisted on writing her own stuff, some thought unwisely. She would employ no ghost as other sports figures did when they went literary for a price. If she had followed this practice the word might have got out sooner. From Bradford later on I learned that something like the following conversation ensued:

"Hello. This is Mrs. Wills. I have to tell you that Helen will not be able to write her article today. I hope you will excuse her."

"Why, of course. Is anything the matter? Isn't she feeling well?"

"No, she is not. As a matter of fact, she has canceled her match today."

"Oh! I'm sorry. I hope it's nothing serious."

"I hope so too. She was in such pain, though, I had to call a doctor. He diagnosed it as appendicitis and took her to the American Hospital right away, perhaps to be operated on. But I do hope it's not as bad as that."

Now, Bradford was a first-class newspaperman, else he would not have been head of that bureau. He knew what he had hold of and he got busy fast. He got the story, at urgent rates, into New York, where it was only midmorning, onto the UP wires and into hundreds of newspapers all across the country before the routine dispatches we had sent from the courts had arrived. Most of the reporters at the club knew nothing about it until next morning, because people did not go about the Paris streets shouting extras, and men released from their labors passed their hours of ease in precincts somewhat removed from news sources.

I learned about it late that afternoon because I was engaged to have dinner with W. O. McGeehan, the sports columnist of the New York *Herald Tribune*, who was on one of his periodic visits to Europe. Bill McGeehan was a renowned newspaperman at this time, and I thought him the finest writer on sports the profession ever had turned up. I have never found any reason to change that judgment either. He had an extraordinary ability to judge matters sporting, or perhaps a sentimental Irishman's instinct for it, and I was soon to learn that his judgment of tennis, of which he had seen comparatively little, was sound.

I had planned to pick up the Sheriff, as he was called, at the Paris *Herald* down in the old Rue du Louvre building in the Markets. I found him sitting beside the phone in the office of Wilbur Forest, the *Herald Tribune* correspondent. Miss Wills, he said, had been in the operating room having her appendix out and he would wait to hear the result before going out for an apéritif. He would need some information about what went on at the tennis club during the day and then, after dinner, we would come back and he would file a column before we would go on to other pleasures. Since New York was five hours behind Paris, it would be possible to file up to midnight and still make the first edition.

McGeehan had been much intrigued by the first Lenglen-Wills affair and was planning to see and write about the second meeting, but he had not expected to go out until they drew closer together in the second week of the tournament.

Bill was eager to speak with Lenglen next day. He was delighted, as I had been, by her slightly venomous statement upon learning of Miss Wills's misfortune. At the time Helen was taken to the hospital Suzanne was playing a mixed doubles with Jacques Brugnon as partner against Miss Bouman and Hans Timmer, also Dutch. None of them knew any more than the rest of us, and when Suzanne heard the news that evening, she first said some spontaneous words of genuine sympathy. It was the formal statement she gave out a little later that contained the bit of acid.

"I am sure," she said, "that France will be just as sympathetic and kind to Miss Wills as America was to me when I was ill in a foreign country."

There was no doubt at all that Suzanne's sympathy was genuine. Bearing a huge bunch of red peonies, she was just about the first of Helen's visitors at the hospital next morning, and Mrs. Wills herself, when I spoke with her, seemed a little overcome by Suzanne's expressions of concern. But she could not resist this little dig, not at Miss Wills, but at the United States for what she still resented as unfair and unkind treatment back in 1921.

We tried to arrange a meeting for McGeehan next day, and when it was not possible I supposed he would lose interest in the tennis and proceed on his pleasant way about the Continent. On the contrary, he went out to the Bois every day right through the finals and wrote columns. It was not only Suzanne who drew him. He was keen to see and write about the Musketeers.

Suzanne, a picture of swooping grace—swooping at the ball, McGeehan said, like a falcon onto a flock of pigeons, killing and killing —moved in her usual way through the remainder of the tournament. In three matches she did not lose a game and in the semifinal she ran Joan Fry, a sturdy, quite good, and very healthy-looking English girl, savagely about the court, placing the ball with marvelous precision.

Mary Browne had beaten Kitty McKane (now Mrs. Godfree), Wimbledon champion of 1924 and to be champion again a month later, both times in Lenglen's absence, with some ease in the other semifinal; but against Suzanne in the final she was helpless. A splendid volleyer, Miss Browne sought the net persistently, but she could win only one game, the second of the match. As the last ball flew past her, Miss Browne drew a delighted guffaw from McGeehan by stomping her foot and exclaiming, "Oh! You're just too damn good."

This was Lenglen at her wonderful best and I do not think anyone who ever saw her in this mood can doubt that she was the finest player of her sex this game has known. It was the last time I was to see her play singles.

"I can see no chance," McGeehan said turning to me, "for Miss Wills to beat Suzanne either here or at Wimbledon. There is no woman player who can beat this champion."

I agreed with this but I was not so certain of McGeehan's opinion of Cochet, even though it was a shock to see how easily Henri defeated Vinnie Richards in straight sets in the semifinal. I was really surprised to see that the little Frenchman was able to generate such great speed of stroke when he needed it. This I had not noted before. It made a much more formidable player of him, for it was this speed he imparted to the ball taken on the rise that gave Richards no chance.

I had new respect for Cochet and it increased when he beat Lacoste, semifinal conqueror of Borotra, with almost equal ease in the final. I knew that Lacoste was not in perfect health that day, but it did not alter what I had seen. I began to wonder just how good this magician of the racket might really be. I got something of an answer from McGeehan as we parted after the tournament.

"This is the one who will beat Tilden. See you at Germantown."

Prophetic words.

CHAPTER TEN

There were three land-sea routes from Paris to London in the 1920s, and although it already was possible to fly, and fly free for a journalist, memories of trips back and forth are inextricably entwined with trains and railway stations. It was a time of luxurious train travel on the Continent and some of these runs have been celebrated by such romantics as Graham Greene, Agatha Christie, Alfred Hitchcock, and Eric Ambler. The Golden Arrow from London, called the Flèche d'Or from Calais on down, connected in Paris with the Blue Train, which ran in lordly splendor to the Riviera, and then there was the famous Orient Express leaving the Gare de l'Est nightly by way of Vienna and other exciting places, for Istanbul, with its load of elegant and often sinister characters.

Le Bourget and Croydon airfields call up nothing to compare with the feeling that comes from remembering the railway stations of London, those romantic monuments to Victoria's reign. There were at least a dozen big stations in London—Waterloo, Paddington, Victoria, Euston, Kings Cross, St. Pancras, Charing Cross—besides innumerable lesser ones. If suddenly the smoky stench of such a train shed happened to blow in my window, it surely would bring once more sentimental recollections of days when storytelling was full of trains with fine names, and a small boy longed above all to be the driver of one of these splendid creatures.

Once while waiting at Blackfriars station for a local train that would take me to Beckenham, in Kent, for a minor tournament, I wrote down the place names carved into the stone of columns before the entrance—Antwerp, Baden Baden, Berlin, Brindisi, Dresden, Darmstadt, Frankfort, Geneva, Florence, Lausanne, Rome, St. Petersburg. What wonderful possibility of choice was offered by these carriers of hope and delight, steaming away to mountains and sea and to delicious unknown adventures in strange capitals.

Super jets now girdle the earth in a few hours and men are hurled

114

into the cosmos to speak to us from strange capsules. Railroads are dull relics of dull times to the young, to whom transportation means, at the very least, sports cars rushing about at a hundred miles an hour. But I think the real world of boyhood is the world read about, and the world of London had been quite real to me long before I first arrived by way of Boulogne and Folkestone at Victoria that June of 1926 for a series of summer adventures that continued without a break right up to the firing of the first gun in World War II.

Like the English character and the English language, London, the world's leading example of non-planning, is the result of a sort of genius for improvisation. There are no cafés where the weary wanderer may pause and rest, but there are manifold compensations, and Londoners themselves are dignified and courageous people. With its historical and literary associations this must be the finest city in the world for strolling, a delightful practice that I followed through sixteen summers' storms and sunshine.

At the beginning of each summer during these years Great Britain, bathed then in the approaching sunset of Empire, would set out on a brief but intense round of gaiety, pageantry, and ceremony that included a series of events, sporting and social, that collectively made up what was and still is called The Season. People spoke of the London Season with awe, especially if they had debutante daughters to present to their Majesties at Buckingham Palace. One got the impression that London opened and closed on schedule as might a country fair, a circus, or an amusement park

On a rather rigid schedule extending through several weeks, and interspersed with presentations at court, were such fixed yearly events as the Derby on Epsom Downs, opera at Covent Garden, cricket at Lord's, the Wimbledon Fortnight, the Fourth of June celebration at the "King's College of Our Lady of Eton Beside Windsor," the Henley Regatta, the race meeting on the Royal Heath at Ascot; the Royal Tournament at Earls Court; the International Horse Show at the White City, and the Trooping of the Color, with its impressive solemnity as the monarch rode up the Mall from Buckingham Palace in royal procession.

These scenes and functions, these out-of-doors ceremonies, were and still are enjoyed by all the people of the Isles. They engage the attention, the interest, the participation, actual or vicarious, of the entire nation, rich and poor, Society, peer, and pauper. These events, therefore, play an important role in British life, linking the present with the centuries. They are part of the social background of the people and by their nature they stand apart from superficially similar events in other countries. And some of the big sports spectacles of the season are especially England's own in the sense that they have grown out of the English temperament, almost out of the soil itself.

The three most significant events of the English summer from this point of view probably are the Derby, Wimbledon, and Ascot. They are unique individually and collectively and could not be thought of as occurring anywhere else. Epsom is a true folk festival of vast proportions to which half a million make yearly pilgrimage. Ascot is a royal pageant where the monarchial nature of England's institutions is reasserted annually and the country is shown very definitely still to have an aristocracy.

Wimbledon stands between these two, neither folk affair nor royal function but partaking strongly of the elements of both. It too enjoys royal patronage, and it draws to its perfect lawns each year for the so-called dedicated fortnight from every sector of British life, including members of thousands of suburban tennis clubs who make up the world's most knowledgeable and most enthusiastic tennis gathering. It is only against this background that Wimbledon may be properly understood, and it is not certain that a foreigner, however devoted to tennis, will understand it completely even then.

The name Wimbledon itself is merely the name of a London suburb in a not particularly attractive borough, half an hour by underground and bus from Hyde Park Corner. But nowhere in all the world is there a place name connected with sports that has the ability so to quicken the pulse and stir the imagination.

It began almost unnoticed in 1868 when four sporting gentlemen rented four acres of ground in the Worple Road "for the laying down of croquet lawns," and formed the All-England Croquet Club. The first croquet tournament was played in 1870, and five years later a part of the ground was set aside for the playing of lawn tennis and badminton. The new game of tennis quickly superseded the old game of croquet, and the name was changed to the All-England Lawn Tennis and Croquet Club, which it has retained to this day. In that year the first Championship was played, four years before the first U.S. title tournament in 1881. Wimbledon then moved, a little slowly at first but inevitably, to its unchallenged position as the world's premier tennis event, the ultimate for players and spectators alike.

After World War I the old ground was seen to be inadequate and the new ground was opened in 1922, stark and gaunt and lacking in eye appeal. But Wimbledon grew in beauty as ivy crept around the walls of the hangar-like center court, and immensely in stature and glamour as gladiators from all the world came to do battle on its famed jousting ground, a sort of Field of the Cloth of Green.

For several tennis generations now people have tried to describe and explain Wimbledon, but success eludes them. Dozens of articles, even books, have been written and all are fascinating because the physical facts themselves are so impressive. An average of 25,000 attend daily throughout the two weeks, and those who go home at dusk often pass long lines of others preparing to wait through the night for the gates to open at noon next day so they can buy standing room. This enthusiasm for the game appears at first glance to be irreconcilable with the following facts:

In the sixty years following 1909, when A. W. Gore won the men's singles and Fred Perry was born, England has had only one winner of the main title, the men's singles, Perry himself. In the half-century since World War I, only three English girls have won the women's title, Kitty McKane in 1924 and 1926; Dorothy Round in 1934 and 1937 and Angela Mortimer in 1961. At the last prewar tournament in 1939 Great Britain had fifty-six, or nearly half the places in the men's draw of a hundred twenty-eight. In 1967 only thirteen from the home country had the ability to get in, yet 1967 was a record year for everything, including attendance.

Wimbledon does not really lend itself to analysis. Too many things flow into it. A thousand little things contribute to the knowledge of everyone who steps inside the gates that this is the pinnacle, the summit of the tennis year. The place breathes its spell over all, native and foreign visitor alike and this place, as is no other place, is haunted by the ghosts of long past champions, even those who never played at the new ground.

Wimbledon never is lacking in grandeur even when the quality of the tennis is low, for its all-embracing history includes all the greater and lesser players since the beginning of tennis time who have trod its matchless lawns. It is the headquarters, the Holy of Holies of the game that is more widely played than any other.

My first Wimbledon coincided with the fiftieth anniversary celebration of the tournament and they had gathered all the surviving
former winners they could round up for the Jubilee. It was a most
confusing two weeks from which a few things stand out clear and
the rest is a blur. A special program was printed for the opening
ceremony and I kept mine, as I suppose everyone who was there
did.

CENTRE COURT

12.30   2.40 p.m. . . . . . . Selections by Royal Military School of
Music (Kneller Hall Band).

2.40 p.m. . . . . Competitors take up positions at the
ends of the court.

2.50 p.m. . . . . Ex-Champions take up positions at the
East side of the court.

3.00 p.m. . . . . Arrival of Their Majesties, the King
and Queen. The King presents medals
to the ex-Champions.

EXHIBITION MATCH

3.20 p.m. . . . . Mlle Lenglen and Miss Ryan
v.
Mrs. Godfree and Señorita d'Alvarez

FOLLOWED BY
B. de Kehrling *v.* P. Feret
C. P. Dixon *v.* H. Kinsey

The ceremony was no doubt very impressive with the King and
Queen passing out to each champion in turn commemorative medals.
They progressed through the champions of earlier years and had just
got down to those of 1924 when Jean Borotra, with whose calculated
dramatics I was to become all too familiar, took charge of the proceedings. Borotra was a great crowd favorite and everybody knew

he was not present at the start. So the crowd was properly keyed up when the moment arrived that his name would be called.

Just as it was rolled out loudly by the voice of Commander Hillyard, Borotra, timing it to the split second, dashed breathless into the arena, making proper obeisances before royalty and well-considered gestures to the crowd's tremendous applause. The story was, and everyone knew it, that Borotra, detained by extremely important business, had flown from Paris, rushed by car from Croydon, changing into tennis togs in the car on the way, and just made it in the nick of time. It was tremendous. The people cheered and cheered and laughed and laughed. The beloved Bounding Basque, with his matchless sense of timing off the court as well as on, had stolen the show. He made his appearance before royalty, the papers said, "literally out of the clouds." Everybody seemed to think it was wonderful, but I seemed to think it just a little too studied and calculated to capture me, and I was never quite able to give my complete approval to Borotra's sideline exploits, either in tennis or out of it, even while always retaining a healthy respect for his ability to win matches, whether by force of stroke or of personality.

I suppose the jubilee program went off as scheduled except for this incident. The King and Queen did come, but I think Queen Mary presented the medals to the lady champions. It was the first time I had seen George and Mary and encountered that extraordinary feeling the British have for the Crown. Noted on the margin of the old program is the fact that, among the living men's singles champions missing were Patterson, Tilden, Johnston, and Lacoste. Patterson was in Australia, Tilden and Johnston did not go to Europe that year, and Lacoste, the champion of 1925, still was not entirely recovered from the severe chill and bronchitis he had contracted in New York in February. Apparently I did not think it necessary to note that Helen Wills was not there either, since her operation had been performed so recently, but she would not have been down on the court anyway. She was not to be a Wimbledon champion for another year yet. As a matter of fact she probably was somewhere there, now I think of it, pursuing her tennis literary career.

The biggest thing at that Wimbledon was the storm, nay the hurricane caused by Lenglen. It practically shook the Empire to its foundations and gave the London papers a field day of "sensation," a word indispensable to the local headline writers. I had to follow the beginning of this development from afar through the papers, because the British Open Golf Championship was being played at Royal Lytham and St. Anne's, right across the country near Liverpool on Wednesday, Thursday, and Friday of this first Wimbledon week. I attended the first two days' play and then left for Lytham, returning to London Friday night after Bob Jones had won the first of three British Open titles.

L'affaire Lenglen began on Tuesday, developed further on Thursday and Friday, and reached its climax on Saturday afternoon, by which time I was back in attendance. My memory of it is bolstered by friendly discussion with F. R. Burrow, referee of the tournament, years later when I had got acquainted with him, and somewhat less friendly talk with Major D. R. Larcombe, the newly appointed secretary of the All-England Club. Both were in the midst of it and most unhappily for them too.

As near as I could straighten out the events leading up to the explosion, Lenglen became miffed because no one came on Tuesday, after she had played her first match, to escort her to the referee's office so that she could be informed of what she was scheduled to do next and approve it. This attendance on the Queen of Wimbledon had been performed for years by Commander Hillyard, the same who had umpired the Cannes match in January, but Hillyard had been succeeded as secretary that year by Major Larcombe. I never was quite clear whether Major Larcombe's failure to perform this courtesy due the Queen was because he had not been informed that it was one of the secretary's duties, because of an oversight, or if it was deliberate and intentional. Major Larcombe was very good at evading questions then and later, but the fact was that he did not wait upon and escort Mademoiselle Lenglen to Mr. Burrow. Feeling insulted, or at least slighted, Suzanne would not come by herself to find out that she was down for a singles match at two o'clock and a women's doubles a couple of hours later. This information, however, was published in all the papers. The time of Lenglen's matches was very important news.

Now, Queen Mary, informed of these times, made a special trip to Wimbledon just to see Suzanne play. The Queen had been on the center court herself two days earlier and had handed Mademoiselle Lenglen her medal. She was very much a tennis fan and had helped open the new Wimbledon in 1922. But Suzanne did not arrive on the grounds until three-thirty, an hour and a half late for her match. Furthermore, she announced upon arrival that she would not play her singles match before the doubles. When it was insisted upon, both because the schedule must be maintained and because the Queen was waiting, Suzanne was reported to have grown hysterical, finally declaring that if she did not have her way, she would scratch from everything.

The officials, placed in a most unenviable position, decided to postpone both matches until Thursday, giving Mademoiselle Lenglen's indisposition as the reason, and agreed that the doubles match should be played first. The papers did not get hold of the true situation immediately, and I returned to Wimbledon on Saturday to find that Mademoiselles Lenglen and Vlasto had played their doubles match on Thursday, losing to Miss Ryan and Miss Browne. It was not played in the center court, however, and rain prevented the singles from being played at all. The singles match finally was played on Friday, also away from the center court, and Lenglen, of course, won it easily.

By Saturday, though, the big storm was coming up rapidly. The London papers had got wind of what had really occurred on Wednesday and went to work on it as only they can do. Probably every British subject felt outraged at the slight to the Queen when he learned of it. The papers demanded to know in bold type why Mademoiselle Lenglen had not been scratched and sent back home. She was, of course, wonderful and all that sort of thing, but I mean to say, old boy, not even the greatest attraction Wimbledon ever had known could be forgiven this. The Championships, the headlines shouted, were bigger than any champion.

All this had its effect. On Saturday, Suzanne was slated to play mixed doubles with Borotra as partner in the center court. Immediately the four players entered—I do not remember who the opponents were—it was obvious that Suzanne's public was not going to receive her as usual. They had turned hostile. You could feel it in the air, and very soon you could hear it too. There were boos. Not loud ones, just low and ominous noises, and there were a few low hisses too as the players walked to the umpire's chair to put down extra rackets and wraps. There was a distinctly unpleasant atmosphere that seemed certain to build up to a most unpleasant outbreak. I wondered if Lenglen might not soon burst into tears and run from the court.

And here at this point, when things seemed certain to get out of hand, Borotra got back into my good graces, for that day at least. He saved the situation by suddenly and cleverly drawing the crowd's attention away from Suzanne and to himself. The Basque, acting the fool in his most inimitable way, called for the balls, declared they would dispense with the usual pregame warmup and, with a loud cry of "Ready!" began the match by serving two of the most preposterous double faults ever seen. Four balls sailed wildly among spectators in the stands, and as each landed, Borotra's expressions of astonishment that such a thing could happen to him on the center court, and his clowning antics, captured the crowd completely. The whole mood of the affair was changed. Everything Borotra did was wildly funny. They roared with laughter. The crisis passed. The match was played through without unpleasant incident. The Wimbledon crowd had adored Borotra ever since his first appearance and he traded on this affection to see Suzanne through. He traded upon it for less worthy reasons at other times, but that is another story. Now they cheered Borotra without restraint and let Lenglen depart without further chastisement. And it was farewell for her. They never were to see her there again.

For seven years she had reigned as Queen of Wimbledon, idolized by these same people with whom she was at last out of favor. Suzanne knew it. She left the center court that day never to return. On Monday it was announced that she had retired from the tournament and a few months later she became a professional to tour with Richards, Mary Browne, and Paul Feret.

From the men's tournament that first year, I remember two matches, Cochet's defeat of Richards and Borotra's defeat of Cochet in the semifinal. Both the Cochet-Richards and the match in which Lenglen also repeated her Paris victory over Mary Browne were played on the second day of the tournament, that being one year before Wimbledon finally got around to a complete seeding of the draw. These results made it hard to resist writing a lead which had the Tricolor waving in triumph over the Stars and Stripes. In fact, I do not think I did resist hard enough. I suppose I really ought to remember something about Borotra's defeat of Howard Kinsey in the final, since I had much enjoyed Kinsey's expertly executed chops in earlier rounds and he was, after all, the only man not a Frenchman to play in a Wimbledon final between 1923 and 1930.

Cochet's defeat of Richards for the second time in two weeks, first on a hard court and then on grass, just about convinced me. After what I had seen in Paris I had little hope that Vinnie could beat this nonchalant little man who seemed to work his magic without half trying, but I thought I might be wrong when Richards won the first set 6–4. I did not take into account the fact that Cochet had arrived in England only the day before and was on a turf court for only the second time that year. He was still tuning up. This casual attitude toward practice was to let Cochet down badly on this same court a few years later, but now the marvelous co-ordination of eye and wrist that he owned got him quickly to his best form.

Very soon then it was seen that Richards had neither the ground strokes for defense against the Cochet volleying attack, which went nearly always toward the forehand, nor a service strong enough to support his own volleying forays. And since Cochet never lobbed, Vinnie was robbed of his two most effective weapons, the volley and the smash. For the first time I grew really excited by Cochet's ability to take the ball on the rise and follow it to the net in one unbroken movement, and Vinnie did not have the counter to such a move, such as the penetrating drive of a Tilden, a Johnston, or a Lacoste.

The Borotra-Cochet match stuck with me for one reason. My extensive but barely legible notes bring nothing back except the fact that Borotra had tried unsuccessfully all through four sets to pin Cochet down in the backhand corner for a volleying coup, and had been passed repeatedly as he advanced to the net. But he never altered these tactics and at the crisis of the fifth set, beginning in the tenth game, Borotra won the match by bringing off this maneuver. A forehand push deep into the backhand corner, followed by a winning volley to the forehand line.

The notes express doubt as to whether this was the result of Borotra's overcoming his driving weakness late in the match, making the forcing shot more forceful, or because Cochet's insolent backhand flip lost both force and precision. I never did resolve the doubt either, but Cochet did. The little Lyonese was very seldom beaten by Borotra after that day. He won the Wimbledon title twice after that, beating Borotra each time in the final match, in five sets in 1927 and in three in 1929.

CHAPTER ELEVEN

W HEN I sailed for New York late in August I didn't really think I was going to see Tilden pushed from the throne he had now occupied for six years. Actually he had already completed his remarkable reign, for he was to be beaten twice within a week, first by Lacoste in the Davis Cup matches in Philadelphia, and then by Cochet in the Championships at Forest Hills.

These were crowded weeks full of rushing about night and day in the full flowering period of the speakeasy era and complicated by the fact that the National Amateur Golf Championship was played at the Baltusrol club over in New Jersey, on exactly the same days as the tennis tournament, and both began only the second day after the completion of the Davis Cup play at Germantown. Then, barely a week after both finals, there was to be the first Dempsey-Tunney fight in Philadelphia.

The nearness of the fight meant that I would see McGeehan only briefly on his stopover in New York between Tunney's camp in Speculator, New York, and Dempsey's in Atlantic City. It was a disappointment not to have the Sheriff's company at the tennis, as we had planned in Paris in June, but he gave me a solid bit of advice which I failed to follow. Get down a little something, he said, on both Dempsey and Tilden to lose their titles. This was heresy and I did not believe it, and so passed up one of the best betting parlays I would ever come across.

The last time I had seen Tilden, Big Bill had played what I thought was the finest tennis throughout a whole match that the world had seen. Nothing anyone said could mar that splendid picture. Two defeats by Frenchmen in five days, however, could make me realize that it was a memory of things past.

But before that, my judgment of the whole tennis situation seemed to be upheld by the way things went at first at Germantown. Tilden and Johnston beat Borotra and Lacoste on the first day with the loss of only one set in the two singles matches, and two of Johnston's sets against Lacoste were won at love. This was a most curious match, since Lacoste also won a love set from Johnston. Richards and Williams then defeated Cochet and Brugnon in the doubles match next day, also in straight sets, and the Cup had been won by the United States for the seventh year in the first three matches.

Williams' play in the doubles was a revelation. I had thought of him as a dashing, reckless, and often careless player to whom all restraint while playing tennis was irksome. Now his was the master hand, the sober judgment, and the responsibility. With what wonderful speed of stroke and cunning he demoralized the French pair! Richards played badly, I thought, but Williams disrupted the Frenchmen repeatedly with the brilliance of his individual strokes and his sudden, original, and unexpected thrusts.

Another pleasant memory from that second day is the extra exhibition match which went on after the doubles. In it were four former champions, three of them left-handed—Dwight Davis, donor of the Cup, and Norman Brookes, against Beals Wright and William Clothier.

On the third day Johnston defeated Borotra, again in straight sets, and so when we came to the final match, the meeting of Tilden and Lacoste, the score was 4–0 in favor of the United States. Up to this point, I thought, the proceedings had been a little dull and disappointing, but then came the match to which we all look back as one of those historic occasions, or turning points. It brought the first defeat ever for Tilden in Davis Cup play. Tilden's first appearance in the worldwide team tournament had been at Eastbourne, in Devonshire, England, on July 8, 1920, when he defeated W. H. Laurentz, of France 4–6, 6–2, 6–1, 6–1. Now, six years and fifteen successful challenge round matches later, another small Frenchman brought this long tenure to an end by defeating Tilden 4–6, 6–4, 8–6, 8–6.

And this match, with nothing at stake so far as the fate of the Cup was concerned, was the "telling" one, or should have been. It told Tilden something and it told Lacoste even more, but I am afraid it did not tell me as much as it should. I dwelt more on the fact that the match was meaningless and that Tilden undoubtedly was handicapped by aggravating an old knee injury in the third set. But the match was not meaningless. I discussed it with Tilden afterward. I mean long after, not after the match.

He said that, seen from the 1930s, it had for him a certain look that it did not have when he was so close to it. He thought at the time that the knee had a lot, if not all, to do with it, but afterward he was able to see that Lacoste had already shown before the knee was hurt, the stroke equipment and, above all, what Tilden called the tennis brain, to extend Big Bill to the very limit. He gave examples of both these things, and I am going to quote him even though it is from memory. It is accurate in substance even if not in actual words:

"I never thought he had much in the way of a service," Bill said, "until suddenly in the middle of that third set, I found I could not start an attack off it. It was not fast at all, but it was aimed devilishly at the short forehand line and so heavily sliced that it spun outward. I could not swing freely enough to punish it. I overdrove it and I put it into the net. It worried me because I soon saw during the play that this small youngster had developed the stroke just for the purpose of using it against me in the important games. This disturbed me a lot because I recognized it as very sound tactically. I wondered what else this fellow might have up his sleeve."

Tilden, who once took me to task for using the word "strategy" when I meant "tactics," also spoke of his match a year earlier with Lacoste on the same court in exactly the same situation, except that it was then the fourth match of the Challenge Round instead of the fifth. I did not see that one, but Tilden said Lacoste had come within a stroke of beating him and had, at match point in a fourth set, hit what he, Tilden, thought was a winning placement. Tilden had served a ball which, he thought, was a good service and Lacoste hit it back out of reach, but it was called a fault and Tilden won in the fifth set after being two-sets-to-love down.

Tilden said that, although the 1925 match was very close all the way and Lacoste might have won it in either three or four sets, he himself never had the feeling that the Frenchman was a good enough player to menace him. He felt, Tilden said, that he could always save himself with the cannonball serve, the sideline passing shot, or the lob carefully pitched.

"I was a sap," Big Bill recalled emphatically. "This was one of the finest tennis players and tennis brains I ever encountered, and I underestimated him. I ought to have had a kick in the pants, and I got one a year later. Served me right."

Tilden meant that he ought immediately in that 1925 match to have recognized the danger; to have seen that here was one of the game's finest and most astute players in the making. He pointed out that in the 1926 match Lacoste used exactly the same methods with one important difference. The Frenchman, who was a first-rate volleyer, did not come to the net except when he felt certain he could make a winning volley.

"He refused to give me the target he had given the year before," Tilden explained. "As the ball got heavier with the slight moisture on the court, he kept mixing up the pace and length from the back of the court, always waiting. I made two serious mistakes, but I didn't know it until the match was over. I tried to hit too hard and I played too much to his backhand. You got a much easier return from his forehand because it was higher and slower and he could not angle it quite so acutely. But I was such a sap I didn't notice this. I kept coming across court with my own backhand, feeding his strongest stroke. I let him maneuver for his opening.

"My knee bothered me but was not the reason I lost. That was because I saw too late that Lacoste had figured a way to beat me. I was about one year late seeing what was going on."

I give all this detail from a conversation held a good ten years after all the exciting performers of this most exciting period of tennis were done with Davis Cup and championship play, and had passed either into the professional ranks or into limbo, because of the bearing it may have on the series of Tilden-Lacoste, Tilden-Cochet, and Tilden-Borotra matches in the three or four years just ahead.

I did not myself see the significance of this match. What impressed me was the ease with which the United States won the series and the Cup. Four matches to one, and it might have been 5–0, I thought. Johnston had beaten Lacoste and Borotra with no great difficulty it seemed, Tilden had beaten Borotra without losing a set, and the doubles also had gone to the United States in three sets. That this was an unrealistic estimate of the situation, Tilden indicated in that long-after discussion. He said that if the French had played Borotra with Brugnon in the doubles instead of Cochet, and if Lacoste had been drawn against Tilden the first day instead of in the final match, France might very well have won the Cup in 1926, a year before it actually was won. But that, he admitted, was hindsight.

I went on from Germantown to Forest Hills knowing nothing of all this and supposing that Tilden and Johnston would contest another final as they had done every year but one since the war. I had the idea, this week of September 13, 1926, that I could see a good part of the golf tournament at Baltusrol and all of the tennis at Forest Hills by shuttling back and forth. This would be possible, I thought, because the golf began early in the morning and ran all day, and they did not begin to play tennis until afternoon. The trip from one place to the other took a long time, though, and I did not really see much of the golf, because I had to leave too early. I have been trying to remember by what route I managed to make it, but it is too far back and the whole of Jersey was unfamiliar territory at that time. Stephen Berrien, one of New Jersey's finest golfers, who also was at Baltusrol as a young player and who later became president of the Metropolitan Golf Association, says that it must have been by bus or taxi to some Lackawanna station; train to Hoboken, tube to 34th Street, and Long Island Railroad to Forest Hills.

This plan, though strenuous, worked out well enough during the early days and I was able to see enough of the golf without neglecting the tennis, which mattered most to me. Jones beat Chick Evans and Francis Ouimet but lost his title when beaten by George Von Elm, two and one in the final. For Bobby Jones to be beaten at that time by an American was sensational, but it was as nothing to what was going on at Forest Hills.

Things worked out there so that for Thursday's quarterfinal round Tilden was drawn against Cochet, Lacoste was playing Dick Williams, Johnston was playing Borotra, and it was Richards versus Brugnon. The four Musketeers each playing one of America's top four. In American tennis history there never has been another day like this one. In the short hours of one summer's afternoon Tilden, Johnston, and Williams were beaten, and Richards went into the discard with them the very next day when Borotra eliminated him in the semifinal.

People got quickly into the habit of calling this day Black Thursday, and well they might. It was the most shocking thing imaginable because no one had been prepared for it. In all the years that the championship had been played, no non-English-speaking player ever had been in the semifinal, and now, here at nightfall of the next day were three of them. Lacoste defeated Cochet in their semifinal and then went on to take Borotra in the final. So the United States title went overseas for the first time since 1903, when Hugh Doherty had defeated William Clothier.

Since Lacoste's victory in the Challenge Round the week before, coming after the issue had been decided, could, as some contended, be considered an exhibition, we may take the Cochet-Tilden match at Forest Hills that remarkable Thursday as the real beginning of that series of meetings between the aging giant and the three young Davids, which made the next few years the most exciting tennis period I have experienced.

From Forest Hills of 1926 through Wimbledon of 1930, Tilden met Cochet seven times, Lacoste five times and Borotra four, apart from a number of matches played indoors in Paris and New York. I was fortunate enough to see all of these matches except those played indoors in New York. Every one was a tennis encounter in which the finest strokes to which the game had attained were on display, and several of these matches were entitled to be classed as outstanding by whatever standards. I am even tempted to apply the word "great" to some, except that I determined long ago to use this overworked and misused term sparingly. I will unbend so far as to say that in more than forty years of watching this game at home and abroad I have seen no more than perhaps a dozen matches that deserved the term, and in about half of them Tilden and one or another of the three Frenchmen were engaged.

In winning the 1926 title Lacoste did not have to play any of the top three Americans, but he did have to beat both his own top two, Cochet and Borotra. He had already been the first to defeat Tilden, however, and he emerged from the tournament as the world's leading player, even though he had actually won only two tournaments all year, one of them indoors. But both had made him champion of the United States, which had been the ruling nation since World War I. Lacoste had taken the U.S. indoor title in February but had been beaten by Cochet in three quick sets while defending his French title in May. In New York he had contracted severe bronchial trouble and played the early European tournaments, including his own at the Racing Club, against doctor's orders. René then retired from all play, forfeiting his Wimbledon title, nursed his cold, and arrived in the United States in late summer a fit man for the first time.

Cochet's quarterfinal victory over Tilden overshadowed everything else that happened during this exciting week. No wonder, since nearly everyone still thought Big Bill invincible. There had been signs and portents even before the seemingly meaningless defeat by Lacoste, but most of us continued to ignore them. I have often heard people who should know better refer to this first defeat at Forest Hills as a final round match, the result of which made Cochet champion. That probably is because the mind rejects the fact that the great champion should be beaten two stages before the end of the tournament he had won for six straight years. And the fact of it was such a shock that it was remembered longer than the possibly even more significant companion pieces that occurred on this remarkable day. It was remarkable enough, to be sure, since Cochet had not even been chosen to play singles for France the week before.

This was, in fact, the first of a series of Tilden-Cochet matches in which the American seemed at times to dominate the play with a whirlwind attack that appeared capable of blowing the little Frenchman right off the court, and was yet ever drawn back into coils from which he could not escape. Cochet played wonderful tennis in this match, reserving his best for the crisis of the fifth set when Tilden, 1–4 down and limping painfully on his bad knee, came suddenly back with the same breathtaking play that had appeared all through the final of 1924 on the same court. This was a characteristic effort by a wounded champion to shake himself loose from the net the little Lyonais had skillfully thrown about him, and save his crown. It brought Tilden from what had appeared to be rapidly approaching defeat to the edge of victory. He won five of six games decisively and stood at 6–5 and serving. He could now win merely by holding his own powerful service once more. It had been magnificent but it failed just short of complete success, exactly as even more brilliant efforts were to fail in the years ahead.

This is the thing to which I kept returning in thought afterward; that Tilden should by magnificent play—as fine as any he had shown in the past—reach a point where one service game separated him from victory, and then be unable to finish the match off.

We had seen clearly in this run of games that Tilden in his prime was more than a match for Cochet, as he had been for all others. But Tilden was not now in his prime. He had gone ever so little past it and that little was just enough to let the Frenchmen come level. The fact that Tilden had been handicapped by the injured knee in both these first two defeats obscured from us the fact of his beginning decline. We preferred to attribute his defeats to the knee, but I think that the Tilden of even a year earlier would have won in spite of that handicap.

We saw something pretty exciting on the other side of the net, too, as Tilden gathered himself at the service line for the big effort. It was clear that he would depend on the old reliable weapon, the cannonball serve, to carry the battle. Alas, after fifty games on a gimpy leg, the weapon was blunted a little. It had lost some of its edge and Cochet was now ready, having faced it so often, to strike it with entire confidence. Standing well inside the base line and taking the ball on the rise, the Frenchman put every serve into play offensively and, in this critical game, hit four cross-court forehand drives for outright winners beyond Tilden's reach. Two of these shots were returns of the service struck off the cannonball, and I still see all four as clearly as on the day they were made. None was hit with extraordinary pace and one was a slow curling shot that nevertheless could not be reached, so sharp was the angle and so near to the net did it pitch into Tilden's forecourt. Having won this crucial game with these shots, Cochet then won his own service at love and won the match by taking Tilden's service again in the fourteenth game. The full score was 6–8, 6–1, 6–3, 1–6, 8–6, and it was a forerunner of perhaps the strangest tennis match ever played, which was to come at Wimbledon next year.

The result was, of course, one of those sensations, and there was a great buzzing among the ten thousand or so present, at the wonder of it, in the interval before Johnston came out to play Borotra. I do not know what the others thought, but I was a little glad Tilden had lost, because now the way was clear at last, after seven years, for Little Bill to be champion again. He had beaten both Borotra and Lacoste within the week, had never been beaten by Cochet, and had never had much trouble with Richards. At Germantown Johnston had used the pace that his forehand could generate, hitting the ball as hard as he could every time. These whiplash drives had the sort of spin that caused the ball to drop quickly downward once across the net, and Borotra had been forced into volleying many of them upward into the tape at the top of the net. This fact alone, I had thought, this inability of Borotra to get close enough to volley the ball into parts of the court from which it could not be returned, or must be hit defensively, had been the key to Johnston's victory, which had not been easy, though achieved in straight sets, 8–6, 6–4, 9–7.

Borotra, like Cochet, had a capacity for brilliant volleying. He had to be forced back onto his weakest ground at the rear of the court sufficiently often to take some of the menace from his raids on the net. The volley was his only weapon, for he was a brilliant specialist. So even a second gained in his advance to the net was vital to him. The service was, therefore, extremely important since it was the blow that began his aggression. This service was never struck by Borotra to score, and he did not really count on a defensive reply. With him it was entirely a question of how quickly he could get to the net after serving.

The match was played late in the day and Johnston, hitting in the same way as he had the week before, appeared likely to achieve the same result. But the first two sets, which Johnston won 6–3, 6–4, had taken almost an hour to play and by the time the third started the moisture was beginning to rise on the grass. This factor began gradually to bring a change in the play. The ball, picking up the moisture, became a little heavier, the passing shot a little slower. Borotra's check volleys were given a little more guile, becoming harder to pick up, and the ones he got a chance to slam could not be handled at all.

The critical period for Borotra came about the middle of the third set when, with a series of desperate lunges at Johnston's drives, he succeeded in making one or two decisive volleys that put him in a position to win the set and earn the rest period. From there Johnston fought a losing battle, and since Borotra in his rushes to the net could be helped by mere fractions of time and distance, I believed the condition of the court alone was sufficient to enable him to win three straight sets from Johnston at Forest Hills, although he could not win even one at Germantown. I think too he was inspired, or certainly helped some, by Cochet's unexpected dethroning of the king, which had preceded. These Frenchmen were forever drawing strength from the exploits of one another in these years.

At any rate, the Basque did win, and twenty-four hours later he completed the rout of America's big four by defeating Richards, also in five sets. Borotra may have been helped even more by the moisture here, for this match too was played quite late. Richards, also the brilliant specialist who could match his man on the volley and over-head, was much less well equipped than Johnston off the ground.

After the defeat of Tilden I thought Cochet would be the French-man to win the title. After the first two sets of this semifinal with Lacoste, which Henri won by the most brilliant volleying I had seen up to that time, I was certain of it. Another instance of misjudgment. I misjudged the total effect of the volleying attack which Lacoste himself launched in the third set to save the situation. Lacoste knew that Cochet, like Borotra, could not be permitted to camp at the net.

I did not see the last match of that surprising tournament, prefer-ring to be at Baltusrol, but it was said to have been one of the quick-est and dullest of finals. Borotra had already played what amounted to two finals in beating Johnston and Richards on successive days, and just about every point had meant something like a hundred-yard dash for him. He never seemed likely to win a set from Lacoste and was beaten 6–4, 6–0, 6–4.

Once more I had the chance to sum up the impressions of the summer on shipboard back to France, and I came to the melancholy conclusion that France had now usurped America's place and that a new tennis cycle had begun. At the end of this summer of 1926 Tilden had been beaten twice by Lacoste, indoors and out, by Cochet at Forest Hills, and by Borotra indoors. Cochet also had beaten Richards twice, and Borotra had beaten Johnston. All these victories had been scored in championship or Davis Cup play and French players now held the national titles on board courts indoors, on hard courts, and on grass outdoors, of France, England, and the United States. They sailed home without the team trophy, but every member of the defending team had been beaten by a Frenchman within a week of the Challenge Round and there was no escaping the feeling that France had put a lien on the Cup for delivery the next September.

CHAPTER TWELVE

I DID not get around to revealing these logical conclusions in print for some months. The occasion for going into the matter was the arrival in Paris in the early spring of 1927 of Tilden on safari. Big Bill had come, he let it be known, looking for big game. He was especially eager to do battle on their own preserves with those upstarts who had contrived in some unaccountable manner to rob him of his crown. He came seeking lost honors and determined to recover them.

This was the beginning of quite the most remarkable tennis year of my experience and, I should think, the most interesting that tennis has known. It was, moreover, the prelude to a three-year period which I think the most interesting period in a long span of observing this game in many places. The Musketeers' long chase after Tilden was nearing its end. They had closed in on him at the end of the 1926 season and now were preparing to finish the job with a three-pronged assault which would end in the capture of the Cup, still the foremost consideration. But they knew that, although they had cornered Tilden and inflicted severe wounds, they had not yet quite brought him down to stay. Like a master swordsman at bay, Big Bill would turn and give battle. But they were too many for him. When one went down another came at him. When one failed another sprang to attack the wounded giant and the one downed was soon on his feet again stronger than before. This is what produced that wonderful series of tennis battles now just ahead.

In 1927, when Tilden was in his thirty-fifth year, he met the three Frenchmen seven times on the Continent, in England, and in the United States, winning three matches and losing four. He was twice within a single point of defeating Lacoste in one match before losing, and in another he stood two sets to love, 5–1 against Cochet before losing in five sets. And with his own racket, almost single-handed, he came very near to denying France the Davis Cup for still another year.

By now, though, Big Bill had been forced at last to begin payment of his due to advancing age. He was now a champion whose powers and whose energies could be calculated. Only to a certain point, though, for Tilden had developed wonderful new plots and stratagems. Definitely past his best, he could be pinned down for a set or two, but could not always be held. The Musketeers had at last found the way to beat him, but Tilden had to slip back a little for them to do so, and they could even then never be quite certain. And how magnificent were the losing battles he fought and how even more luminous were the triumphs the old master now and then brought off!

From his arrival in France in April of 1927 as a deposed king seeking to destroy the usurpers in their own stronghold, until his triumphant return to Wimbledon as champion for the third time in 1930, Tilden played a total of eighteen matches in France, England, and the United States against Lacoste, Cochet, and Borotra. He won only eight of them, all five from Borotra, two from Cochet, and one from Lacoste, but these matches were for me among the great moments of tennis history, and I do not think there are so many such moments as there used to be.

Tilden had not visited Europe since 1921, when he had successfully defended the title won at the old Wimbledon a year earlier, and had played also in Paris. At that time he was already recognized as the world's best player, but he had not yet reached full development, had not ascended to that towering place where he was to stand alone during three or four years of complete, unchallenged supremacy. He was actually, though unbeaten anywhere in the world, still an improving champion in 1921–22.

During the years of his supremacy Tilden had felt no urge to visit Europe. European tennis had not in those early years of the decade quite reached the point where a round of the Continental tournaments could be an excessively profitable venture for a man of Tilden's potential as a drawing card. By the standards of pay established later on for players to whom Tilden could have given thirty, both as player and showmen, Big Bill would have been worth no less than $1,000 a week.

But Tilden did all right at home during those early years of the Lawless Decade. He had inherited money and if it could all be added up he probably made more money as an amateur than any other player. He spent more too, no doubt, than any other, including those early millionaires who started the whole thing and carried the game around the world.

Another thing that kept Tilden home in these years was his intense interest in the stage. It was almost as great as his interest in tennis and he longed to make his mark as an actor and playwright. He wrote plays, produced them, and acted in them, invariably losing all the money he put up. These were terribly frustrating experiences for Tilden, for he was so bad that people laughed. It is not likely that any one who saw Tilden on the stage can forget the experience. It was certainly embarrassing and for me it was even more. I felt ashamed for him, almost humiliated. Tilden himself, of course, never knew how incredibly bad he was as an actor. In admitting that he had perhaps been foolish to waste so much money in that way, he attributed it only to bad luck, never to lack of talent.

So Tilden had many good reasons for not going to Europe. He was very busy at home. Let them come to him. And that is exactly what the Frenchmen did. They wanted to play Tilden as often as they could to improve their own games by exposing them to the best, to probe and study, to see if they could not get close to him and finally to find a way to beat him. That is why the lot of them, all four Musketeers, had gone to New York in February of 1926 for the U. S. Indoor Championships and for a Franco-American team match they had arranged.

They sought every opportunity to meet Tilden and, since he would not come to them, they went to him, observing, discussing, and comparing notes on what they experienced. In this they had the support and advice of Suzanne Lenglen, who saw before anyone else the road leading to tennis supremacy for France. I believe it was she who set the Musketeers upon it.

The gist of the collective French logic went something like this. You must try to make Tilden serve the cannonball every time he toes the service line. He must not be allowed to hold it in reserve. He will be fifty years old, Suzanne once said, and you still won't beat him if he can hold back that big service. The little black book in which Lacoste kept his tennis observations noted that Tilden's cannonball hit the mark eight times out of ten when he could use it sparingly or only in critical situations.

In order to make him use it more frequently you must make him play long games when you yourself are serving. Try to put him in a position where he must use the cannonball to shorten his own service games in order to conserve his energy. Then, after you have faced this terrible service for a set or so, it becomes possible to take it on the rise, to put it into play, and start another long rally. You get gradually adjusted to it, and constant use has taken something from it.

But by this spring of 1927 the situation had changed around. Tilden was no longer the pursued. He himself was the hunter and part of his mission in Europe this year was to find out how great was the danger to the Davis Cup. Now, on his return after six years, Big Bill, though refusing to admit it to himself, had already passed over the divide and begun the long journey down the far slope. Europe thus never did see Tilden in all his majesty, only as he was rising and at the slow decline. They had many fleeting glimpses of this mightiest of players at his best, both in France and England, during 1927 and 1928, and were amazed at the quality of the tennis, declaring that they had seen nothing like it in their lives. Nor had they.

For Tilden still was a great player. We should not be mistaken about that, for it would be unfair to the Frenchmen who brought him down. Time had given him only the gentlest tap on the shoulder but, as we were soon to see, time, though seemingly afraid to touch him, had not passed him by altogether the way he himself pretended for a while to believe.

The publication of my thoughts and conclusions regarding Tilden's decline, coinciding with his arrival in Paris, made my next encounter with him a rather violent one. Big Bill had come over with Frank Hunter as doubles partner and had stopped off in Paris enroute to Berlin, where he was to play in series of European team matches arranged by the United States Lawn Tennis Association before playing in the French Championships and at Wimbledon.

I approached him at his hotel, the Carlton on the Champs Élysées, and immediately received a severe chastisement right there in the lobby for my audacity in writing that the great Tilden had slipped. The piece had been printed in the Paris *Herald* that morning and Tilden seemed infuriated by it. He shook his finger and his voice rose high and loud into practically a shout.

I was terribly embarrassed for myself and a little also because I felt he was making a fool of himself in public without knowing it. It was perfectly dreadful, he said, that uninformed people, and therefore people with no basis for judgment, were permitted to write such tripe in disparagement of their betters.

Tilden had himself been quoted in the papers after Forest Hills as saying, most graciously, much the same thing, but over the winter he had apparently convinced himself that it was not true. He was, after all, the greatest, and he had not got that way by underestimating his own ability. Like actors, the egoism of great athletes is part of their talent. Now he berated and lectured me on tennis values, hurling his thunderbolts from his great height.

After a while the storm abated a little and he came down the mountain to my level, inviting me to have a cup of tea, of which cheering brew he had himself been about to partake when I entered. All this had taken place while standing in the lobby with an interested audience, but soon we were settled for a calmer and more rewarding talk. And damned if he didn't pretty nearly convince me.

I found Tilden in repose an intense and most intelligent man, and in our occasional encounters during the next twenty years and more we enjoyed a kind of friendship. It was never close and I had always a feeling that Bill maintained for me a precarious balance between unwilling approval and a sort of half contempt. He never once had the slightest praise of anything I wrote about him, however complimentary it might be, and he was often furiously critical. Tilden accepted praise as his due and resented anything even slightly the other way. And yet he was quite generous toward his opponents, often praising them beyond their due, I thought.

I value this particular interview for the light it threw on Tilden's development as tennis technician. I was curious about his strokes and the long period of gestation. After we had established a basis for unemotional discussion, I asked about those years of preparation before he became champion. He spoke freely about this, giving me much material which I appreciated and used profitably over the years.

"Look," he said, holding me with his eye, "I worked hard, darn hard, for five or six years until I was twenty-five. And I was pigheaded. All the experts I knew and all my friends in Philadelphia tennis kept telling me I had to decide whether I wanted to be a backcourt player or a net player and go to work on one or the other. I didn't believe them. I wanted to be both. I wanted an all-court game.

"You wouldn't think so, but I was an imitator. I believe in imitation. You can't reproduce another man's strokes exactly, but in trying to do that you can discover a good stroke of your own. My forehand drive at its best is the nearest thing I could make it to the forehand of the Australian J. O. Anderson. I realize it actually has no resemblance to Anderson's but that's where it came from. That's the basis on which I worked long and hard.

"My sliced backhand, the defensive one, was given to me by Joe Armstrong, who was intercollegiate champion (from Harvard) at the time when I was trying to improve my game. I started out by trying to imitate Armstrong's fine slice, only the one I finally perfected did not resemble it much."

This sliced backhand, with which Tilden could do extraordinary things, was an important part of his repertoire of strokes, but I wanted to know about the other backhand, that electrifying bang that had already at the time we spoke lost a little of its glitter but had been one of the greatest of all tennis strokes. This one stroke, as noted earlier, made it impossible for any contemporary to keep him on the defensive for long. I believed it to be the finest single stroke developed during my years of watching tennis. I said something of this to Tilden and, pleased, he was glad to talk about it.

"When Bill Johnston and I began our long rivalry in the Nationals, in 1919," he said, "he beat me so easily I was shocked. I had beaten him in unimportant matches [Newport and the East-West series] and thought I could do it again. What a shock I got! I never had a chance. He pounded that backhand and tore it to pieces. I couldn't handle him at all on that side.

"All through the match I was saying to myself that I had to have an offensive backhand or give up. So I got it. You've probably heard the story and it's true. I went to Providence that winter and worked indoors all day four days a week on nothing but the backhand. This was the most intensive work I ever did and it made the difference. The new shot made it possible for me to win Wimbledon, all Davis Cup matches, and the American title in 1920. Johnston pounded the backhand again, but I had just barely enough to win. He never has beaten me again in the Nationals, and I think it is just that one thing that gives me the edge over him."

In this way the encounter, which had begun so violently, wound up as the pleasantest visit I ever had with Tilden. I think he always did enjoy our subsequent encounters, although there usually was a certain amount of disagreement, now and then violent. His mind was quite sharp, and I think he enjoyed striking it against something that would give off a spark.

Tilden said that day that he already was in training for St. Cloud and Wimbledon and was eager to do battle with the Frenchmen again. There had been two factors involved in his 1926 defeat by Lacoste and Cochet, he explained over the teacups. Two causes, both of which had since been eliminated. First, he had been badly handicapped by the injured knee. I did not remind him that he had discounted this factor at the time, for I realized it was in accord with his idea of sportsmanship never to detract from an opponent's achievement.

I wondered, however, if he had not exaggerated the injury afterward in his own mind to make his defeats acceptable to himself. He certainly had been below his old best at Germantown and Forest Hills and, if you thought about it long enough and were looking for excuses, it all could be attributed to the knee. Elaborate such wishful thinking and it becomes not only acceptable but convincing.

In the second place, Tilden said, he foolishly had taken both Cochet and Lacoste too lightly. They were better than he had thought. This was a serious mistake, not to recognize danger, and it served him jolly well right that they beat him. He didn't realize they could both make certain shots under pressure and he had no idea Lacoste was such a smart tennis player.

"René [he pronounced it Rainy] has a tactical sense of the highest order," was the way Tilden put it, and he said it was inexcusable not to have known it from playing him in 1925, when Lacoste came so close to winning.

"But he was only a schoolboy then," Tilden continued. "I knew he couldn't beat me. I was a fool. He came back with a special service he perfected just for me. In that first one he was figuring things out all the time. He outsmarted me."

Tilden intimated that being outsmarted was the unpardonable sin and he would chastise Lacoste severely for having the effrontery to do it. Anyhow, all that was in the past. No more mistakes. He knew exactly how to beat them now. Forewarned was forearmed. But he had to be in the very best shape possible. Absolutely top condition. Part of the training program was skating and I could come with him, if I liked, to the Palais de Glace, a popular rink of that day in Paris. I did not like, and he left me, saying, "I'll be back for St. Cloud and you'll see."

He was back right enough and I did see that he was perfectly correct in saying that he knew how to beat them both. He was wrong about being in top shape physically. He would never again reach that perfection of conditioning that he had known and that had made him one of the most remarkable athletes of all. That was to be the difference from now on. Big Bill had passed into his athletic twilight. It was to be a long, lingering twilight with occasional brilliant, almost blinding, flashes from his setting sun, but the signs of age were to become ever more plainly visible now.

He arrived back in Paris on schedule toward the end of May, but my hoped-for second visit with him was not possible because of another unscheduled arrival of a young man named Charles Lindbergh. The tennis tournament turned out to be not quite as important an event as it might have been. Held for the last time in the sylvan recesses of St. Cloud, these French Championships of 1927 remain the most confused and the most difficult to straighten out in my mind of all tournaments.

It was, in fact, an exciting two weeks of tennis, but I have to go to the files to get any true picture of what happened before the climax. With the aid of what was written at the time I can reconstruct the final in which Lacoste defeated Tilden, a match that was called by me and others the toughest ever played on the European Continent. That may seem an extravagant statement, but it certainly was mercilessly taxing on both.

To reach the final, Lacoste defeated Hunter and Borotra, and Tilden beat Cochet in the semifinal. It is the latter match I would like to recall because it was their first meeting since Black Thursday, but sometimes I wonder if I actually saw it at all, although I know perfectly well I did. Tilden's book *My Story*, written more than twenty years after, says merely, "I scored decisively over Cochet in the semifinal." I feel confident he did so, although the book has many misstatements of fact.

The files tell me that the scores were 9–7, 6–3, 6–2, and that I myself quoted Cochet, after the match, as saying, "Those who said

Tilden was through have another guess. I said already last year that Big Bill would come back stronger than ever."

Tilden's recollection of the Lacoste match was not exact. The score he gives is quite wrong, but he certainly was correct in saying he knew how to beat Cochet. He showed very clearly once more that the best Tilden would beat the best Cochet, another indication that he had passed his peak when the little man from Lyons started tormenting him through the next few years.

Lindbergh landed on Saturday, May 21, a day when the preliminary skirmishes of the tournament were being played, and I did not even get out to St. Cloud until the second week. The final was played on the second Sunday after Lindy's arrival and somehow the erroneous word got around that he would go to St. Cloud to see Tilden play Lacoste. People stormed the place to see Lindy and if they did not see him, they did see one of the very finest of that series of encounters between these two players.

Lindbergh went instead to a luncheon of the International League of Aviators at the Pré Catalen in the Bois. Invitations were worth gold and very hard to come by. I owned one and was eager to make contact with the hero about whom I had been writing for two weeks. I thought I had a greater desire to attend the luncheon than to see the tennis, the details of which I could, in any event, pick up later because of the difference in time between Paris and New York. I discovered though that in the end I preferred the tennis. I gave away my luncheon ticket and I have been happy ever since that I had the good sense to do so.

I had expected to have another talk with Tilden on his return, but the hullabaloo over Lindy made it impossible. Bill had been giving off confident statements about regaining his place at the top of the heap and they appeared to have some basis. He was said to be in devastating form, and in common with many thousands of Frenchmen I was eager to see this battle with Lacoste. With Suzanne gone and Cochet beaten, people looked to Lacoste to humble the haughty American before their own eyes, as both Cochet and Lacoste had done before Tilden's compatriots in America last year. So Cochet's defeat by Tilden had made a very great affair of the final. The French had not yet brought home the Davis Cup and this match was looked to for an indication of whether or not their hopes of capturing it this year was to be fulfilled.

It was a hot day for Paris and Lacoste set out deliberately, I think, to make the match a real test of Tilden's physical resources. They battled for more than three hours before one of the most demonstrative tennis gatherings ever assembled, for this was the first really big tennis occasion for France, forerunner of five years of excitement to come. Suzanne's greatest exploits had been outside the country, or at any rate away from Paris, and French tennis was only now becoming international in the true sense.

Lacoste suffered severe leg cramps but recovered to win from a losing position. Tilden played one of the finest matches of his life but lost in the sixty-first game after serving what appeared to many to be a winning ace at match point, two games before the end. And that ball, which would have won for Tilden, was called a fault by Cochet, who had taken the outer service line for the final.

Tilden's intense personality exerted a striking influence on both the play and the crowd throughout this incident-filled match, and at the end there was a demonstration of joy and enthusiasm such as I don't think I have since witnessed on a tennis court. It was all friendly enough, simply an overflow of enthusiasm after tension. Lacoste was, after all, a home-town boy and, as a champion who had conquered heavy odds, he gave them assurance of even greater things to come. We were to have plenty of incidents, and unpleasant ones, in the years ahead, but all was now good humor, including the way Tilden took his defeat after almost unbearable strain. I doubt that there ever has been a tennis battle waged with more perfect sportsmanship under trying conditions, or with greater mutual admiration between adversaries.

The play began, however, with Tilden showing nervousness and petulance. The court was soft from rains and also from a hose wetting, and Tilden preferred a faster surface to minister to his speed of stroke. He objected to movement in the crowd, demanded that photographers be ordered out of the court enclosure, and seemed wholly unable to settle down to business. The heat was excessive, his nervousness continued after play began, and Tilden lost his service in the first game without winning a point.

He got hold of himself quickly, though, and then for the next three hours Big Bill gave still another demonstration of how completely his personality could dominate and give flavor to a tennis match. Lacoste had nearly perfect touch, and Tilden's task was seen immediately to be of the sternest sort, but Tilden managed somehow throughout to give the impression that nothing could stop him.

Lacoste, quietly confident, revealed early that he had given much thought to this problem. He served a spinning ball of medium pace to the forehand line, confirming Tilden's observation. It did not surprise Big Bill now, but it did seem to restrict his freedom of action and to worry him a little.

Tilden went to a lead of 4–2, nevertheless, with each game providing long exchanges and streams of wonderful backhand strokes from corner to corner. Lacoste squared the set by carefully calculated play and then won it after taking Tilden's service with as fine a passing shot straight down the line as ever was hit.

The loss of four games in a row after he had established a winning lead indicated to Tilden what he was in for and he reacted quickly and characteristically, capturing the second set in ten evenly and fiercely fought games until near the end, when Lacoste came to the net on the wrong ball and was promptly passed. The two sets had taken almost an hour and they were still dead level.

Tilden's reserves of strength seemed to be superior in the third set, which was even more fiercely fought, when he imposed such a strain on Lacoste that the Frenchman was attacked by cramps. Contributing to this condition, at least in part, was Tilden's relentless accuracy and his ability to force Lacoste to chase deftly placed drives endlessly. Lacoste lost two games he seemed on the point of winning because his reduced mobility left his court exposed.

Tilden went to 5–3 and here Lacoste, unable to move freely, resorted to the chop and the drop shot to save his legs and I have never seen more clever use of these slowing tactics. For two games the Frenchman stroked the ball perfectly and placed it exactly to spots from which Tilden could not reply effectively. When he squared the set at 5–all the cheering was a deafening roar.

But Lacoste's intentions, concealed for a time, were now revealed to Tilden, who, anticipating a drop shot at a vital point, was running toward the spot as the ball was struck. Tilden had not invented the drop shot but he had perfected it as an offensive weapon. He knew that the most effective reply to it often is another drop shot and, using this reply, he won Lacoste's service and the third set 7–5. Tilden had thus won a set in which the Frenchman seemed to have established a strong tactical advantage and in doing so had placed further strain on his opponent.

Lacoste, returning after the interval restored by massage, sent the crowd into new uproars by taking Tilden's service so confidently and so effectively that, after losing the first two games, he won six of the last seven games for the set, 6–3. Now they entered the fifth set and the strain of it was great for both players and spectators as fortunes rose and fell. The heat was even greater now and each time they changed courts up to 4–all, Tilden poured drinking water over his head from a pitcher under the umpire's stand.

Another of those lovely, slowly curling backhands down the line brought Lacoste to 5–4, but Tilden, gathering himself for the effort, replied with three service aces. Lacoste went ahead 7–6 and 8–7, but Tilden, hitting deep to the corners and coming in to volley, finally won the Frenchman's service and led 9–8 with his own service to come. Twice he reached match point with only one cannonball between him and victory. The first one was angled toward the right line and the player never lived who could have got a racket on it. It seemed a winning ace. Tilden thought so; Lacoste appeared to. But it was called out, a fault.

From the railed-off press section high in a corner of the stand, I could just barely see Cochet in his chair against the back wall as he threw out his left hand, indicating that the ball had pitched beyond the line. He made the call instantly, without the slightest hesitation, and when Lacoste looked inquiringly toward him, Henri extended his arms, palms inward about an inch apart, telling everyone that the ball had been out by that much, the tiny difference between victory and defeat. Tilden did not question the call but worked back to match point again. There he missed an easy shot, an ominous sign. Lacoste then squared the set and soon was ahead again himself at 10–9. And then he won the American's service, and the match, when Tilden served a double fault at the first match point against him. Big Bill probably had been upset by the Cochet call after all, but he made no sign.

There followed a tennis demonstration I have never seen repeated. People stood and shouted for minutes and swarmed onto the court to hail the boy champion now grown to a man's stature. This had been a test of nerves as well as of tactical skill and technique, and it was

Tilden who had faltered when in sight of victory, although his reserves did not appear to be depleted. Bill had been called on foot-faults several times, a rare thing with him, but otherwise he seemed to have been very nearly at his resourceful best. I decided reluctantly that the difference really had been in the ages of the two men.

CHAPTER THIRTEEN

Wहile the leading tennis players of the world were occupied in mid-June of 1927 with preliminary grass court play in and around London leading to Wimbledon, I was making the first of many visits to St. Andrews, in Scotland, the shrine of golf, to see Bobby Jones carried off the final green of the Old Course by enthusiastic Scots. Bob had just won his second straight British Open title with a record score of 285 and it was a real mob scene, by which I believe I was more overwhelmed than Jones, who had captivated the Scots by his play and his manner.

I brought back only emotional thoughts of this historic golf occasion, but the 1927 Wimbledon, to which I returned immediately, remains for me the most exciting and dramatic tennis tournament I have known, and the easiest to remember. I think all who were there would say the same. This was partly, no doubt, due to the fact that it had been building up in the minds of the public for weeks because of the return of Tilden and his effort to repeat at the new tennis grounds his victory of six years earlier at the old.

In spite of his defeats by the Frenchmen, Tilden was still regarded in England as the world's greatest player, and it was thought only fitting that his "comeback" should be achieved at the headquarters of the game with all the Frenchmen in the field against him. They were all there, and the seeding had been arranged with a Tilden-Cochet semifinal and a Tilden-Lacoste final in view. It didn't work out that way. Neither Tilden nor Lacoste reached the final, and it was Cochet who authored most of the excitement as he survived a week-long series of crises to become champion.

It is unlikely that the public interest in this tournament right from its start ever has been exceeded and this was in a country where no home player was good enough to be among the eight seeds. When I arrived at the grounds on opening day there were at least five thousand in line waiting for what we call the general admission sales windows to be opened. Of course all reserved places had been sold months before. The sustenance with which many in line had provided themselves indicated that they had been there for many hours. This was a whole week before the quarterfinal matches could be played. So it was, all through the first week, and when the real excitement began with the second Monday, we passed long lines when we came out at the end of each day. They were prepared to camp out all night to be sure of getting tickets at noon next day that would permit them to stand all afternoon on the concrete terraces of the center court. And there are very few nights even in an English summer when it is pleasant to sit in the open air for very long.

By the second Monday the unseeded Frank Hunter had come through to the quarterfinal against Cochet, and here began the astonishing series of matches that brought the little Frenchman through to the title. In each of his last three matches against Hunter, Tilden, and Borotra, Cochet lost the first two sets, was each time in sight of defeat, and then won the next three. After his narrow escape against Hunter on Monday, he had to play Tilden on Wednesday and Big Bill, who had beaten him in Paris only a few weeks earlier, had been playing the most magnificent tennis.

This meeting of Cochet and Tilden was, of course, one of the most famous tennis matches ever played. I can still speak of it in detail because I kept the point score and notes made that day, but I could not explain it then and I cannot now. Tilden, having noted what happened to Hunter, went all out from the start to win quickly. He unleashed a withering attack of unanswerable speed. Drives from both wings, either "flat" or carrying top spin, were hitting the lines, out of reach or too swift to return, and the service often brought no reply at all.

Here was Tilden in all his majesty, "blowing his opponent off the court" with irresistible gusto, and at the end of the first set, which he won 6–2, I made a note to the effect that probably all but a very few of those looking on must have been amazed at the quality of the tennis, since they never had seen anything like it. Cochet seemed overwhelmed. Tilden's great pace and accuracy of stroke from any part of the court gave the little Lyonese no chance to organize a defense and no time in which to bring his own best weapons into play.

The Frenchman became a little more venturesome as the second set began and his confidence increased enough so that he could at least attempt a counterattack. He tried a crisp forcing shot to Tilden's short forehand, inviting the return across the body that could be volleyed out of reach. This got Cochet four games, but Tilden still won all the critical points and games, and it was clear that if Big Bill did not begin to make errors, all would soon be over.

And then, with the beginning of the third set, Tilden launched his most devastating attack. Never on that side of the Atlantic had he struck with such real violence. Cochet searched in vain for an effective weapon to stem the tide as Tilden went steadily on, literally hitting through his man, dominant, domineering, and arrogant. It was the Tilden of 1921–25 back on top, piling up the games. He seemed in a big hurry to get it over with. After banging his way to 5–1 with a cannonball that Cochet could not reach, Bill threw the two balls remaining in his hand over the net behind the service and could hardly wait for Cochet to gather them in and serve what we all thought would be the last game. In the competitors' stand just below the press box I saw Hunter hurrying out to be there when his doubles partner should come victorious from the arena. But Frank had still another hour to wait and no congratulations to give at the end of it.

For now the incredible happened. I have to keep referring to that point score, which I know to be accurate, to reassure myself. From 15–all in the seventh game, Tilden, going all out for a quick finish, hit three of Cochet's serves with all his force but all three sailed beyond the lines, out of court. What matter? Tilden's service was to come and Cochet had won only two points against it during the third set.

They changed ends and Tilden waited impatiently, three balls in his left hand, for Cochet to take his place. But Tilden's sudden overhitting in the other game had not been due to his haste to get it over. Something had gone wrong. The cannonball missed the mark also, missed it rather badly, and Tilden hit every other ball out or into the net. He could not win a point. He lost the service at love and then another love game as Cochet served. Tilden was still trying to hit winners, and doing it with all the old pace, but now every ball went wild. The earlier stream of winning points became a stream of errors. From 15–all in that seventh game Cochet actually won seventeen points in succession, going from 1–5 down to 5–all and 30–0 before Tilden won a point, and yielding only four points altogether before winning the third set 7–5. Three of these points were in the last game, which Tilden managed to force to deuce when control of his cannonball returned momentarily.

People could not understand what had happened any more than I could. Tilden had said before going into court that he was "not going to let that little fellow get me into a long match," emphasizing the pronoun. And now, after seeming to have timed it perfectly, this had happened.

There is no rest period at Wimbledon after the third set, as there is at Forest Hills, and they went directly into the fourth set with no more than a quick mopping of brows. The match was not over. Tilden got back some of his effectiveness. The sudden check in the numbing attack, however, had given Cochet's own assets, smothered under the avalanche of lethal blows, a chance to operate. With the pressure off, he could work out a plan of campaign. He offered easy, soft strokes, refusing to give Tilden the pace from which to generate counterspeed.

Tilden pressed more and more to recover his accuracy but the initiative passed to the Frenchman, never to return. There were some periods of fine play in the last two sets, but they came when Tilden made desperate rallies to recover lost ground and the physical strain on him was great. He recovered from 2–4 down in the fourth set to 4–all, but the reaction was immediate and Cochet won the set 6–4. Tilden had played the set very well, but he had expended great energy only to lose it, and the possibility that he might win a fifth set now, it seemed clear to all, had gone.

Cochet, still fresh, took the net more often now to bring off his volleying coups. Tilden's formerly incisive passing shots had lost pace and Cochet, increasing the speed of his own forcing shots, was calling the tune in almost every game. Tilden, with a great effort, rallied again to win the enemy service in the fifth game and led by 3–2, with his own service to come, but the effort cost him so much he could do no more. It was the last game he could win. He was done physically and his face showed it. Two double faults followed immediately, two more in the eighth game and three errors in the ninth.

Tennis writers have a way of speaking of results which they did not expect as "stunning surprises" and in this case at least the use of the words is justified. People certainly were surprised, and I was, if not stunned, completely bewildered. I have discussed this match many times with many persons, one of them being Tilden himself, and I never have arrived at a satisfactory explanation of what happened, of why the greatest player of all could not win just one more game after the most brilliant play of a long career had taken him to the verge, as we say, of overwhelming victory. He could not win even one single point until it was too late.

It had not been an exhausting match at all up to that third-set collapse. There had been rain earlier and the day was cool. At one moment Tilden, in full possession of his physical and mental powers, seemed to be crushing his opponent with a withering attack, and in the next he was done, all control had left him, and he was in distress.

Tilden declared vehemently some time after the match that the whole explanation could be found in Cochet's rising brilliantly to great heights in the face of defeat. This, of course, was nonsense, as Tilden very well knew. Some said that Tilden, having demonstrated beyond doubt twice within a month that he could beat Cochet, wanted to make sure that the little wizard would be chosen to play Davis Cup singles. This was, likewise, moonshine.

Another popular theory was that, when leading 5–1 in that third set, Tilden had noticed that the King of Spain had just entered the Royal Box and he decided to prolong the match a little to give Alfonso, a great fan, some tennis. And then, having relaxed, he couldn't get it back. Tilden assured me later that he had never been conscious at all of the royal visitor's arrival, and I believed him. I had not been conscious of it myself.

I think now that the explanation might be found in a remark Tilden addressed to me immediately after the match, or as quickly as I could reach the dressing room. "Maybe you were right," he said and he said it with what I thought was scorn, but in a voice that carried a certain hatred too. He was referring to the statement that he had now passed his best years and could no longer call on that matchless stamina. Still he defeated Cochet in four sets later that year and Lacoste in five sets more than a year after.

F. R. Burrow, after eighteen years as referee of the tournament, remarked that the fact that Cochet ever got to the final "was the most astonishing event that has happened in my time at Wimbledon." That Henri ever won that final is even more so. Borotra had beaten Lacoste in the other semifinal, in which the Basque had used the crowd and its emotions almost as a weapon of victory. Against Cochet in the final Borotra had six match points, the third of which also is a part of Wimbledon history.

Leading 5–3 and 40–30 in the fifth set, Borotra served and dashed in. Cochet hit the return down the middle and also closed in. There followed a lightning-like exchange of volleys at close range. It ended when Cochet scored with a stroke which I thought he had "scooped" up with a double hit. Others thought so too. The players looked to the umpire's chair and we all expected the call to be "Not up. Game, set and match to Mr. Borotra." It never came. Instead the umpire called "Deuce." The stroke had been ruled legal. Borotra served again and had three more match balls, losing one on a heart-breaking net cord, while Cochet was climbing to 5–all. Cochet eventually won 7–5 and the third Musketeer had become Wimbledon champion.

That was the end of my most memorable Wimbledon, but before the climax there was a women's match I cannot ignore since it looms so large in memory and was, in some ways, the finest I have ever seen. Helen Wills, after an absence of two years, returned to win the first of eight Wimbledon titles. Her final round opponent was Lili de Alvarez, the Spanish girl who, though never a champion, was one of the most exciting and attractive players of her sex the game has known.

That the señorita, dark and handsome and with flashing smile, played tennis wholly for fun was as obvious to me as it had been that Dick Williams did. And since they both gloried in the half-volley, preferring it even when the extreme danger of using it was apparent, I am wondering if there may be some special joy to be had from employing this stroke. In a game where girls not excessively talented take themselves with such deadly seriousness and sometimes even burst into tears on the court, the lovely, carefree, exuberant Lili was a refreshing change. I greatly admired her way of playing, and watching her has given me as much real pleasure as the play of any other girl I can think of. With it all she was a person of rare and charming femininity.

Lili was good enough to be Wimbledon finalist three years in a row, and this was the middle one of them. It was a quick match of only eighteen games, which Miss Wills won 6–2, 6–4, because both her strokes and her physique were the more sturdy. But I doubt if any match ever played by two women could equal it for sustained attack on both sides of the net and the quality of strokes employed over such a long period.

This relatively short encounter was attack from first stroke to last. Both girls could hit winners off shots that themselves appeared to be winners, and in the whole match astonishingly few defensive strokes were employed. Miss Wills won the first set in a session of glorious hitting. The señorita instinctively favored the half-volley and she could bring off this time-saving and exciting shot from anywhere in the court equally as well at her level of play as Cochet and Williams could at their higher level.

At the beginning of the second set Lili brought out a maneuver that I never was to see any other girl, with the one exception of Lenglen, attempt against Miss Wills. This was to exchange full length drives from deep court and then to draw Miss Wills forward with a short, almost insolent flick to the forehand line. With this plan, the señorita went to 4–3 after a series of unforgettable exchanges. But she was at advantage three times before she got the game, and by the end of it Miss Wills, though she had yielded, had caught on.

Miss Wills now set out to defeat the plan by sheer speed of stroke, which made the final half-volleying coup impossible to bring off. This brought them to the crisis of the match, the eighth game. It was an extraordinary session of tremendous hitting, and the last point of it produced a rally the equal of which I have never seen again in women's tennis. Such sustained hitting and such gorgeous shots by two girls had never taken place on this court or, I imagine, anywhere else. Twenty strokes by each girl were counted, each hit to score, speed countered by more speed, until finally the señorita, perhaps in desperation, attempted once more to trap the other girl with her favorite coup and failed. The backhand half-volley curled out of court and the score was 4–all.

Both girls placed racket heads on the court for support and leaned exhausted over them while deluges of applause enveloped them. It was the end. The señorita could not recover her breath. She could win only one more point and, half-volley she ever so well, she never could win a set from Miss Wills. But for speed of attack and counterattack, for quality of stroke employed over a sustained period, I am wondering if women's tennis did not here reach its highest point during my time. I have since seen flashes of perhaps similar brilliance by individual girls, but never a succession of games in which two girls played with such virtuosity of stroke at the same time.

CHAPTER FOURTEEN

I HAD been looking forward all summer to crossing in the same ship with the French team, but this became impossible for me when they decided to sail for the United States immediately after winning the European zone final in Copenhagen the week following Wimbledon. Great enthusiasm attended the sailing of the *Paris*, and all the papers carried interviews full of hope and confidence. The whole French nation seemed involved in this Sixth Crusade and Les Mousquetaires were heroes going forth to fight for the honor of France and bring home the spoils.

Year after year these young men had gone across the ocean in search of the Davis Cup and had returned empty-handed. They had made five trips trying to win the trophy that had become, in that era of anti-American feeling because of controversy over the unpaid war debts, a symbol which it seemed everyone in France desired greatly to possess. Now at the start of this sixth journey the feeling was very strong in France that it would be the last.

It was a real disappointment not to sail with them, but I did speak briefly with the players before the boat train pulled out from the Gare St. Lazare, and at some length with Pierre Gillou, the captain and manager of the team who was to take a later ship. Then I wrote a lengthy analysis of the situation for my paper. The long road that these young men had traveled over the years, ending always short of success, extended back from Copenhagen through Rome, Bucharest, Eastbourne, Prague, Barcelona, Cabourg, Noordwijk, Évian, Dublin, Deauville, and Boston. These were the places where they had fought Davis Cup battles.

With Lacoste and Cochet as the babies of the squad, Borotra and Brugnon as the elders, they had set out upon the long trail in 1922 as juveniles and now, five years later, with even the youngest grown to tennis manhood, the goal appeared to be in sight. I wound up with a cautious prediction of a victory though by no means convinced.

Both Tilden and Johnston had been beaten by Frenchmen, so they no longer appeared invincible. Frenchmen had won the individual national titles of Great Britain and the United States with Tilden in the field. But Tilden might be a very different proposition, I thought, on his own courts before a home-town crowd and with the Cup at stake. No Frenchman had yet beaten Johnston in Davis Cup play, and Cochet never had even played Little Bill. I thought that the French were being overly optimistic, but I rather hoped they were right. Since I was then domiciled in Europe, I could contemplate with traitorous selfishness the presence of the Davis Cup in Paris, since with it would come the most important tennis of the following years and the French Championships would themselves become a major event.

When I rejoined the Musketeers at the Germantown Cricket Club in Philadelphia a few days before the Challenge Round, they still were in wonderful spirits. They had played in the invitation tournament at Southampton on Long Island and in the national doubles Championships at the Longwood Cricket Club, Boston, where they also had beaten Japan in the inter-zone final of the Cup series. Lacoste said he was particularly pleased with his match against Takeichi Harada, the Japanese number one, because "Harada played very much like Johnston" and he, Lacoste, was able to try out a new way of playing Little Bill.

I remember this because the remark puzzled me greatly. I could not see the resemblance, and I did not discover what the new plan was when Lacoste played Johnston on Thursday of that week. But I had by now begun to develop respect for Lacoste's judgment, even a little awe of his ability to weigh tennis matters. I had been close enough to this group to know that it was to Lacoste they all looked for advice about how this or that situation should be met.

I could not go the whole way with the Frenchmen in their predictions about the coming matches. They were certain Johnston could be beaten by both Lacoste and Cochet, and were in doubt only as to where they would get the other point necessary to win the Cup by three matches to two. It could come, they said, either from the doubles on the second day if Tilden did not play in the match, or if Tilden played both singles and doubles, from defeating Tilden in singles on the third day. Tilden had played some sort of tournament every week, except when on shipboard, since early spring, often singles, doubles, and mixed doubles. They thought he had played too much tennis to be fresh enough to wage a third successive long battle on the third day.

The French confidence was not really as solid as it appeared on the surface. Tilden had, after all, been twice within a point of beating Lacoste in June, had beaten Cochet easily in one match, and had been within a couple of points of overwhelming victory in another. But for some bad luck he might have won all three matches. In defeat he had been magnificent, and he seemed to be playing magnificently in practice for the Cup matches.

The French were counting heavily on what they hoped would be a favorable draw. Lacoste explained, not at the time but later, that very much depended on his being drawn to play Johnston the first day and then having a day's rest before meeting Tilden, who they were sure would play the doubles match on the second day. René said he had worked out especially the strokes and plan for beating Johnston and felt certain of success, although he had lost to Little Bill in the two previous years' Challenge Rounds. But with Tilden he felt he might need the help of cumulative fatigue and strain. He would not, he said, feel at all confident of beating a fresh Tilden on the first day, but on the third day Big Bill's power to conduct a long, tiring match, which Lacoste would try to impose upon him, would be considerably reduced.

The draw worked out exactly as the Frenchmen had hoped and they took it as a good omen. I thought of all these things on the train back to New York the night before the matches and spoke of them with Bill McGeehan on the ride back to Philadelphia the next day. McGeehan had been writing in his column that the Frenchmen probably would win the Cup and that it would be a very good thing if they did. Now he also said that the one who played Tilden on Saturday would beat him, and he was very interested to know how Lacoste had played Tilden at St. Cloud.

This was the first Challenge Round since the war in which there had been even a slight feeling that the Cup might be lost, and probably for this reason we found the crowd at the old club highly partisan. About thirteen thousand were in the wooden stands rising high around the court, and they did not try to conceal their feelings when Lacoste and Johnston came out to play the first singles match. But the first shock came immediately.

At the very first ball Lacoste attacked with more force than I had ever seen him use, and he never stopped applying all the speed to the ball he could command. The amount of pace the Frenchman could generate also was a surprise. This surely was the plan Lacoste spoke of later that he had worked out for use against Johnston, and very soon we saw how certain it was to work. Lacoste hit the ball hard to the corners, and Little Bill could not get there in time to deal with it effectively. That was the whole thing. Johnston missed with the backhand, and if the first of the famous forehand shots came back, as it did very often now since its pace was reduced, he missed that too. No more than a handful of games had been played when the result could be plainly seen.

Lacoste, perfectly trained, was driving the ball deep and true with a relentless, rhythmic smoothness and was serving to Johnston's wide forehand the same spinning ball that had handicapped Tilden a year earlier on the same court. The Frenchman was applying to Johnston the same principle of strong attack, which really constituted solid defense because it could not be countered, that Little Bill had forced upon Lacoste in other years.

It was a sad thing for those of us who loved Little Bill to see Johnston, the former fierce attacker, now helpless before a lesser attack than his had been a short time before. He was still the wonderfully appealing figure we all had known, but this was really the last stand of a great little fighter. The crowd did not recognize this at once, for Johnston actually was only fractions of a second slower than he had been the last time they had seen him. But tiny fractions of time are like miles to an athlete and some of us did see it.

There was the point that gave Lacoste a 5–2 lead in the first set. Johnston, chasing a beautiful backhand that Lacoste had shot down the line all the way, arrived so late in the forehand corner he could only lunge almost pathetically at the ball. Vincent Richards, now a professional and occupying a seat in the press box as a journalist, looked over and caught my eye. His lips formed one sad, tragic but almost eloquent word, "Legs." An occasional blast from the old Johnston forehand roused the crowd, but the end was swift and inevitable, for Lacoste had only to let the mistakes occur to win 6–3 6–2, 6–2.

The other match was very different. It was a testing fight all the way, and Cochet, though beaten in four sets, was able to cause

Tilden so much strain that the result of the Davis Cup may have been settled there and then. Lacoste had thought the whole result might turn in France's direction in this match that France lost. Everyone, of course, had in mind that strange affair at Wimbledon, and we all thought of it throughout the four sets, watching Tilden for any sign that he might be losing touch again.

Tilden was not so crushingly good as in the first two sets of the earlier match, and Cochet was very much better. The Frenchman was, in fact, so good that when he had taken the second set, by timing his advances to the net perfectly, one felt that he might win even if Tilden had no strange lapse this time. Tilden won finally, but under great stress and expenditure of energy, because of the importance of this match after Johnston's defeat. Particularly did he throw his strength into the service, and he brought a great roar from the crowd by finishing with an ace in the fourteenth game of the fourth set. The scores were 6–4, 2–6, 6–2, 8–6.

Because of what had happened to him earlier in the summer, Tilden dared not risk a fifth set against the best long-match player in the world, and the effort to avoid it undoubtedly took its toll. This was, incidentally, Tilden's last victory over Cochet as an amateur.

The Frenchmen were happy over the first day's results. They were sure now that Cochet would beat Johnston on Saturday and were equally sure that if the doubles had to be sacrificed to Tilden and Hunter, Tilden would have expended energy that he would not be able to recover. The weather also was a factor. It was very hot for the doubles. Nearly an hour and a half of hard play was required for the first three sets, with the United States leading 2–1 at the interval. The American counter to Borotra's brilliant display, which captured the first set 6–4, was a lobbing campaign to slow the game and deny the Basque and his partner, Brugnon, the speed on which they thrived.

One saw again what a consummate lobber Tilden was. His tosses were often so perfectly judged that Borotra, one of the greatest of smashers, could not get a full swing at the ball but had to push it back defensively. These tactics won the second and third sets, but they consumed much time in the heavy humid air.

When they returned after the rest interval, I noticed that Brugnon now stood at the back of the court while Borotra was receiving service. The lobs were allowed to bound before Borotra pounced upon them and the early capture of Hunter's service was the key to a squared match and a fifth set. I learned later that it was Lacoste, during the interval, who had suggested the new alignment, insisting on the great value to France of playing a fifth set even though it be lost.

It was lost, for Tilden was magnificent and ruthless, and Brugnon faded toward the end. So the United States led in the series, two matches to one, and need win only one of the remaining singles on Saturday to keep the Cup. But Tilden, on whom everything now depended, had played nine sets in two days in the heat, while both Lacoste and Cochet had enjoyed a day's rest.

The last day of the last Davis Cup Challenge Round that would be played in the United States for a decade or more, was, from the standpoint of both crowd and contestants, perhaps the most emotional of a long experience of these matters. When the stands they had set up at Germantown were full, there still were several thousands outside the club grounds clamoring to get in. Finally they were let in to sit on the grass around the edges of the arena, in the aisles, or to find standing room where they could. I had thought on the way out that tennis people, generally speaking, still had great confidence in Tilden's ability to carry the day. It seemed to me that nearly everyone still thought Tilden invincible in defense of the Cup, ignoring both the record, the inexorable passage of time, and what he had gone through on the two previous days.

Everyone could see even on Thursday that Johnston already probably had passed into the shadows and would surely lose to the wary and tough Cochet, ten years his junior. But by that time the Cup would be safely won by Tilden's victory over Lacoste. It seemed to me on arriving at Germantown that this was the mood of the crowd on that hot and sultry Saturday noontime, with thunder muttering in the distance.

After a while I realized that I was wrong. I think most of these people retained their hope, but were clinging to that alone. They thought that Tilden might bring it off, knowing that if he failed the Cup was lost. So when Big Bill made his magnificent but futile bid for victory, the excitement reached a rapturous emotional pitch I have seldom experienced at a sports event. And then when Tilden had spent his remaining energy grandly in his vain effort, gloom settled over the crowd, for we all knew that we were next going to witness not only the departure of the trophy, to which so much sentiment was attached, but also the passing of Billy Johnston, one of the most loved figures of American sport.

Tilden, weighing the values, apparently had decided to stake all on a frontal attack from the start in the hope of a quick victory. He threw everything into his service, using the cannonball for the second ball when he missed with the first. He served a dozen clean aces in the first set and lost it 6–4. Lacoste, imperturbable, almost lazy-looking but certain of his method, wasted no energy. He was the cat that waits, and the cat that springs, tireless in defense, instantaneous in attack. When he first won Tilden's service and then held his own without difficulty, all the dynamic American blasts that followed could not save the set.

The speed on Lacoste's ground strokes was appreciably greater than at St. Cloud, when he had sought to prolong the match. Now he was hitting with surprising power and extraordinary accuracy. It was not to score always, but to induce a defensive return or an outright error. The defense against the whirlwind attack of the earlier encounters with Tilden had now changed from merely keeping the ball in play to prolong exchanges, to pace that would in itself constitute defense. To the cannonball he opposed the slower spinning service with a distinct "break" which, if it did not draw an error, gave Lacoste control of the following exchange.

Nevertheless, Tilden led 3–0 in the second set and then settled back to keep that lead with the service. He won the set 6–2, but it had cost him. Lacoste had made him pay dearly for, after serving all through with great fury, Tilden had been made to run many times back and forth across his base line. And now in the third set the web that Lacoste was weaving grew stronger game by game. The Frenchman remained in back court except when drawn in by a drop shot, which Tilden used in desperation in an effort to break up the relentless driving. Now and then there came from Tilden a shot of the old unanswerable kind, but except on service they never were consecutive.

Tilden won his service games to 3–all and then Lacoste, never varying his plan, won the American service to lead 4–3. This was only the second time in the match that Tilden's service had been lost and he had won Lacoste's twice, both in the second set. But it was an ominous sign, for it indicated that Tilden's main weapon was being blunted by overuse. The end was near as Lacoste ran out the third set to lead 2 sets to 1.

Tilden lost the second game of the fourth set by serving a double fault to give Lacoste a 2–1 lead. He saved the next game from 40–love, and all the people cheered, but Tilden now was approaching the absolute limit of his physical resources. Lacoste went out with beautiful scoring shots off Tilden drives that had lost their sting and won the match by 6–4, 2–6, 6–3, 6–3.

That made it two matches each, and it seemed somehow unfair that the final burden of defense should be placed upon the frail shoulders of Johnston, in whom signs of athletic old age were now all too visible. Tilden left the court haggard of face but smiling. He and Lacoste changed and then came back to sit side by side to watch together the last act of the drama.

Wistfulness came into the court with Johnston, nervousness with Cochet. They stopped a moment by the umpire's chair to deposit extra rackets, and as Johnston walked slowly to the back of his court to begin the preliminary warmup, a woman's voice from the crowd called softly, but distinctly, "God bless you, Little Bill." Not many heard it, but all who did no doubt were feeling the same.

Everything depended on these two now, and they never had played each other. Cochet's nervousness remained with him for a few games and Johnston went ahead 4–1. Then the Frenchman ran five games in a row to take the first set 6–4 and the hope that had risen quickly expired. Johnston raised hopes again by hitting with some of the old fury to win the second set 6–4, but he was helpless in the third. And then with Cochet at 5–2 in the fourth, and twice within one point of winning the match and the Cup, there came back for one brief moment the old fighting Johnston.

Hurling those wonderful old forehands across the net and volleying with the old skill, Little Bill won two games and the crowd was aroused once more to intense enthusiasm. It was a picture to remember, for this was the Johnston we had known and admired for so many years, but it was all too brief. There followed a sequence of errors for which Cochet patiently had waited. He had not long to wait nor had we.

The scene when Johnston hit the last ball into the net, giving the Davis Cup to France, was extraordinary. Cochet threw his racket into the air, Lacoste and Tilden stood up and solemnly shook hands.

The crowd began to swarm over the court and surround the Cup, sitting on a table at the one side, pictures were taken with the Cup as background, the French players and supernumeraries embraced one another in the traditional French way, and in the press box dozens of experts who had been wrong searched for words to describe the pathos and the drama of it all.

CHAPTER FIFTEEN

W HEN the boat train carrying the crusading French
Davis Cup team of 1927 to the liner *Paris* had begun to move slowly
along the platform at the Gare St. Lazare that pleasant July morning,
Henri Cochet, cocky, handsome, and appealing in his small-boy way,
stuck his head through a compartment window and called, "First the
Davis Cup and then the American Championship. We bring them
both back this time, yes?"

Behind his shoulder someone remonstrated in explosive French,
cautioning against saying such things. They might bring bad luck.
But there was no bad luck at all. The prophecy was fulfilled on September 17, inside the concrete stadium at Forest Hills with a capacity crowd looking on. In the final match of the United States National Championship played that day Lacoste defeated Tilden 11–9,
6–3, 11–9, and won for the second year the title no other save Hugh
Doherty in 1903 had taken overseas.

Lacoste and Tilden were to meet three times after that. Two of
these meetings resulted in tremendous tennis matches, and Tilden
was to win one of them. But many people think this last match they
played on American soil, a match in which Tilden did not win a set,
was the finest of all. I do not know. I saw all of their matches in·this
country, France, and England, except the one in the Challenge
Round of 1925, and every one was intensely interesting, often highly
dramatic.

This last one at Forest Hills had certainly one element which set it
apart and made it forever memorable. It is the thing that I remember
from that tournament, played directly after the French had won the
Cup at Germantown. I concede that is was one of the finest exhibitions of tennis techniques and skills ever seen, but the really impressive thing was something else.

Tilden, never popular in victory and often actively disliked, acquired here in defeat something beyond popularity. Although he

could not win a set from Lacoste, he won from the crowd something approaching the feeling we all had for Johnston. It is not likely that anyone ever really loved Tilden in that same way, but he certainly did manage here to establish some emotional connection with them that was more than admiration. Something of the same thing was happening in these same months with Jack Dempsey, the unloved heavyweight champion, whose immense popularity with the public began to grow as soon as Gene Tunney had brought him down from his throne.

For these reasons I have always felt that this final of 1927, the last we ever were to see of Lacoste in this country, may have been Tilden's finest hour, for he was magnificent in adversity and defeat as he never had been in triumph. I could share the crowd's collective feeling for him and, at those critical moments when they called to him such things as "Come on, Bill" and even "Good old Bill," it seemed that it was I who called.

There were critical moments aplenty. So many they could not be counted. The calls from the crowd disturbed Tilden, destroying the fierce concentration he sought and needed, but when he recalled them long after, they seemed to give him an intense sort of pleasure.

It may be that my memory of this match, in which I recall more of the surroundings of it than of the details of play, is influenced by the fact that I was not required to write about it immediately after. I think that the necessity of describing such a contest without delay requires one to look at it, to watch it differently than if one were merely a spectator. The translating of visual images into words is not as easy as it might seem. A certain detachment undoubtedly aids observation but I have wondered at times if it does not also reduce somewhat the pleasure to be had from uncomplicated and undisciplined watching of games so highly charged with nervous strain as this one and so brilliantly conducted from the technical standpoint. In tennis the spectator must of necessity always follow the flight of the ball, but it is actually impossible to know the how and why of the success or failure of shots unless the eye now and then lets the ball go on its way and remains with the bodily mechanics that produced the shot.

At this particular match I was spectator pure and simple. I can reproduce in myself almost the exact emotions I felt during its progress, but I would have to go to the files to know its details. I do know that Tilden, attacking wonderfully, was ahead in every set, that he won Lacoste's service first to establish a winning lead and then lost his own.

I remember that this happened several times and that each time Lacoste's service was won I thought, Now Tilden will win the set. And then Lacoste won Tilden's service immediately to get back even. Tilden had chances to win each set, the first and third more than once, and could not. I thought, This is the end of Tilden. He can never beat Lacoste or Cochet again.

I remember that the stadium echoed for many minutes with the tribute that crowd rose and gave to Tilden at the end of the match, and that the people who could not get in after the gates had been closed, with many sitting in the aisles, had waited around outside to hear the result. It seemed to me there were several thousands of them but it may have been only hundreds.

So Cochet's boat train prediction came true. The Frenchmen took home both the Cup and the title, and for the next ten years the center of the tennis world was to be on the other side of the Atlantic.

The Cup had hardly reached the shores of France before they began planning a new tennis site in keeping with their new position as champion nation and, as might be expected, they came up with the most attractive tennis ground in the world. They chose a tree-shaded spot on the edge of the Bois de Boulogne not far from the Auteuil race course, and, where other tennis plants had been planned from a purely utilitarian point of view, this one was laid out with an eye to preserving as much of the natural beauty of the site as possible and even adding to it.

Some of the courts were hidden among spreading trees around behind an old, old house which was itself partly concealed by growing things. I seem to remember that there were eight courts but, turning the eye backward and inward, I can actually see and count only seven. I have known any number of people who went regularly to the matches in those days who cannot recall for certain where three of the courts were situated. How different from Wimbledon or Forest Hills, where they march like soldiers in rows side by side.

The old house was carefully preserved as a clubhouse for eating, drinking, and dressing purposes; and they left plenty of room for strolling about, sitting at tables, and ordering things brought in glasses, tall and small. Everywhere there were flowers, informal and unofficial.

They surrounded one of the khaki-colored courts with poured concrete stands and, although about as many could be seated as in the other places for watching tennis, it seemed much smaller. Its architecture was simple. Just a plain stand along each side and each end of the court and all running together at the corners to form an oblong box with no top. This simple arrangement managed somehow an informal quality that made the people seated in it seem very near the players and the players nearer one another. The arena effect of Wimbledon and Forest Hills was entirely lacking.

They named the place the Stade Roland Garros, for what reason I must have known at the time but have long forgotten and I wonder if many Frenchmen now remember what connection the name had with the game in their country. But by whatever name, it was for the next half-dozen years the center of the tennis world as the nations stormed its citadel in vain, seeking both the French national title and the Davis Cup. Have there ever been pleasanter tennis years than just these?

Even before they had got the place completely ready, and wooden scaffolding to support the concrete still rose around the court for the first defense of the Davis Cup in 1928, there was something special about the place that set it apart. It may have been the result of a happy accident. If its elements could have been separated out and studied as they do with chemicals in a laboratory, probably they would have been seen to be the same as found elsewhere.

The crowds at Wimbledon were much larger, about as cosmopolitan, and just as "dressy" too, if you disregard the ever-present models the leading dressmakers always send to such places to parade the new frocks like showgirls in a Ziegfeld revue. Everything seemed to combine, however, at Auteuil to produce something unique in sports, and I am wondering if the catalytic agent may have been gaiety. The French knew how to be gay in those days.

They were now on top of the tennis world, likely to remain there for years, and war was still a small, remote cloud on a distant horizon. Year followed pleasant carefree year as the summertime came round again and we all went to Auteuil for the French Championships, the inter-zone matches, and the Challenge Round. There was for me always the faint feeling that I was entering upon a setting for a musical comedy and that all the people wandering about chattering in a dozen languages were extras carefully chosen and costumed to form a background against which the main actors would perform.

The place retained its charm even after the Musketeers had departed and another great player, Fred Perry, had come with Bunny Austin to take the Cup across the Channel to Great Britain. That reduced France to a second-class tennis nation again, but it left their Championships still a delightful event. Before Perry came Ellsworth Vines, and then Jack Crawford and Gottfried von Cramm, and finally an even greater player than these, Donald Budge, to dominate play at Roland Garros. These tennis weeks of early and midsummer, stretching through the decade that preceded World War II and back into the end of the 1920s, were experiences about which it would be easy to grow overly sentimental. But let me not be guilty of the sin of overindulgence in nostalgia and an overreverence for days gone by.

I will let it go with the observation that I loved going to Auteuil for the tennis and happily was present at some of the high moments of the game's history, both comic and tragic. For on the porous surface of this center court with engaging intimacy in a sylvan setting, tennis of a quality comparable with the best of Wimbledon and Forest Hills was played.

There was always excitement. It began during the very first match of the first Challenge Round ever contested on European soil, when the wooden part of the new stand not yet removed from the concrete caught fire. How this occurred no one knew, but thousands knew how to put it out. They shouted advice from all sides in that wonderful way the French have of taking active part in everything.

This incident at the start of the new tennis era seemed to set the tone, and the shouting of advice to officials and players on the court became a recognized practice. The French simply ignored the traditions of genteel watching that had grown up around the game in England and America. They had no traditions and they made their own rules as they went along. They dispensed with custom altogether and some of the remarks shouted from the stands were very funny and very bawdy. One naturally expects Latin races to express excitement with a rich output of vocalism, but this was something special. The French spectator, more demonstrative and more articulate, responded quickly to the drama of the match, and English and

American visitors often were shocked by the ejaculations and exhortations from the stands.

There began on the day of the fire a running verbal battle between the crowd and a fat, fabulous Alsatian character in a huge Texas hat named Redelsberger. He sat in the umpire's chair at all important matches in this court for the next decade, calling the score in a mixture of English and French that often roused the crowd to violent protest.

Let him call out *"Quinze-love"* or announce "Ow-OOT" instead of *"Dehors,"* and there would come a roar from the crowd with shouts of *"Cause Français, vieux tomate! Cause Français!"* (Speak French, old tomato).

At times Redelsberger would exhort the crowd, plead with them, demand *un peu de silence* in a menacing voice, and threaten them with eviction and worse. They would then taunt him with inelegant insults, telling him where he could go and what he could do when he arrived. They would call out the price they had paid for their tickets and demand to know how much he had paid for his.

This exchange of indelicacies was repeated so often it seemed a rehearsed act and was accepted as part of the show. A very popular part of the show it was too, hugely enjoyed by both parties to it and by the less demonstrative and more elegant part of the crowd in the boxes at court level. Even by officialdom and important guests in the large committee box raised higher above the court at one end beside the smaller press box. In such an atmosphere it was inevitable that Jean Borotra should perform brilliantly, and there were to be many demonstrations of his histrionic talent on this stage.

Extraordinary things kept happening in this enclosure year after year. Two of our own greatest players, Ellsworth Vines and Alice Marble, collapsed during matches on this court and were carried out unconscious. Vines had it happen while playing Perry in the 1934 inter-zone final, which the United States lost to Great Britain 4–1. Miss Marble fainted during a French-American team match and was ill for many months after.

There was the final day of the Challenge Round of 1932 when Borotra, putting on one of the finest acts of his entire career, using the volatile crowd as an instrument on which to play and as a weapon against his opponent, was said to have "stolen the Cup" after serving what clearly appeared to be a double fault at match point to

Wilmer Allison. This incident has been made much of and a certain amount of distortion has come into it in the retelling. I am convinced myself that the ball Borotra served was well beyond the line and that Allison should have been declared the winner of this fifth set and the match. But I am not at all convinced that it would have meant the winning of the Davis Cup by the United States team.

This was the fourth match of five and France was leading by two matches to one. Borotra had beaten Vines, and Cochet had beaten Allison, each in four sets on the first day, and Allison and John Van Ryn had beaten Cochet and Jacques Brugnon in a brilliantly played five-set doubles match on the second day. So that the victory of Borotra over Allison, which gave France the series, would have left the score tied at two matches-all if the ball in question had been called out. Then the final match, in which Vines defeated Cochet in five sets after losing the first two, would not have been merely an exhibition. In that event I thought, watching the play, that Cochet, drawing inspiration from the crowd and the situation, would have played less carelessly and probably would have won one of the three sets he lost.

In the first match of the series Borotra really had played one of the finest matches I can remember from him in defeating Vines 6–4, 6–2, 3–6, 6–4. It was a glittering display that he gave, for he was thirty-five years old and this was to be his final Davis Cup appearance as a singles player. He played with great cleverness and great energy for a man his age, and when he had uncovered a weakness in Vines's backhand corner, his road to victory had been mapped out. To this sector he played a low ball with spin, and my old notes say that Vines never once was able to hit it safely down the line in the whole match. He was forced to play it across court and directly at the finest shot Borotra owned, the volley pushed straight down the forehand line and far out of reach. Even so, Vines could not make this cross-court shot effectively very often, and the defect in his backhand corner was glaringly revealed.

Vines had come straight from Wimbledon after defeating Bunny Austin 6–4, 6–2, 6–0 in the final with a withering attack that had astonished British observers and caused them to rate Vines as probably the greatest player of all time. I had seen that performance and had been very impressed by it too. Since Cochet had been beaten by Allison at Wimbledon two years earlier and had not survived the second round there in either 1932 or 1931, beaten each time by second-class players, we all crossed to Paris in the full expectation that the Davis Cup would be won back for the United States. The shock and disappointment of what then happened at Auteuil may have led some of us to judge these encounters incorrectly and to give credence to that "stolen Cup" theory.

The confidence with which an aging Borotra handled the Vines blasts, and gradually led his man into error and even to double faulting, was the first shock. Borotra's conduct during this match was above criticism, and there could be only praise for his dazzling display of virtuosity. He knew the task he faced and he never faltered in pursuing his plan. Since we had been so certain of winning this point, the disappointment was great, but we had to admit that Vines was not yet the complete player we had supposed. But Allison had beaten Cochet in straight sets on his way to the Wimbledon final of 1930 and would no doubt get his country back even by doing it again two years later.

The same tactics of consistent attack got him the first set at 6–3 after he had been 3–5 down, but he never won another, and Cochet, coming back to the form he had shown in earlier years, had Wilmer in control in a fourth set. And so, after the doubles had been won by Allison and Van Ryn, we came on a hot, sultry Sunday afternoon to the controversial match.

Allison now had played nine sets and a hundred and nineteen games on two days, and he had to beat Borotra before this extraordinary crowd and under the most trying conditions imaginable. Else the series would be lost. France needed only one more point to retain the Cup. And this surely was one of the most unusual and dramatic tennis matches ever played with so much hanging on the result of it.

First of all the court had been watered down until it was almost muddy, and it still was slow and heavy when play started. This was no doubt done to take some of the sting from the lightning strokes of Vines and to aid Cochet, in case the whole thing should go down to the final match. But in hampering Vines and favoring Cochet they apparently forgot about Borotra, for he was terribly hampered at the start. The Basque could not get to the net behind his service in time for his volleying coups, and the bite was taken from his shots off the ground, which had been so full of guile against Vines on Friday. Allison, hitting winners all about the court and forcing errors, ran away to a two-set-to-love lead, with Borotra winning only four games. Of course, this did not fool anybody. Borotra was not beaten so easily as this and Allison was sure to react from his nearly flawless play if the thing could be prolonged. Moreover, the sun was very hot. It had been drying and baking the court and, at the end of his eleventh set Allison's stamina may have been drained a little. At 3–all in the third set Borotra won Allison's service for the first time and all of a sudden the old Bounding Basque was back in court, leaping about and throwing the crowd into ecstasies, and running out the set.

The rest interval restored Borotra, but Allison's game had dropped far below the level he had maintained during the first two sets. His length was poor, his speed reduced, and he could no longer pass the volleyer. Borotra not only won the fourth set 6–2 but began here to lay the foundation of his fifth-set performance with a mild histrionic show. The Basque had come into court wearing a pair of those rope-soled beach shoes called espadrilles. These articles are not meant for so strenuous a pursuit as tennis and Borotra had burst one pair midway through the set and changed to another. Toward the end his toes came out again and he made a great show this time of not changing. All this was done to great head wagging by Borotra and delighted shouts from the crowd. Borotra knew very well how to stir an audience to response. He pretended to be shocked at their display. He shook his finger at them and the more he pretended to quiet them the more they roared.

Allison was greatly depressed by all this, but he threw it off and the stand he made is beyond praise. Borotra, seemingly now in command of the situation on the court as much as he was of the crowd, had gone to 2–1 in the deciding set. With a great effort Allison brought back his best game. Once more he was cheating the great volleyer and coming forward to hit winners himself. He was steady and calculating, and he went straight to leads of 4–2 and 5–3. And now came the first of those crises that caused the match to be underscored in tennis annals.

At 5–3 Allison three times came within a point of victory. On the first match point Borotra, lunging at a ball that seemed to have him beaten, struck the net tape with it and watched it drop safely on the American side of the net for the luckiest sort of salvation. On the next two match balls, however, the Basque played characteristically and boldly. He forced the errors on Allison and, winning the game, had a chance to serve himself back even at 5–all.

The saving of these points had stimulated Borotra and, serving shrewdly, he went to 40–0 in the tenth game. And here Allison turned the thing right around by bringing off a series of shots that stopped Borotra. Then the American appeared on his way to victory as surely as could be when suddenly Borotra stopped play and called attention to another burst shoe with the toes sticking out.

The crowd set up a wild shout for him to change. Someone had brought a new pair to the court and was displaying them plainly before the people. Borotra's actions said just as plainly, "No, no, no, never would I do such a thing while play is in progress." But, with the score at deuce, he finally consented to yield to the overwhelming pressure of the crowd. Allison stood a little disconsolately at the back of the court while the change was being made, and I suspect he was beaten right there.

Just the same Allison worked back to match point again when Borotra returned to serve. At this fourth match point to the United States, Borotra's first ball was into the net. The second, from where I sat directly above the service court, appeared to have hit so far beyond the line that there could hardly be any question that it was a fault, and Allison had won. But the linesman said it was good and, since Allison had let it go by without even offering at it, the score was deuce. Soon it was 5–all in games and then 7–5 to France, and Le Basque Bondissant had pulled yet another lost cause out of the fire.

This performance probably was Borotra's finest moment before the adoring home crowd, for it certainly was he who kept the Cup in France for another year. The Basque had many moments here at Roland Garros, and there was only one occasion when his histrionics were not fully appreciated and when his act fell a little flat. That was during the second year of the French reign as champion nation, when the Challenge Round of 1929 was being played, with the United States again the challenger.

This whole incident, which involved Alain Gerbault, the lone mariner, was slightly fantastic, and if Borotra miscalculated, so too did the whole French nation. Although France still was on top of the tennis world in 1929, the country was rather badly in need of a hero. National pride demanded it. This was the era of transatlantic flights and other spectacular exploits such as Channel swimming, and no

Frenchman had done anything spectacular in a long time. Then suddenly one day Gerbault appeared literally on the horizon.

Six years earlier Gerbault had sailed away in his tiny boat measuring less than thirty feet. Nothing had been heard of him since, but now in mid-summer the word came that he was off the Azores and on the way home. France whipped up great excitement, and a triumphal welcome was planned. They made him out to have been a tennis player of an earlier day comparable almost to the Musketeers, and such old tennis-playing friends as Coco Gentien and Pierre Albarran were in the official delegation that went to Le Havre to welcome him home to what amounted to a planned national celebration.

Gerbault took his little boat into Le Havre through a heavy overcast on the afternoon of July 24, which was a Wednesday. A great crowd had been waiting many hours for his fog-delayed arrival, including the Minister of Marine and a representative of the President of the French Republic bearing a citation of officer of the Legion of Honor.

When Gerbault stepped ashore he was barefooted and his only article of clothing was pair of dirty dungarees. He was bare from the waist up and while champagne corks popped and speeches were made, he just stood there saying nothing, clearly bewildered and seemingly a little disgusted. The great reception collapsed and hung limp like a sad child's balloon that has been pricked with a pin at a carnival. The French press tried valiantly to make the best of it, but their hero would not go along. In a sense he simply walked out on them.

The sequel to this curious occasion, which brings it into the annals of Roland Garros, occurred the following Saturday, the second day of the Challenge Round. Gerbault, back in the clothes of civilization now, turned up unannounced at the tennis stadium. Someone recognized him and he was rushed to the imposing committee box, full of important personalities. Down on the court Borotra and Cochet were playing Allison and Van Ryn in the Challenge Round doubles match. There was great excitement when the crowd, realizing that Gerbault was present, turned its attention from the court to the box.

Suddenly, Borotra, also catching on, ran with a chair to the base of the wall below the box, jumped to grasp the top of it and scrambled up and in. He then embraced Gerbault with a great show of affection and many dramatic gestures. And there, before the eyes of his subjects, the great Bounding Basque likewise got the complete brushoff in a wonderful way that one thought Gerbault meant for the whole nation and the whole silly business of proclaiming heroes.

Borotra climbed down, a little chastened, and the United States won the doubles 6–1, 8–6, 6–4, but lost the series 3–2, since Cochet beat both Tilden and George Lott, and Borotra lost to Tilden but also beat Lott. While the doubles match still was going on, I went around into the box to try to get a word with Gerbault, and I also got the quick brush. I tried to remind him that we were both friends of Sam Hardy, and at the mention of the name he smiled, for there had been a genuine link between them. But the only response I got from Gerbault was: "I came here to see Tilden play. For nothing else. I shall return to the sea very soon."

He did not see Tilden play and he did go back to sea, drawn by some inner necessity to run away from civilization. He baffled his countrymen and they saddened him. They could not understand his passionate and mysterious interest in the sea, because it has been so rare among Frenchmen. Finally they shrugged and dismissed him as a crackpot. He slipped away again to roam the seas alone in his tiny craft, still looking for whatever it was he sought. He was soon forgotten, and he had been dead for nearly three years when, among the war dispatches of 1944, there came a small item telling about it. Gerbault had died of a fever on Portuguese Timor in December 1941, just about the time of Pearl Harbor.

The papers put together obituaries to go with this one-sentence dispatch. They made far too much of Gerbault as a tennis player and too little of his other qualities. They did not even mention the incidents at Le Havre and Roland Garros, where he gave the back of his neck to a nation trying to make a hero of him, but these are what I remember best.

Of course it was not all comic opera by any means at Roland Garros in these years. The hilarious and comic incidents were surrounded by some very fine tennis matches, the finest of all, I think, the very first Davis Cup Challenge Round match, played before a huge and boisterous crowd in the still uncompleted stands, which seemed not only likely to burn down but to come tumbling down under the surging emotions of the people in them.

This was France's first defense of the Cup after the glorious victory at Germantown, and the great Tilden was to open against Lacoste, the home-town boy who was now generally regarded as the world champion. But even this meeting, which surely ranks near the top of all their matches, was preceded by an international uproar straight out of *opéra bouffe*.

Only a few weeks earlier Lacoste had beaten Tilden at Wimbledon, and they were calling that semifinal one of the very great battles of tennis history. I am in agreement with that judgment, and I am not sure it wasn't an even finer match in some ways than the one now to come. Lacoste won it in five sets after withstanding a rain of the hardest blows I have ever seen delivered on a tennis court.

Lacoste then won his second and last Wimbledon title by defeating Cochet in the final, and there was something about this last victory on the turf where the French players had refined and perfected their skill that I must mention because of its overall bearing on the tennis of the period. It had a bearing on Tilden's final victory over Lacoste in Paris, and it again revealed Lacoste's analytical ability and his genius for working out the solution to tennis problems.

René had played Tilden on Wednesday, and since he was not engaged in the doubles, he had a free day on Thursday before meeting Cochet, who only recently had deprived him of his French title in the first tournament played at the new grounds in Auteuil. In that encounter Cochet had attacked Lacoste on the forehand wing and had been able to volley the cross-court return successfully at crucial points of the match. Lacoste knew that success at Wimbledon depended on the trajectory and pace of the short forehand across the body of the man crowding the net.

On this Thursday it happened that I arrived at the grounds quite early in the day because a date to play golf on the adjoining Wimbledon Park course had been canceled. I had somehow not learned of it until I reached the clubhouse, and when I walked across to the All-England Club there still were more than two hours before the gates would be opened at noon. I remember I had a good deal of trouble finding somebody to let me in but finally saw through the fence an old sergeant of the Guards who had been press box attendant for some years and in return for past favors, including an occasional half-crown and a regular offering to which he always referred as "a spot and a splash," he stood sponsor for me and got somebody to unlock. Since I had so much time to kill, I wandered about and found

Lacoste on a far court with one of the other French players, Pierre Landry I think it was. I sat beside that court—Wimbledon provided comfortable green benches beside outer courts at that time—and watched Lacoste practice one stroke and no other for hours. I wandered away several times, came back, and he still was practicing the same stroke, although Landry had been replaced by another member of the French group.

The stroke was the cross-court forehand, sharply angled and quickly dipping as it crossed the net before the inrushing volleyer. Lacoste hit this shot endlessly from every angle and from everywhere along the forehand line and he practiced no other. If the ball came to his left side or too near the middle of the court, he ignored it. He was acquiring a new stroke, and the next day I saw him win the Wimbledon title with this very stroke he had acquired for the purpose, a shot whose lack had cost him his French title a month earlier.

I thought that day of how Tilden had said that Lacoste had acquired a special service spun slowly to the forehand line just for use against Tilden in the Challenge Round, and I wondered then how many hours of practice had been required to perfect it. And I wonder now if there ever has been another tennis player able so quickly and easily to detect a flaw in his own equipment and so willing to work toward perfecting the missing weapon. Lacoste always did practice an hour or two in the mornings when he had a big match coming up the same afternoon, and I regret that I did not pay close attention to all of these sessions, for they surely would have added greatly to my store of tennis knowledge.

With this memory fresh I had no doubt that Lacoste would beat Tilden again on Lacoste's own court in the Challenge Round which followed Wimbledon, and I was not prepared at all for what happened. I was not prepared either for the uproar that preceded the first big tennis occasion for France as holder of the Davis Cup.

CHAPTER SIXTEEN

ALL during Wimbledon Tilden had been writing pieces for an American syndicate commenting on the play. Now, just before the inter-zone match between the United States and Italy, the European winner, which was to be played in Paris, the word came that the United States Lawn Tennis Association had suspended Tilden for violation of the amateur rule. This action was a little hard for us to understand in Paris, since the President of the U.S.L.T.A., Samuel Collum, was then with us in Paris and had taken no part in the decision. He seemed, on the contrary, indignant, and I never did understand how the action could have been taken without consulting either Collum or Joseph Wear, the chairman of the Davis Cup Committee, who also was with the team and also was indignant.

But neither of these gentlemen was as indignant as the French. They began to roar, and they kept it up all through the inter-zone matches, which were played a week before the Challenge Round, from which Tilden was withdrawn. The newspapers roared and the crowds at the matches roared, cursed, and shouted abuse, some of it obscene, at American officials, who fortunately did not understand French.

These people felt that after all these years of striving had finally brought the Cup to France, they now were going to be cheated of the chance of seeing the great "Beeg Beel" beaten by their Mousquetaires. They felt affronted, even insulted. All the old epithets about Uncle Shylock were pulled out again and it really was developing into an international incident when the Quai d'Orsay, the French Foreign Office, decided to step in. They made representations to Myron Herrick, the well-loved American Ambassador.

I think we all made a little too much of the international incident angle at the time. The way the story was told was that Herrick got in touch with the State Department in Washington, which spoke sharply to the U.S.L.T.A., which then lifted the suspension. I do not think that is quite correct, though it made a good story at the time. I think Herrick merely called Collum and asked him, as president of the association, to reinstate Tilden like a good fellow and get the French off his, Herrick's, neck. At any rate it certainly was Collum who put Tilden back on the team, and there was much rejoicing.

The United States team, with Frank Hunter and John Hennessey playing singles, and George Lott joining Hennessey for the doubles, defeated Italy easily 4–1 and, with Tilden restored to the team, the crowd was in a happy mood on the first day of the Challenge Round. The sky was overcast and there was a strong blustery wind blowing the sand on the court's surface into people's eyes, but everybody was in holiday spirit on this first Davis Cup occasion. Billy Johnston had retired now, and everybody looked upon this Challenge Round as Tilden standing alone against the Musketeers. It turned out just about that way too.

Tilden had been drawn against Lacoste in the opening match and Big Bill received what must have been the greatest ovation of his life when he swept into the arena with the air of a conqueror instead of a man who had been beaten by Lacoste the last four times they had met. Tilden seemed at first surprised by this reception, but then his manner indicated that it was, after all, his due. I had the impression though that he was as pleased as surprised, and I confirmed later that he was immensely stimulated, even inspired. I think this fact influenced what followed.

Everyone settled back to enjoy a tennis treat with the inevitable result of another Lacoste victory. Of course there never had been any question about the other American player. He would be beaten twice, that was certain. But Tilden and Hunter were to play the doubles, and so the crowd would get to see the great man in three matches. Victory over Tilden three times would confirm before their own eyes the fact that Lacoste, Cochet, and Borotra were the world's best players and France the champion nation.

But Tilden defeated Lacoste 1–6, 6–4, 6–4, 2–6, 6–3, and considering all the circumstances surrounding the affair, I am disposed to rate this the finest victory of Tilden's brilliant career. Bill began the match in his old way of furious hitting, but the ball hit with little spin is hard to control in the wind, and this wind was so strong and so unpredictable that balls were sometimes blown crazily. Tilden's drives and service both were woefully unreliable, and when he could win only one service game in the first set it had the look of a rout. The crowd was disappointed. This was not the Tilden they had heard so much about and seen something of at St. Cloud. They never were to see that Tilden, but they were to see now a performance from the greatest master of spin the game has known, the like of which no other tennis gallery probably ever has witnessed.

For Tilden, realizing that he could not hit Lacoste off the court on such a slow surface as this, a surface, incidentally, especially prepared to reduce just that likelihood, now placed his trust on steadiness from the back of the court, on the use of slice and spin, and especially on the use of the drop shot. I have before me as I write a note made during the progress of the second set to the effect that this was the silliest procedure ever heard of, wholly unworthy of Tilden's long match-play experience.

The theory behind this brilliant observation was that, in forcing the twenty-three-year-old Lacoste to run miles, Tilden would be putting an impossible strain on his own thirty-six-year-old legs, and was bound to come out second best in an endurance contest. Outsteady Lacoste in a long match on a slow court? How foolish! And how wonderfully certain we all are of our own judgment!

There now followed two sets of tennis as interesting as any I have seen. Tilden never once hit a full-blooded shot and, using the wind to check the ball now and then, he spun it toward the corners and sliced it just over the net, drawing Lacoste forward, pushing him back, and because of the way the ball came off the floor, causing the Frenchman to take extreme care with his strokes. We had never seen Lacoste hesitate so after the bound of the ball before striking it. He was waiting to see what it would do, whether it still was spinning, or if the court had taken the guile from it and left it hanging dead in the air. Never had Lacoste hit so many balls into the net. Never had he misjudged the bound so often, and never had he been forced to stroke with such care and such uncertainty. Tilden depended almost entirely on making Lacoste miss altogether or send a ball so indifferently hit as to invite immediate destruction. Bill rarely hit with the expectation of scoring outright, and he used the heavily cut twist service exclusively. That he could wring so much spin from that stubborn surface in the high wind was astonishing, and gradually we began to realize that if Lacoste did not soon find the answer Tilden was going to win the match.

Exactly an hour, according to my notes, was required to play the second and third sets. Lacoste won four games in each but Tilden was in control of the play at all critical points and went off for the rest interval leading by two sets to one. Tilden had appeared more tired than Lacoste when they left the court, but he returned apparently refreshed and began immediately to hit out as he had done at the beginning of the match. And once more he began to fall behind. In very short order Lacoste had squared the match at two-sets all.

I think Tilden, feeling he had the energy in reserve and that Lacoste was more tired than he, thought that he could finish off the match with a burst of the old flat drives and cannonball serves, and when he realized his mistake it was too late to end the match that way. Toward the end of the set he reverted to the chopping, forcing Lacoste to work hard for games he had won easily while countering the hard hitting. This accomplished, Tilden set out to repair the damage of the lost fourth set in the fifth.

It was really a desperate struggle all the way. Lacoste had not quite found the way to counter Tilden's tactics, but he was getting ever closer, and Tilden was missing a good deal at times now. There is no doubt that Tilden had some luck in recovering from the early loss of his service, but he was ahead at 4–3 with Lacoste serving when the crisis came. With the score 15–all, Tilden hit a beautiful spinning ball down Lacoste's backhand line. It was the sort of shot that earlier Lacoste had always played short and not too near the lines for fear of overhitting in the wind, but he had learned to judge the spin better now and he hit deep and hard to the backhand corner, closing in to the net to cut off the reply on the volley.

Tilden, seeing the shot in time, was there ahead of the ball. The ball, hit crisply, invited a crisp reply and that is what we all, including Lacoste, expected. But Tilden, with plenty of time, did not have to take the shot on the run. He hit a slow, curving, spin-invested backhand slice straight to Lacoste's forehand. It was a masterly stroke and it, in reality, won the match. Lacoste, set to take a hard straight drive and angle it sharply out of reach across court, as he had done any number of times earlier for a winning placement, had to check his volley, stroke the ball more, and cut it. This cut gave the ball a slight check as it hit the court and gave Tilden, who had turned and run back across court as soon as he had hit the ball, time to reach it. He had to go beyond the sideline to take it, but he was there and he never in his life hit a finer forehand, flat and with the old familiar crack. It passed Lacoste, still standing there at the net, so fast he could not make even a motion toward the ball with his racket, and this reply from an obviously tired man so shook the Frenchman that he served a double fault on the next point. So Tilden got to 5–3 and then threw everything into the final service game, to which Lacoste now had no effective reply.

The dressing rooms, which later would be under the concrete stadium, were at this time over in the old house in the trees. When I arrived there some time after the match, I found Lacoste still in his tennis clothes, sitting with a towel tightly wound around his neck. He was a forlorn-looking figure from which the energy seemed to have drained. His hands were between his knees and as he began to talk of the match in response to questions, tears came into his eyes.

He was not crying for loss of either the match or the series, for he knew very well that this one really had no bearing on the final result, which was a victory for France by four matches to one. René had just gone through a severe emotional experience and he was reacting.

"Two years ago I knew already how to beat him," he said sadly. "Now I do not know any more. Now on my own court he beats me. Is he not the greatest player of all? I never knew how the ball would come off the court, he concealed it so. I had to wait to see how much it was spinning. Sometimes it didn't spin at all. I thought the wind would bother him too much, but he played the wind better than I."

René seemed eager to talk about Tilden and in no hurry to end the conversation. He brightened considerably after a bit, and as we all left him, he smiled at last and said, "*C'est incroyable, n'est-ce pas?*"

It seemed so at the time, but in retrospect it is credible enough. Tilden and Lacoste were to play one more match, in the semifinal of the French Championships, on this same court a year later, and Lacoste was to win it with comparative ease. It was not only their last meeting but the very end for Lacoste who, threatened all along with tuberculosis, was forced to give up tennis altogether soon after. Tilden went on, and some thought an even greater achievement than his defeat of Lacoste in 1928 was his victory over Borotra on his way to his third Wimbledon title in 1930, ten years after his first victory there in 1920. It could be. That match had elements no other that Tilden played possessed, and as he had beaten Lacoste by outsteady-ing the steadiest player of the day, he defeated Borotra, the finest smasher of his time, with the lob.

Tilden was beaten by Cochet in three sets on the final day of that 1928 Challenge Round and was then suspended again, so that he could not play in his own Championships at Forest Hills, where he very likely would have won again, since he did win in 1929.

CHAPTER SEVENTEEN

From the day of her first Championship at Wimbledon in that wonderful final with Lili de Alvarez, Helen Wills, like Tilden, enjoyed absolute supremacy for six years. She was, in fact, an even more dominant champion, since Tilden, though never beaten in a Championship match, was often challenged. By 1933 Miss Wills had won four Wimbledon titles, seven United States and four French without losing a set and she was unchallenged anywhere in the world. No tennis player of her time, man or woman, stood out so far ahead of her contemporaries.

And like Tilden also, several of Miss Wills's most dramatic and most memorable encounters came after something had gone from her game and she had lost the power to rule without question, and when, in fact, she had begun to decline. With the exception of the Cannes match and the 1927 final with Alvarez, which are unforgettable, all of Miss Wills's matches about which I can remember anything worth remembering came after 1932. That was the last year in which she was untouchable and other girls were struck with awe in her presence.

I remember very well, of course, seeing the teen-age Miss Wills for the first time; but between the 1927 Wimbledon final and her last appearance on that center court in 1938, I remember Miss Wills only when she was in difficulty, if not actual distress.

The women play a greatly inferior game, comparatively speaking, and I think there were scores of good men players who never were ranked at all who would have been able to beat Miss Wills at her best. Any really good consistent club player, I suspect, would hold his own with most of the girls who are ranked near the top. Nevertheless, at their own level they have had many exciting encounters, but the thing about the girls is that with them, personalities count as much as skill. So now and then elements other than pure tennis enter into a match or a tournament, and women's tennis raised to a plane of equal importance and interest with men's.

If you think back over the women's matches that are mentioned whenever outstanding contests are discussed, I think you will mark these. Suzanne and Molla at Forest Hills; Suzanne and Helen at Cannes; Helen Wills versus Helen Jacobs in the two matches at home and abroad; and the final at Forest Hills in 1962 when Darlene Hard, twice a champion, broke down and cried on the court while being beaten by Margaret Smith, the sturdy Australian girl who won the title that year and again in 1965.

Miss Wills had not Lenglen's ability to give you pleasure by the beauty of her method and the glitter of her personality, but she had a manlike speed of service and drive that gave her superiority over her rivals. There was an immaculate quality about her play. Never much of a strategist, her progress through a tournament was seldom exciting, but the steady placidity of her play, unvaried against all opponents, never seemed to bore her. She never sought new ways of dealing with and defeating opponents as Lenglen did, but she never had to do so for a long time. A quick guess and a bit of mental arithmetic indicate that I must have seen Miss Wills play about fifty matches during the six years of her untroubled reign as Queen of the courts, but of them all I really remember only those to which she came feeling not quite up to strenuous effort, as happens periodically to girl athletes.

During these years there was this British tennis journalist, Powell Blackmore, who kept book on the girl players and he always kindly informed me when Miss Wills's time was due so that I did not miss these interesting occasions. They were interesting because she was so good she could win standing still, you might say, while the other girl ran miles. If there came a ball that was out of reach and was to beat her, well let it. There would be others that could be dealt with, for Miss Wills, standing in the middle of the base line, was so persistently accurate and so forceful that she seemed actually to attract the ball to her racket, to force the opponent to play back to where she was standing or else to miss altogether.

One often wondered why the silly girl did not make Miss Wills run, until one realized that the silly girl had more than she could do merely knocking the ball back down the center. It was certainly interesting to see Miss Wills operate during these few times of comparative discomfort, but otherwise I do not even remember the names of the long list of victims she disposed of as easily as shelling peas.

But in 1933 one noted for the first time a change. This year was for Miss Wills what 1926 had been for Tilden, and, as it also was with Tilden, there is little doubt that it is to this fact of Miss Wills's slipping back a little that we owe three of most dramatic scenes of women's tennis. After this year she was, like Tilden after 1926, no longer held to be invincible. Girls were not so afraid of her. They felt she could be beaten and took courage.

The first sign of any wavering in Miss Wills's glittering if unemotional and uneventful reign came for me in the Wimbledon final of 1933. She defeated Dorothy Round, a splendidly athletic English girl who was to become champion in Miss Wills's absence the next year, 6–3, 6–8, 6–3, and this middle set was the first Miss Wills had lost at Wimbledon since 1924. It was not the actual loss of the set which revealed that Miss Wills was at last vulnerable, so much as the circumstances surrounding it. The loss brought in its course one of the strangest reactions I ever have experienced at a tennis match.

Miss Wills lost this set after Miss Round, leading 7–6 and serving at 30–40, game point to Miss Wills, drove a ball toward the American's forehand corner. Miss Wills, running to retrieve, saw it pitch well beyond the base line and stopped. The umpire immediately called 7–all, but the linesman's arm was extended, indicating the ball was good. Miss Round, who knew the ball had been out, came to the stand and asked that the point and game be awarded to her opponent.

But the scoreboard showed deuce. Both girls and the crowd felt this to be wrong. Everybody seemed unhappy about it, and Miss Wills, badly upset at the loss of this critical point, lost the next two and the game and set. I had never before seen Miss Wills in the least upset, and I wondered if she were not aided in winning the decisive third set by the strange thing that now developed.

Something had gone from the occasion. Miss Round, the very popular home girl who had played so well, actually got only perfunctory applause for winning the first set the champion had lost in nine years. Where great enthusiasm for the girl who had played the champion so evenly and so bravely had been, now there was sympathy for Miss Wills. The incident had a depressing effect on both the crowd and the match itself.

Up to the disturbing incident there had been a match so level that the possibility of Miss Wills's defeat by an English girl was always there. Miss Round had shown in both sets that she actually might have the stroke equipment to dethrone the champion. She did not know how to go about it, but she revealed for the first time how Miss Wills might be beaten. At the same time she showed that the serene champion's physical resources were no longer proof against exploitation. Miss Wills was tiring in that long second set and was fortunate, I thought, that Miss Round did not play well enough in the third to extend her. The third set, which might have been a splendid climax to a notable occasion, was just a more or less routine victory for Miss Wills.

Miss Round had led 2–1 in the first set and went to 30–love in the fourth game. She got there by hitting forceful forehand and backhand drives to the corners where Miss Wills was arriving a little too late to meet the ball squarely in the center of her racket as was her wont. It was something new to see Miss Wills rushed. She was not controlling the game as she always had done, and her inferior footwork was exposed. It was glaringly exposed when Miss Round inserted the drop shot judiciously. But Miss Round used this shot too often, taking from it the essential element of surprise, and she also began to hit beyond the lines. A dim note in pencil informs me that Miss Wills won the first set in the tenth game by picking up easily a drop shot and putting it away.

Miss Wills came near to winning the second set when she led 5–4, and I thought she lost the chance because of the running she had done in the first. She had run so much it was said afterward that she had badly blistered feet. Some of the exchanges had been long, and she had to hit many more drives than she liked, to win some of the points. Her play had, in fact, been more defensive than was her custom. But Miss Round played quite badly in the third, making frequent errors and doing the wrong thing persistently, so that Miss Wills could once more go about the business of winning in her normal way. In a hotly fought deciding set the champion might have been in serious trouble.

Although she came easily in the end to her sixth title, she had shown signs of fatigue and nervousness. The conclusion was inevitable that the younger girls were closing the vast gap, or rather that the champion was coming back to them as Tilden had come back to his pursuers, and I thought we might soon see some interesting girls' tennis once more. In fact, this Wimbledon final was the prelude to misadventure.

When Helen Wills returned from Wimbledon in 1933 with her sixth title, she already had been champion of her own country seven times, and it seemed more than likely she would increase the total before she was done. She was to add two more at Wimbledon, the last one five years later, but her reign as champion at home already had been completed in 1932, when she did not defend, and Helen Jacobs began a run of four straight victorious years, three of them in Miss Wills's absence. Miss Wills was, nevertheless, looked upon as world champion all through these years, and all things considered, she probably still was.

These two girls, Helen Wills and Helen Jacobs, from the same town, Berkeley, California, had met already half a dozen times in Championship finals with the seemingly inevitable result that Miss Wills always won with routine ease. Now they were to meet three times more in finals, and there was nothing at all routine about these encounters. All three were, on the contrary, highly dramatic, and I think that it is out of these meetings, the first at Forest Hills that same year of 1933, the last at Wimbledon in 1938, that the "feud" between two nice girls was manufactured.

I did not see the first and most celebrated meeting, during which Miss Wills abandoned the court, but I saw the other two and wrote at length about them. I never spoke to Miss Wills after the Cannes experience in 1926, although there was later on an exchange of notes, but I have been friendly with Miss Jacobs for many years. I do not believe there was any feud at all. Both girls denied it, Miss Jacobs directly to me, and I don't think it could have been built up at all if the girls had come from different home towns and had not each gone through similar experiences of having to abandon a match to the other because of injury under strikingly similar circumstances. We heard a great deal more about the feud after it was all over and both girls were done with tennis than during their years of court rivalry.

Certainly they were rivals, as were Miss Wills and all the other girls she kept from being champion. And certainly they were not particularly fond of each other and never very friendly. Their backgrounds and temperaments, their individual attitudes toward the game and toward opponents, and the dramatic occasions which brought them together all fostered the rivalry of these two Helens and made "feud" almost inevitable in newspaper and magazine accounts of them, especially in retrospect. Thirty years after, people were still retelling the saga of it, with elaboration.

There was, obviously, a certain coolness between them, even in Wightman Cup matches where they were team partners, but I am convinced there never was any active dislike. Miss Wills was, I think, too calmly confident of her superiority, which made her seem almost phlegmatic at times, to have so unregal an emotion as active dislike. Miss Jacobs was too open and outgoing, too friendly and understanding of others. There was a strong melancholic tinge to Miss Jacobs' temperament. She undoubtedly was most courageous on the court and off it, but I often had the impression that she could burst into tears of frustration and disappointment. Of course she never did, for she was of much too strong a character for that. But she clearly was of a deeply emotional nature as she revealed plainly in her most generous attitude toward opponents.

One could hardly imagine Miss Wills crying, certainly not in public, because she concealed all emotion behind outer calm. One could more easily imagine Miss Wills feeling disdain for an opponent than dislike, for it seemed most of the time she scarcely noticed them at all. She seemed detached both from them and from the crowd, wrapped in her own thoughts, concentrating wholly on the job in hand, which was to impose her game and get the matter over with as soon as possible.

And yet it surely must have been an illusion, purely bred from watching her play tennis, that Miss Wills was really cold and calculating. She was an appealing young girl, full of a young girl's hopes, fears, and dreams, when she set out on her fifteen-year tennis career, and she was only twenty-seven when she encountered her first setback. She had in success, however, given an impression of a certain haughtiness, and I am sure that is why there was a lack of sympathy for her in adversity.

There had been vague reports early in that summer of 1933 that Miss Wills was not well, and some said the loss of a set to Miss Round at Wimbledon confirmed it. Then, when she withdrew from the Wightman Cup matches, scheduled for Forest Hills the first week in August, it was said that she had injured her back. Some felt that this was the end of the great Helen Wills, that she was through and would not play again. This talk may have annoyed Miss Wills. I do not know. The report was that she had been forbidden, or at least advised against it by a doctor, to play in the Championship that followed, but, determined to show she was not through, played anyhow and reached the final without strain. And there in that final, the first and most celebrated of the three meetings with Helen Jacobs, occurred the incident that has become perhaps a little distorted, as a chapter in the history of tennis.

Miss Jacobs won the first set 8–6 and it was the very first set she had ever taken from the other Helen in years of striving. Miss Wills won the second 6–3. With the score 3–0 to Miss Jacobs in the third, Miss Wills walked to the umpire's chair, picked up her sweater and calmly announced that she was in such pain she could not continue. For this Miss Wills brought down upon herself the wrath, the scorn, and the criticism of press, public, and many tennis people, who seemed delighted at the chance at last to criticize, if not actually to berate her. Miss Wills was, in fact, quite badly treated, and she retreated to California with the ugly word in her ears, as Suzanne had heard it twelve years earlier.

Since I was not present at Forest Hills on this occasion, I have no opinion about the play. Since I never knew the extent of Miss Wills's injury and her pain, I cannot judge of her wisdom in abandoning the match and thus, as they said, cheating Miss Jacobs of a complete victory. Miss Wills herself was the judge of that, but it is my own opinion that if she was in pain she would have been wrong to continue, that her action was perfectly justified, and that the verbal beating she took was no way to treat a girl who had been an exemplary champion seven times. I was myself severely criticized by way of the United States mails for defending her.

Miss Wills sat out 1934, but in early May of 1935 she started out from California on what we sportswriters delight to call the comeback trail. After arriving in England to get ready for Wimbledon, she was beaten by Kay Stammers, a pretty left-handed English girl, in an early grass court tournament. And she was very nearly beaten by a Czech girl named Cepkova in the round of sixteen at Wimbledon. She lost the first set to this girl of no great previous achievement and came twice within a point of being 1–4 down in the second. The set was saved, however, and Miss Wills was calm as ever in the third.

Normally whenever Miss Wills survived a crisis, usually more mild than that, you could leave her in complete confidence and look elsewhere, but this year all her matches had to be watched carefully and everything noted. I was afraid to leave her with Miss Cepkova, and I wished I had a more favorable seat than the No. 1 court press box afforded so I could observe more closely what Miss Wills was doing wrong, if anything. For she had been open to attack by a girl of no reputation but one no longer afraid of the great former champion. I remember that this interested me greatly. Perhaps it disturbed me. Anyhow, I had not seen it before and it made me wonder.

By the time Miss Wills reached the final, though, she seemed to have found the old champion's form once more, and I put the thought aside. Miss Jacobs reached the final too with the most impressive play she ever had been able to command at Wimbledon, and I thought as they entered the famous arena to fight it out once more 6,000 miles from home that for her the long trail full of frustration might at last be nearing its end.

A hot sun was shining almost straight down on the court and I wondered if this might have some bearing on the outcome. Miss Wills, taller and heavier, wore the familiar eyeshade, a sleeveless dress with a jacketed top, buttoned coat fashion down the front, and a skirt that came to her knees, and over it a coral-colored coatee. Miss Jacobs, bare of head, wore a dark blue sweater to match the stripe in her neat shorts. The costumes that tennis girls wore were considered part of the news in those days and that is why I noted these things.

The center court was packed, with many standees, for people had anticipated the match, knowing it was the first meeting since Miss Wills had walked out at Forest Hills, knowing too what they thought lay between the two girls. The atmosphere already was tense before the first ball was struck. Everyone thought, certainly, of the long rivalry and of the last encounter. Only Miss Jacobs stood between Miss Wills and the completion of her return to the throne, her desire to wipe out the memory of the Forest Hills of 1933, to make people take back the ugly word. It is strange how these things work out and how destiny plays into our lives. On this same court a dozen years earlier Suzanne Lenglen had her vindication in her next meeting with Molla Mallory after she too had walked out at Forest Hills and been called quitter.

On the other side of the coin, only Miss Wills stood between Miss Jacobs and realization of the greatest ambition of her life, to be crowned champion at Wimbledon, an honor for which she already had fought three times in finals only to fail. To become a champion at Wimbledon is the ambition of all tennis players everywhere, the thing they dream of from the time they first become serious tournament players. It is the highest honor the game can bestow. Failure at Wimbledon dims the luster of triumphs elsewhere.

Miss Jacobs no doubt began dreaming of Wimbledon when as a small girl she went to the Berkeley Tennis Club. There she found Helen Wills, three years her senior, developing the game that already had made her the best player of her age in the world. It may be that while playing against Miss Wills at the home club of both, Miss Jacobs first realized that she also could be very good. But from that day onward it was ever the fate of Miss Jacobs to follow in the shadow cast by the other Helen, playing, one might say, a minor supporting role to the game's greatest star. Miss Jacobs became a better player than all the other girls in the world, but Miss Wills had always stood between her and the top. She had by now been three times champion at home but never, except for that one unsatisfactory occasion, in a year when the other Helen competed.

Now it seemed as they prepared to do battle again on this famous tennis ground so far from home that the gap had closed, that Miss Jacobs had at last caught up or Miss Wills had fallen back. But they were so grim and determined during the preparation for their battle on alien turf before an alien crowd that one felt that other things than tennis might decide the issue so important to both. It hardly seemed they were preparing for a mere game of tennis. No game could be so grim as this promised to be.

Imponderables, portentous factors, thoughts of what had been, should have been, or might have been seemed to be intruding into a game of tennis between two attractive girls. For Miss Wills, now that she had been in the shadows for two years, had brought back with her the capacity which had been missing before of investing all her comeback matches with a sort of electric current and this was picked up and communicated throughout the stands.

Finally the call "play" came from the chair, Miss Wills toed the service line in her dainty but strong way, and everyone sat forward. For the next hour and forty minutes there was no relief from the tension that had taken hold of both players and those who watched. Receiving the first service, Miss Jacobs brought into play the chop stroke she had made her own, and Miss Wills, replying, swung into the ball and hit for a corner of her opponent's court. There in the first exchange was revealed the plan each had decided would bring victory; the one willing to fence with the purely defensive chop and wait a chance to attack, the other hitting to score. Neither was able to stick to plan. Miss Wills often found herself defending rather desperately; Miss Jacobs' solid defense was not always good enough.

Miss Wills, apparently well prepared for the match, began in such perfect attacking form, however, that she ran quickly to a lead of 3–0. This was the way it always had been in the past with that one exception. The champion's deep forceful drives to the corners could not be offset. But Miss Jacobs knew that things were not really the same any more. She knew that fight could now accomplish what defense had failed to do in other years. Now she began to force and maneuver, not waiting for attack to falter of itself. She abandoned the chop on the backhand, using a flat shot effectively.

Throwing Miss Wills off her rhythmic driving with this change, Miss Jacobs won the next game and then eleven points in succession to stand 0–40 against the Wills service in the seventh game. She was six times within a single point of a 4–3 lead. She never got that lead and it might have made all the difference if she had. Six times Miss Wills, scrambling a little frantically to defend now where she had been all attack before, saved the game point, the importance of which both girls and all the rest of us fully realized. Miss Wills finally won the game to go 4–3 herself and immediately resumed the attack to take the first set 6–3 while Miss Jacobs was reacting.

Now Miss Wills seemed beyond menace and most of us thought a quick two-set victory would follow. But we underestimated the value of Miss Jacobs' service, the accuracy of her passing shots, and the fight that was in her. I think Miss Wills also made this miscalculation. She seemed surprised when, advancing to the net behind good length drives, she was passed cleanly. She retreated to the base line and was beaten by sharp, short volleys or a smash as Miss Jacobs took over the forecourt position.

Miss Wills, surprisingly, seemed uncertain how she should deal with this surge, how she should play, and before we realized exactly what had happened, Miss Jacobs came to 5–2 and set point. There she served a double fault and lost the game. She won the next game and the set 6–3, but both this failure at set point and Miss Wills's uncertainty were alive with portent of what was to come.

Now with the beginning of the set that was going to decide the issue there came a burst of very fine women's tennis, almost brilliant one would say. Both girls played for a while remarkably well considering the strain under which both worked. Miss Jacobs, defending tirelessly and seizing her chances boldly when they came, got the first service break and led 3–2. Then, serving about as well as it is possible for a girl to serve, she went to 4–2.

The seventh game, which followed, was the longest of the match. Miss Wills, using the service as the initial blow in a series of attacking shots, drove Miss Jacobs from corner to corner. Miss Jacobs, hurrying and scurrying back and forth across her base line, chopping away, kept getting the ball back and finally, with Miss Wills seeming to tire, won the game to lead 5–2 with her own fine service to come.

Now the end of the long road was in sight. Now ambition, long frustrated, was about to be realized. Miss Jacobs, playing magnificently, had richly earned the prize. Now she had only to hold her service once more and she would be champion. Alas! Had only. These are the saddest words in the lexicon of sport. How many have there been who "had only" to do this or that but could not do it. Miss Jacobs lost her service. She tossed away this wonderful chance because at the crisis her aim faltered, her shots missed the mark. Miss Wills won the game by careful play and the score was 5–3.

But still another chance would come. Miss Jacobs could still serve herself out even if Miss Wills should hold her own service for 5–4. Dare she wait for that chance to come? She decided not and went after victory in the ninth game, Miss Wills serving, with the greatest resolution. With a steady hand and what seemed complete confidence Miss Jacobs came to match point with, I think, the finest smash I have ever seen a girl make. Hit off a lob so carefully thrown over her left shoulder it made Miss Jacobs leap from the ground for the shot, she replied with an absolutely untakable shot. As it bit into the turf at the back of Miss Wills's court, I thought that any girl who could make such a smash at such a time had a steady nerve and deserved her long delayed reward.

Miss Wills faced calmly the first match ball against her since Cannes in 1926—far more calmly than the thousands who were looking on. But she could not prevent Miss Jacobs from forcing her, in desperation, to throw up another lob. This one was weak and short. Miss Jacobs stood under it along her forehand line as Miss Wills scrambled back leaving the court open for the easy winning shot. Miss Jacobs decided to let the ball bound to make doubly sure before striking it sharply across court.

It was a fatal decision. In just those tiny seconds while waiting for the ball to come shoulder high the thought no doubt came to Miss Jacobs' mind that now at long last she was about to beat Helen Wills. And she could not accept the thought, could not stand it. Miss Wills stood helpless at the back of the court. It was the simplest sort of shot any club player could make nine times out of ten. Miss Jacobs was unable to make it. She struck the ball weakly into the net, almost at the bottom of it. It was one of the saddest things imaginable. We all ached for her that she should thus fail at the very moment of victory and I think I realized instantly both that Miss Jacobs would never get another chance and that I had wanted rather badly for her to win, without knowing it.

Miss Wills, thus reprieved after she herself certainly knew she was beaten, became immediately the champion of old. It is a way champions have. Let them up off the floor, let them escape from a tight corner into which they have been pushed, and they are all over you. Miss Jacobs, looking backward, reacted badly and soon we were all back where we had been when Miss Wills used to win easily against any defense.

I never did see Miss Wills play as well again as she did in going straight out 7–5 with a run of four games in succession. I don't think she ever did play anywhere near that well again. Miss Jacobs recovered her composure before the end and made some fine shots, especially volleys, but she was up against the best now and could not hold it back.

Miss Wills, finishing as a champion should once again, permitted herself at the final point a most un-Willslike gesture. She threw her racket into the air and, for the first time in my experience, she "dashed" for the net. Moreover, she put her arm around Miss Jacobs' shoulder, and I think this is something it is nice to remember about Miss Wills. She was very tired and probably she could not have continued much longer, but it was good at last to see Miss Wills express something spontaneously.

Wimbledon welcomed back its Queen with a burst of cheering not often heard there. I had got the impression all through that the crowd favored Miss Jacobs, so generous were they to her. I think they did want her to win and she earned their sympathy too, but it was very clear at the end that they were very glad Queen Helen was back on her throne. I was too, after thinking it over. It seemed right that she should set at rest the impression that she would quit. And there must have been something that prevented Miss Jacobs from making that easy smash, she, one of the finest smashers, who one point earlier had brought off a superb example of this stroke. Destiny perhaps? Certainly destiny did take a hand in their final meeting of all there on that same court in 1938.

In making her comeback of 1935 I do not doubt that Miss Wills was influenced by a desire to wipe out the memory of her retirement at Forest Hills and to erase the ugly word from the minds of those who did not prefer her to all others. She took something of a chance that she would not retire for good as champion and we have seen what a close thing it was. But with that seventh victory she exceeded by one the six titles won by Lenglen and tied the record of Mrs. Lambert Chambers, which had stood since 1914. With that Miss Wills took rank without question alongside the Suzanne, who had been called incomparable as the greatest of women players.

What then induced Miss Wills to try again three years later when she very definitely had passed her best by several years? She must have known that there were girls about then who would beat her if she were not completely fit. What had she to gain? There was a report around the English tournaments that summer that Miss Wills had decided suddenly to come after a transatlantic-transcontinental phone call from Wimbledon to Berkeley in which certain sums of money were mentioned, inducements offered, and terms met. I do not know about that, since it could not be checked out with anyone in authority, and I was not on sufficiently intimate terms with Miss Wills to ask her. I do not either presume to understand the mental processes of athletes, especially those of female games players, but I suspect that the 7–7 tie with Mrs. Chambers had a lot to do with it. Of course, I do not mean to imply that Miss Wills paid her own way from California to London to Dublin, where she also played in the Irish Championships, and back to Berkeley. However, she did feel affluent enough upon her return to give back to the U.S.L.T.A. a check for $1,309 which she had been advanced for expenses while abroad.

Although the money was only for the trip abroad, Miss Wills felt she should return it, since she would not play at Forest Hills. Some people are so suspicious that they said this was not money to pay expenses at all but payment for playing in the Championships at home and that Miss Wills was obligated to return it when she decided to pass up Forest Hills. At any rate she did all right financially while abroad by writing for the London papers, the same thing for which Tilden had been set down ten years earlier. I heard at the time what the figure was for the pieces, but I have forgotten, although I still am able to report that tennis champions were paid at a much higher rate in those days for reporting tennis than regular tennis reporters. In fairness to Miss Wills I must say that they were very well-written pieces and I was assured that she wrote them herself, entirely without professional help. I was quite impressed with her literary talent. I never did get straight the deal that took Miss Wills to Dublin after Wimbledon. It seemed a bit complicated, for I was told she asked for and received social and entertainment considerations besides having her expenses paid.

All this was part speculation and part gossip. There were a surprising number of people about that war-haunted summer of 1938 who seemed glad to say derogatory things about Miss Wills, but the observable facts were interesting enough. There is no need to go beyond them to establish motives, financial and otherwise, that persuaded her to try again. The principal fact is that she chose to place her glittering record in jeopardy against all the fine players who had risen since that faraway day when she had come swinging out of the West, pigtails flying, to herald the approach of the finest player of her time. She had already three years earlier looked defeat squarely in the eye, for that "imposter" had come as close as ever he could without taking over.

But Miss Wills had not been afraid then and she was not now, although she certainly was aware that there were a number of girls capable of beating her on certain days. Miss Jacobs, especially, had become Wimbledon champion at last in the meantime and certainly was a better player than when she had stood with only one easy little smash between herself and victory. And Alice Marble, already rated one of the finest of players, had beaten Miss Jacobs to become United States champion in 1936.

Miss Wills must have pondered all this and still she came, risking very much to gain only a little more. If she had failed she would have had to step down from equality with Lenglen. If she succeeded she still must share honors with Suzanne. By winning again she could only make more secure a position already won.

By going to Wimbledon, though, she injected an element that made it possibly the best women's tournament ever held. Donald Budge's victory in the men's singles was placid, almost routine. In seven matches he did not lose a set, and there were only forty-eight games in all. The women's tournament overshadowed the men's because it had Helen Wills, seven times champion, in a field of girls from all over the world, each now eager to meet her and hopeful of being the first to beat her on the center court since 1924.

Although Miss Wills did not lose a set, her progress through the draw to the final was not untroubled. She won no match in the old way and anybody could see that time was catching up with her. But she did arrive in the final and there for the fourth time she found waiting Miss Jacobs, who had gone from strength to strength, beating among others Miss Marble, who was to be the last prewar champion at Wimbledon a year later.

This was the tenth time these girls with the same name and the same home town had contested the final round of a National Championship. Always, with that one exception, Miss Wills had won. Now Miss Jacobs, because her play throughout the tournament had been so much superior and because she had clearly outplayed Miss Wills before losing the 1935 final, was entitled to believe that she would finally gain a clear-cut victory to write finis to the long rivalry. Almost everybody else thought so too.

But Miss Wills began the match with a burst of her old deadly accurate hitting off the ground, and another desperate struggle developed immediately. It was a brief one, ending in the ninth game. At this stage Miss Jacobs, within a point of a 5–4 lead and serving, drove to Miss Wills's backhand and came to the net. Miss Wills hit a fine sharply angled backhand across court and Miss Jacobs, twisting her body awkwardly to the left in an effort to volley the ball, came down heavily on her right leg. A muscle was badly strained, and we could see that Miss Jacobs was in pain.

There followed an interval in which several people, one of them Hazel Wightman, donor of the cup, tried to persuade Miss Jacobs to abandon the match. Surely she ought to have done so, but remembering the storm of criticism Miss Wills had stirred up by walking out on that other occasion, she refused to do so. It could be seen from the stands that she was shaking her head stubbornly and finally all the people who had come onto the court left. Play was resumed. Miss Jacobs did not win another game, hardly another point. She could not move without pain and Miss Wills hit every ball she could for a winner to get the painful and now embarrassing affair over as soon as possible.

This incident caused almost as much controversy as the other, when the roles had been reversed, and I was again attacked by letter for reporting it without taking sides. People who did not favor Miss Wills but loved Miss Jacobs thought I should have blasted Miss Wills as a heartless person who showed no consideration for an injured opponent. Those who thought Miss Wills could do no wrong, and their number surprised me, blasted me for not pointing out how right she had been on both occasions.

As a matter of fact I do think Miss Wills was right both times. What angered people, I think, was that Miss Wills made no observable gesture of sympathy so that the bewildered crowd might see that she was concerned over Miss Jacobs' condition. I thought too that if she were a different girl she might have shown a little more concern, but I could find nothing in her conduct with which to reproach her. She just kept concentrating on the job in hand, which was Miss Wills's way.

I thought Miss Wills did the right thing in both instances and that Miss Jacobs was mistaken in not retiring rather than risking permanent injury. There can be no stigma attached to quitting in such circumstances, and the American notion about it is silly.

The result may well have been different if Miss Jacobs had remained sound throughout, but by whatever means, Miss Wills became Wimbledon champion for the eighth time that day. It is a record that may stand as long as the game is played, certainly until there comes along a girl who can reach the high plane on which we must, up to this point, place only two, Wills and Lenglen, and this theoretical girl must begin to win titles in her teens.

In fact this did happen. Maureen Connolly, another California girl, did start winning in her teens a dozen years later and winning so impressively that there has been speculation ever since as to what she might have become if she had not been forced into retirement before she got out of her teens by a leg injury. As a teen-ager Miss Connolly had won three titles each at Wimbledon and Forest Hills, was French champion twice and Australian champion once. In 1953 she won all four and she won every one of these four most important titles in the game at her first try. She arrived on the tennis scene as a schoolgirl of sixteen and was never beaten in any of the four.

There is no record in women's tennis to compare with that, and it is certain that we never saw Miss Connolly at her best. Good as she was, she still was improving and there is no telling how good she might have become. Since Helen Wills had won eight Wimbledon titles by the time she was thirty-three, it is most interesting to speculate on what Miss Connolly might have done in the thirteen years between her retirement and her own thirty-third year. She might have racked up more titles than any girl before her. Probably would have, because no better woman player than she already was appeared during those years.

Still, she did not, and although she belongs among the great ladies of the game and like them had that rare quality of consistency, she cannot quite be placed alongside the greatest of them. And there is about Miss Connolly's career the unfortunate fact that she never did take part in any particularly dramatic match that lives in people's memories. This saddens me because I think people have forgotten, or will forget, what a wonderful little person she was.

Miss Wills's eighth victory in her thirty-third year was her last appearance at Wimbledon. The following year saw Alice Marble win her only Wimbledon title. Because she reached her full development just as World War II began, when she was twenty-six, and then became a professional and was not seen again in tournaments, there has been a reluctance to accept Miss Marble as one of the greatest of women players. I have no reluctance and no hesitancy in saying that she owned an array of strokes never surpassed in quality by any woman player. On several occasions she played briefly a brand of tennis I never saw excelled by any player of her sex. She was so fluent and easy she never seemed to be hitting the ball hard, being like Lenglen in this respect, and I think, on the whole, she had the most nearly perfect way of striking the ball.

Miss Marble was a better server and smasher than either Lenglen or Wills and a far better volleyer than Wills. Probably she was a better volleyer than Lenglen too, but Suzanne had other qualities that overshadowed the volley, such as her marvelous control off the ground and her leaps and pirouettes. She was a fine volleyer too, though less pleasing than Miss Marble.

The Marble first service often was as hard as a man's, the second a "twist" with plenty of pace and kick that many men would envy. Tilden served that way too, and Miss Marble's was just as effective against her opponents as Big Bill's had been against his. Miss Wills had a good hard serve hit to a length with her body lithe in the delivery. It was nearly always certain. Lenglen seemed merely to be putting the ball in play until you noticed her rare judgment of pace and spin and the variety of her direction. Miss Wills, in their one meeting, was the only girl who attacked the Lenglen service successfully for all that it seemed so comparatively innocuous.

The Marble forehand, taken by her so easily, could be hit with fine pace to the base line or angled, for she had in common with Lenglen that wonderfully telling shot, the short forehand cross. Both used the court properly and all of it, having regard for the many angles which put the opponent in difficulty. The Wills forehand was a resounding whack at the ball, not taken too early, not pretty but absolutely certain, fluent, and severe.

The Marble backhand was a highly individual shot, a peculiar stroke delivered with a slack wrist. It was well produced, and though it seemed of equal quality with her forehand, it was slower, less certain. The Wills backhand was safer, as safe as could be. She could hardly be made to miss with it across court, the shot she played nine times out of ten whatever the situation, but it was often taken off the wrong leg and, as a stroke, did not compare in appeal with Miss Marble's version. Lenglen could take the hardest shot ever hit to her backhand in the exact center of her racket every time and place it unerringly where the eye directed.

The Marble range of volleys and smashes was marvelous, a most excellent line. Here there is no comparison. Lenglen could put a smash away about as well when the way had been prepared, and she showed in mixed doubles what she could do with a volley, but for all her flamboyant nature and eye for the spectacular she had not Miss Marble's flair in the forecourt.

There was for years a theory that Miss Wills could be beaten by drawing her into the forecourt, but no girl ever could control the play off the ground precisely enough against her to do so. Miss Wills didn't mind at all trotting about the base line from side to side, but she did not relish darting to the net, because she was a slow starter.

She did not own the pretty volleying touch of Miss Marble, but she could get the racket on the ball and she usually scored the point because her preparation had been so good. But Miss Marble, being a genuine volleyer, liked to close a rally by advancing to the net. Here there was a vast difference, for Miss Marble played with a dash that was a delight to see and is a pleasure to remember.

If Miss Marble's development had been normal and uninterrupted from girlhood onward, I do not doubt that we all would be forced to acknowledge her as the greatest. It is well known to all interested in tennis that this girl, just as she was becoming very good in the twenty-first year, suffered collapse and could not play at all for nearly two years.

I first saw Miss Marble in that spring of 1934 at the Stade Roland Garros, and the clippings tell me that I was impressed and delighted with her style but not overly impressed with her potentiality, which may have been the greatest ever seen. The impressions were gained mostly from practice sessions as Miss Marble, with other girls on the Wightman Cup team, was tuning up for a special team match with French girls and for the French Championships. She played only a little while competitively at that time. In her first match against Sylvia Jung, the French number two, she slumped to the court in a faint after a few games. They carried her to the American Hospital in Neuilly, and I did not see Miss Marble again until the National Championships of 1936 at Forest Hills, where she became champion for the first time, defeating Helen Jacobs in the final. In the meantime I had forgotten all about Miss Marble, but the American public dearly loves a "comeback" and here was a classic example.

They had told Miss Marble soon after her collapse that she had anemia, pleurisy, and even tuberculosis, and now here she was champion two years later. The people loved it and her. There never was a more attractive woman athlete than this tall, graceful girl with fair curly hair, large eyes, and a wide smile. It was great fun watching her play, and I saw every stroke she made in that 1936 Championship. Every stroke too at Forest Hills and in Europe during the next three years, when she won three more United States titles and one at Wimbledon.

With all her undoubted excellences why cannot Miss Marble be placed at the top above all other girls? It is because the record will not support such a rating. There were times when she seemed to stand out above her contemporaries just as Wills and Lenglen had done, but they were not, I think, of the same quality as the opponents the other two overcame with such certainty. I do not think Miss Marble's challengers were as strong as Molla Mallory, Mrs. Lambert Chambers, Elizabeth Ryan, Mary Browne, Kitty McKane, Lili de Alvarez, Helen Jacobs, and Dorothy Round. Probably most of these were better players than Miss Marble ever met, but Lenglen won six Wimbledons and never lost a set after her first final except in 1924, when she was ill and had to withdraw. Wills won eight Wimbledon titles and seven in the United States, and for a period of six years neither did she lose a set nor come near it.

Against a lesser group of opponents Miss Marble was not really consistent. As defending champion in 1937 she failed to survive the fourth round at Forest Hills, beaten by Dorothy Bundy, the eighth-ranked player. Two years after she had first become champion she was beaten in the semifinal at Wimbledon by Helen Jacobs and thus missed a chance for a title match with Helen Wills. Returned to Forest Hills that same summer, Miss Marble was twice within a point of being beaten by Sarah Palfrey.

The saving of the match against so fine a player—Sarah was herself twice a champion later after Miss Marble's retirement—was a brilliant effort, but Miss Marble had to play thirty-six games, three 7–5 sets, before winning. The other two, Wills and Lenglen, never were placed in jeopardy even by players somewhat better than Miss Palfrey. Nevertheless, I feel sure that no woman ever played better tennis than Miss Marble did at times in this same match, especially near the end of it. A round earlier she had needed thirty games to beat Kay Stammers, that quite good and very pretty left-handed English girl, but in the final set, which she won 6–0, Miss Marble played tennis of a quality which I do not think Miss Wills ever at any time matched or Lenglen ever surpassed.

Again, in winning her one Wimbledon title in 1939, Miss Marble had those beautiful strokes on dazzling display, but also again it was against such opposition as Miss Stammers could provide. Miss Stammers was capable of excellent play "on her day," as the London writers used to say, but she was not of the top class.

Because her play gave me such enjoyment I would like to place Miss Marble above all others, but I am unable to do that. Under other circumstances she might well have attained the highest peak and have occupied it all alone. As it is, though, I would be afraid, because of her lack of consistency, that both the other girls would have beaten her. Her volatile nature could explode in dazzling flashes, but she made too many loose shots after working up a rally to a climax. Lenglen and Wills never missed the crucial, or finishing, shot of a rally.

We will have to leave it, I think, that Miss Marble was, like Maria Bueno twenty years later, one of the most pleasant and beautiful players but only "one of the best." Miss Bueno, incidentally, also was hampered by severe illness. Even as late as the final round of the 1963 women's Championship at Forest Hills, this beautiful Brazilian player showed a flash of tennis no girl before had bettered, in going from 1–4 down in a second set to 6–4 victory. I thought at the time that this equaled anything I had seen, but on reflection I realized that it was played against a yielding opponent, Margaret Smith, the Australian girl who, though a champion herself, could not resist Miss Bueno with counterattack.

Nothing could be more beautiful in tennis than the way Miss Bueno played on this occasion, and each time I have seen her I was conscious of the fact that she was the nearest thing to Lenglen we have had. Always I was reminded of the Incomparable Suzanne in the way Miss Bueno struck the ball, the speed with which she got it off the racket, and the grace with which she moved about the court when winning. She had neither Lenglen's consistency nor her ability to disrupt the opponent's game, but Miss Bueno could impose her own game on the other girl when playing very well.

The difference was that Lenglen, like Wills, always played very well—Miss Bueno and Miss Marble only on occasion. And to be placed at the very top in the company of the truly great demands, I think, that a player maintain greatness, not merely touch it.

CHAPTER EIGHTEEN

THE comparing and rating of athletes who were not contemporaries and did not encounter one another on important occasions, is a trap in which no tennis reporter of experience should be caught. The temptation to make lists, neatly numbered from one to ten, is great, but the experienced observer resists the urge. He knows that it cannot be done in any satisfactory way. Probably it is a harmless practice, but the most I would permit myself is to declare that I do not think any player I have seen between that youthful Davis Cup experience of 1914 and the late 1960s could have beaten the best Tilden.

Beyond that I do not care to go, for I do not subscribe to the theory that everything was better in the old days. For those who cannot resist the temptation to make these lists, however, I can suggest a study that might help. Scattered through the years are certain key matches whose results can be revealing. These are "telling" tennis encounters and they merit careful examination for the light they can throw on relative skill.

The maker of lists should, however, be cautioned in looking back into the past of this game, or any game. We all come young to our sports, and at that time of life things always are pretty wonderful. Our sports heroes can be heroic indeed, as I well know, and although we acquire a certain perspective as we grow older, we must guard against the tendency to go along with our own generation. As the span grows longer the view grows wider and experience of games makes us more critical. We demand more, forgetting perhaps that in our younger days we may have been blindly undiscriminating in our hero worship. The sports figures of our more mature years may thus be compared unfavorably with the glowing figures of our youth. This may be the secret of the good-old-days-old-timer complex.

On the other hand it is just as easy to be sentimental about the present as about the past, as easy to overestimate as to underestimate.

A certain amount of careful observation and thought is required if we are to distinguish in any game of skill between players of the first and second classes and between these and what may be called the championship class, the exclusive society of the truly great. There is confusion, I think, as to what constitutes an athlete's form as distinct from his class, and if this distinction is not understood it is not easy to separate the classes for rating purposes.

An athlete's form, specifically that of a tennis player, may be off on a particular occasion for any number of reasons—his liver or his glands, loss of sleep, poor digestion, family worries. Any of these might prevent him from reaching his best form at a particular time. Class, on the other hand, does not vary from day to day. If he is a first-class player he remains one when right off form. Thus it is that a champion, such as Ben Hogan in golf for instance, could seem to be playing quite badly in a certain round and yet get a decent score, say a 73 or 74, whereas your merely good man would be up in the 80s. In the case of a tennis player, he may play badly, fail altogether to touch his true form, yet still beat a player of a lower class.

But the first-class man, even in his very best form, cannot exist at all in the championship class any more than the second-class opponent can stay alive with the first. This is the thing about class as opposed to form. A very definite line separates one class from another, and while form is variable, class is constant. A man may play much better on one occasion than on another, but however well he plays, he cannot get beyond his class once he reaches his full development and that class has been attained.

I have passed many pleasant hours at tournaments and games of various kinds trying to decide what it is that separates class from class and I have had discussions with those among my colleagues inclined to ponder such matters. The most profitable of all these talks were with John Pollack, who was Paris correspondent for the London *Morning Post* during the late 1920s and early 1930s before that fine paper expired. John had been a real devotee of games-playing in his younger days and a real student of techniques. He had written a very good book on tennis called *Listening to Lacoste* and many lucid magazine pieces on other sports. I engaged in a continuing discussion with him on this matter of class among athletes as distinct from form, and the conclusions drawn from these talks he incorporated in a series of pieces for some British publication whose name I do not remember. I remember the talks, though, and I am now in the process of "picking his brains," as the saying is, in retrospect.

Tennis, where the superior skill of one player, his ability to counter, is imposed directly upon the opponent, where thrust is met by immediate counterthrust, is, I think, the best place of all for such a study. Fencing probably would offer much the same opportunity, but I never learned enough about that sport to compare intelligently. I recall John, who did know about fencing, once saying that Peter Amphlett, rated one of the world's finest swordsmen in the 1920s, had told him that against Lucien Gaudin, the French champion, he had been helpless, even when Gaudin was out of competition several years during World War I.

The thing I remember particularly is Amphlett saying that Gaudin did not seem especially fast. You could, he said, see the attack all the way from its beginning until the button landed on your jacket but, so perfectly was it executed, you could do nothing to prevent it.

From this and other instances Pollack concluded, and I agreed with him, that what distinguishes one class from another is the ability to direct a sequence of well-executed movements until they place the player in a position to deliver a thrust, blow, or stroke that cannot miss being successful. Any reasonably good player may, on occasion and if the opportunity is presented, score with an ace, a drive into an unprotected corner of the court, or a volley to an unreachable spot. It is the master alone who can so lead up to these things that none can prevent him from bringing them off. Only in those of the real championship class do we find this ability to impose the game on the first-class opponent and not accept his game.

The second-class player must concentrate on his execution and is happy when it does not let him down. If he has a defect, the first-class man will inevitably search it out and expose it. The first-class man, certain of his execution and beyond worry that the mechanics of his game will betray him, may concentrate on tactics and he may even improvise. When the first-class player is opposed to the master, it never is the faultiness of his execution of any particular stroke that defeats him, for his strokes are hardly of lesser quality, and he will make them even under stress. This may well account for the fact that the great ones so often seem to defeat the very good ones more easily than they do the second-class player. They know that the first-class man must be treated with respect but with such uncompromising severity as to assure victory. The strokes of the first-class player are often as good as, in some cases better than, the master's. It is his inability, when playing the master, to apply these strokes to the execution of a "series" of moves that lead to the inevitable result.

Bobby Riggs, that enormously talented little gamesman who came to the top just as World War II began, is the outstanding example here. Without a really big serve he was yet a better and more consistent server than all but a few of the big blasters. He could serve an ace too when he needed, for he understood the principles of good serving and how to put them into use. His other strokes were his own, neither elegant nor powerful, but sound in every detail, and his footwork, as distinct from mere speed about the court, probably never has been surpassed. Riggs almost never missed unless made to, and he was full of guile whenever given a slack rein. That is why such men as Cramm, Budge, and Kramer never monkeyed around with him. They knew he had to be beaten, for he would not beat himself, and that he would be all over them before they knew it if they let down. But they did not let down, and Riggs could not beat them when they played their best.

It is the unorthodox more often than the master who amazes us with what he does, but we must not for this reason expect to find him among the great. Being what we call unorthodox is merely doing things in your own way, and it not only can lead to profit but can be the very essence of happiness. Even in failure the unorthodox are interesting and the game of tennis is better for having had many of them. Still, they do not reach the top. Both the first-class man and the master follow the narrow path of correct execution. It is the foundation upon which they build. They do not seem to be doing anything extraordinary most of the time because their perfection of movement leads so easily to the successful result, which often seems quite simply brought about. And all the really eminent have had this certainty of stroke, this ball control, in spite of a great variety in styles.

Since there is a lack of unanimity as to what constitutes the proper method, there also is a misconception as to what is the wrong way. It was said often in his day, and written even more often by the unthinking, that Fred Perry, the last British player to win major tennis titles, was unorthodox. That was nonsense. Perry, possibly the most underrated of all fine players, was individual, not unorthodox. All the great ones have been individuals. They do not fit a pattern. Perry was entirely individual, but in his thoroughly orthodox way he gave as fine an exposition of forehand driving as the game has known and on that sound and secure foundation he built one of the most beautiful all-round games I have ever seen. So far from being unsound, he showed us what a great forehand is; that it need not be a fierce slog but a ball exactly controlled to a nicety as to pace and length—the thrust down the line, sudden, fast; the long, dangerous slice right into the backhand corner, the deadly short cross court with the opponent at the net. The real excellence of Perry's forehand was easily apparent when supplemented by his eager, panther-like dash for the net and his very high skill as a volleyer.

The Perry backhand, though less spectacular, was equally as beautiful a stroke for one able to observe it closely. His manner of taking it was what fooled most observers and persuaded them that he was "unorthodox." The trouble was that they did not watch his feet at all. He would run almost past the ball and in the body's turn sweep it away with real pace, cunning accuracy, and perfect control.

It worked beautifully. When the volleyer sought the net, apparently with a safe point to come, he would be robbed by a lovely passing shot. It might be a slow, acutely angled shot across the body that cut the line inside the service court, or a straight, swift spinning shot down the forehand line, hugging the line, the intent disguised until the last instant.

Perry also gave us a beautiful exhibition of one of the game's rarest strokes, the smash from right to left. This is the unusual direction, and I have wondered why we do not see it more often. Most players smash from left to right although the other way would seem to be the more natural stroke. It is not apparently "natural," nor is it natural that, given a good service, a good smash follows. Tilden was the owner of the world's finest, most consistent, and most varied service, but he never owned a great smash. He was perhaps the safest smasher of all, but he would never bring off the devastating, electrifying thrust of the real smasher, the leap, the graceful bending back of lithe body in perfect timing of a perfect stroke. John Van Ryn made this stroke as few others have, and he did it so easily, and one saw it so often, it seemed something inevitable and usual. It is, however, a comparatively rare stroke in this perfect form, and although its principles are known, putting them into practice is not often achieved, even by the very best players.

Perry was a fine server, acing his man now and then, as well as great overhead. His game was his own, disconcerting, able to upset the other man's rhythm. This was because he could take a ball so early, could volley so well, and above all because of his marvelous speed about the court. Perry moved so rapidly he made even very quick opponents seem slow, although he never seemed to hurry in bringing off his coups. The completely equipped driver seldom is in a great rush to get to the net, but I do not think even Tilden covered the court so easily as Perry, who also had one other asset, his own matchless stamina, the same quality that brought Tilden through on so many occasions.

That most observers who saw him in his prime do not consider Perry one of the finest baffles me as much as their insistence that he was unorthodox. It cannot be merely because he was different, for the great performers in any sport invariably are "different." All the great ones learned grammar without losing their own individual accents. Some players, such as Sidney Wood, the Wimbledon champion of 1931, never achieved the greatness that seemed possible to them but were nevertheless players of exquisite culture who put the bloom on the orthodox. Fred Perry achieved greatness while doing the same thing, because he did it even better.

There are other players who went very far in the game, and gave us some of our most pleasurable moments, not so much because they really belonged on the highest rung of the ladder but because they were such indomitable fighters. Ted Schroeder and Vic Seixas come to mind immediately. Each had a heart and spirit that took his game well past the very high standard it reached on pure capability.

I was propounding these ideas one day in the mid-1930s among a group of professionals, when an extraordinary thing occurred. This was at a tennis center in the Auteuil section of Paris, where the touring pros used to hang out between exhibitions and tours, and where they taught such pupils as they could fit in. Four hard courts, glass-covered, heated, and lighted, fanned out, two along the street and two at angles behind, from a semicircular area occupied by a smallish combination restaurant-bar-lounge.

Sitting around this common room that day, some drinking, some eating, some just killing time, were half a dozen well-known pros of the time and a few lesser-known teaching pros who used the courts for lessons in the winter season. Present were Tilden, Albert Burke, Martin Plaa, and Robert Ramillon. I have a vague notion that Vines may also have been there, but Elly never was talkative and I cannot be sure.

I had taken what in golf are called playing lessons from Burke and Plaa and had got to know the others quite well too. The talk had been of styles of play. Tilden made some most interesting and revealing comments on his own game, and the discussion had got around to outstanding matches and great individual performers. All these men except Tilden had been professionals the whole of their adult lives and really had seen few tournaments. Since I had seen more play over the years than anyone present, except possibly Tilden, and was presumed to have sound judgment, I was asked to give an opinion as to the finest match ever played, or the finest I had seen.

I replied that, since I could not even decide which was the finest match I had seen with my own eyes, I was certainly in no position to name the finest ever. However, I was in no doubt about the finest stretch of tennis I had ever seen played. That, I said had been in the first set of a match in the Pennsylvania Championships about ten years earlier, and it had been played by Dick Williams. The effect of this statement on Tilden was astonishing. He leaped to his feet, threw out his arms, and stalked up and down the narrow passage shouting, "No, no. It cannot be. It is not so. It is impossible. Unthinkable!"

The others looked their surprise and Burke said, "For heaven's sake, Bill, sit down. This is not a theater. What the hell's the matter?"

Stopping dramatically in front of me and pointing his finger, Tilden declared, "I don't believe it, but there sits a tennis writer who knows what he's talking about. Imagine it! He speaks the truth."

"All right," said Burke, amused. "Now sit down and tell us about it."

Tilden did then sit down and without more histrionics told of how on that day of which I spoke he had been at the top of his game and playing as well as ever he played, and yet had been helpless before Williams' incredible artistry. In that first set, which he won 6–0,

212

Williams made only one error and Tilden made exactly five points, three of them on service.

"It was fantastic," Tilden said, using a favorite word of his. "I was playing my best whenever I could get my racket on the ball and I could do nothing. I tell you such tennis was never played [Tilden won the match in five sets]. No matter what people say about the finest tennis player, the finest tennis ever played for one set," Bill continued, underscoring the word "one," "was played by Dick Williams. I mean the finest tennis ever played by anyone. I have said it before and I will say it again."

Tilden was vehement about the fact that most lists of great players leave Williams' name out. "He should be at the top," Bill declared in his extravagant way. That was in the 1930s. Alas! On a list of the twenty outstanding players of all time that Tilden published not long before his death, he placed Williams at the very bottom.

I was thinking of this dramatic byplay in the Paris club as I rode down to Philadelphia on a blustery winter day in 1959 to have a visit with Williams. The wind was whipping across the ample pavements of Broad Street, ruffling the pigeons, and driving a fine mist down Locust to lay its smut on a noble building Philadelphians probably intend to visit one day but seldom ever do. This was the old home of the Historical Society of Pennsylvania, and Williams had been sitting in its director's chair for years, acquiring bit by bit, manuscripts and such things to fill gaps in the national archives.

This man who had carried the game to its peak, there to leave it for some future genius to equal or surpass, was within sight of his sixty-eighth birthday, and he had lived all the years in between in Philadelphia. The black hair that had been worn long and brushed back in his playing days was cropped close now and was almost white. But some of the old excitement still clung to him, and he still suggested in the quick movement of the hands and the soft, strong speech the vitality and exuberance that were so pleasant a part of his play long ago. He could still suggest the dashing young man of Cannes, and as I sat there in his office forty years after, an almost intolerable nostalgia flowed between us.

I told him of the little gathering in Paris and of what Tilden had said. I spoke of what he, Williams, had represented for me, a bridge leading over to a past I had not known. I said that Tilden, the greatest of players who believed that Williams had played the greatest tennis, had been a reaper of harvests, building his wonderful game on what had gone before, showing in his play the logic of growth, development, and progress. But Williams, I said further, was unique, springing seemingly from nowhere, so that those who saw his game, along with those who stood against it, believed that Williams had played, if only occasionally and then only briefly, such tennis as no one before him had played and none since.

I reminded him that in the same year of the Tilden match he had defeated Borotra, the Wimbledon champion, 6–2, 6–2, 6–2 at Forest Hills with comparable play over an "entire" match and that Borotra had said it was the greatest, the most astonishing tennis he had seen in his whole tennis life.

Williams listened to all this quietly, leaning forward with arms on desk, twirling a pencil in his fingers, a thoughtful expression and a half-smile on his face. When I had done he smiled fully and said very quietly and quite simply, "This is very interesting, but you know, I don't really understand what you are talking about. I don't really know what you mean. I don't remember this match you speak about at all. We had a number of matches, Tilden and I. Certainly I enjoyed them all. It was always fun playing Bill. I can see this disappoints you and I am sorry. But I do not remember."

I certainly was disappointed. I wanted to speak about that first set in detail and hear what he would have to say about it. That's what I had come down for. And he didn't remember. Later I thought that perhaps it was better to leave it that way. It may be that Dick Williams had more fun playing tennis than any other leading player who ever lived, and that's why he didn't remember. Perhaps it is just as well not to rub out by analysis this picture of Williams as the link connecting us with the youth of the game, the bridge spanning the gap between tennis as the comparatively private pastime of the few along the Eastern Seaboard and the exciting public spectacle enjoyed by thousands and played by millions.

Dick Williams never seemed to be playing for anything so definite and calculated as his reputation or a ranking. To keep track of his aces, placements, and errors seemed to me like counting the grace notes in a Mozart sonata or the crotchets in a Bach fugue. He played as he did simply because he could play no other way, taking great joy in the lightning fast co-ordination of his own eye, brain, and muscle. There has been no other of our time like him. He is now in the lasting care of fond memory, and for me his star has never set.

This would have been a subject into which Tilden could throw himself with enthusiasm, but I did not bring it up that day in the Paris club. Instead I asked him what he thought was the finest tennis ever played for an entire match.

"Certainly, I can tell you that," he said. "It was by Vines in Madison Square Garden against Fred Perry. That was their second New York match, not the first. When they came back from their tour. Nobody ever equaled it. You don't agree, of course."

Bill said this last with contempt, as though it stood to reason so ignorant a fellow as I would be bound to disagree. I did not agree then and I do not now. Nor did Tilden stick to this judgment any more than he did to others he gave off with that Olympian air. Years later he even denied having given such an opinion. Even so, he may well have been right in a certain sense.

Vines, like Williams, played incredible tennis at times, and people who care about such things are in danger of forgetting it, although Vines probably would have a place in the top group of any of those lists we were discussing. His matches bear closer study, however, than most people who make lists give them. Vines's place among the tennis greats really is based to a considerable extent on his defeats of Cochet, the man who first brought down Tilden in an important Championship match. Elly defeated Cochet in the final of the United States Championship at Forest Hills in 1932, at Wimbledon in 1933, and in the Davis Cup Challenge Round of the same year in Paris.

All these were impressive victories over a player universally rated very high, but I cannot persuade myself that they rate as outstanding achievements. It should be kept in mind for rating purposes that Cochet had been beaten in Championship play by quite ordinary, or at least second-class international players years before Vines ever saw him. Players named Ian Collins and Nigel Sharpe had beaten Henri in the first and second rounds at Wimbledon and Wilmer Allison, unseeded, won a quarterfinal match from the Frenchman on his way to the Wimbledon final of 1930. We should not, of course, rate Allison an ordinary player, for he was first class in every way, but we must not either give too much importance to his victory over Cochet as late as 1930. Something of Henri's astonishing co-ordination of hand and eye certainly had gone by then and possibly a little of his quickness too.

I do not think I have seen anything in sport much more exciting than those days when Vines raked the enemy court with those wonderful drives that barely cleared the net and struck near the lines with such force that no player of any time probably could have handled them. I saw this many times from Vines as amateur and professional, and in this mood, when he was able or was permitted to do this, I really do think he was unsurpassed. This is the Vines that Tilden remembers when he writes, "I have seen and played Vines when he showed the most amazing tennis I have ever seen. It was stupefying; there was absolutely nothing I could do to stop him that day. It was hard even to see the ball, let alone hit it." And yet the forty-six-year-old Tilden did beat the twenty-seven-year-old Vines for money in a professional tournament at Wembley in 1939, and there were a number of times when Vines was not permitted by others to work his will, or was unable to do so. These occasions also are part of the record.

The Wimbledon final of 1933 between Vines and Jack Crawford, the beautiful Australian stroke maker, is recommended to those who would place tennis players in neat lists numbered from one to ten. I consider this match the best final I ever saw at Wimbledon, and one of the most interesting matches seen anywhere. Vines came to it hailed by the British press as the greatest player of all time. They were thinking of his crushing victory over England's best player, Bunny Austin, in the previous year's final, finishing off with a love set that took less than ten minutes to play. Such powerful and controlled hitting over the last two sets of this 6–4, 6–2, 6–0 victory had, I believe, never been seen on a tennis court. It was simply devastating and probably no player of past or present could have matched it or stood up to it.

This was the picture we all still had in mind when Vines, having beaten Cochet 6–2, 8–6, 3–6, 6–1, in the semifinal, came out as champion to defend his title against the challenge of Crawford, the classic model of a tennis player. Crawford's game had a stately-domed sort of grandeur. It seemed as British as a three-volume novel in the paneled library of a manor house, as pre-World War I as a hansom cab. Though a very large man, he was a graceful and seemingly effortless mover, a fluent easy-footed driver with a strong, impressive personality expressed through a rare and charming amiability.

The Australian was a master strategist and a deadly aggressive attacker with a mild manner but, with all his aggressiveness, so sure an artist, so stylish and so courteous. He had command of every essential stroke and, attacking from the base line, could use the entire court as few have been able to do. But for the asthma with which he battled through his whole tennis life, he probably would have been rated among the great. I do not think any tennis player has given me more genuine pleasure than Jack Crawford.

In his long sleeves and immaculate flannels Crawford made an impressive picture, in strong contrast to Vines, who was tall, slim, and athletic enough, but slightly gangling and shambling for all that.

Certainly we did not suppose on the day they met that Vines would deal with Crawford as he had dealt with Austin, for the Australian was of a higher class, but we doubted that the beautiful stylist would be able to survive such an attack all around the court as Vines could launch. Vines did launch such an attack. It was just as severe and at times just as controlled as it had been against Austin. But Vines was beaten in a fifth set 4–6, 11–9, 6–2, 2–6, 6–4, and I doubt that anyone who saw the match would argue that Vines was not at his best. Crawford found the way to circumvent and counter Vines's far more powerful hitting and bring his own somewhat less spectacular assets to bear.

This was really a tennis match about as near heart's desire as I can remember, a thoroughly enjoyable thing in which the emotions were not so involved as to forbid a sort of detached admiration of both players. I am sure it must rank with the very best matches because of the pure pleasure it gave. For superlative play on both sides of the net, the blending of stroke and strategy, the unrelenting speed of service and considered counterstroke, I cannot remember another to place above it.

Conditions were perfect, a rare thing, when they entered the court and began at a rather leisurely pace what was to be a marathon of fifty-six games. Then suddenly Vines, having won his first service game with ease, almost casually, stepped up the pace. He hit the base line and deep sideline with two forehand drives no player could have returned, captured Crawford's service, and led 2–1. Then came streams of service aces and more forehand drives that made the chalk fly. As the last ball flew untouched and untouchable past Crawford to give Vines the first set, Jack smiled and bowed toward his opponent in acknowledgment, and we all wondered how the Australian could possibly check this enormous fire power long enough to bring his own less explosive but still deadly weapons into play.

We did not really think it possible, and at this point I was sure Vines would win, probably in straight sets. The burst of hitting had been so impressive that I was certain of it even though I knew well Crawford's artistry and resourcefulness and had learned long ago not to judge the outcome of a tennis match by the way it began.

Crawford was one of the finest of servers, but he seldom tried for an outright ace unless the point was critical. And he could take a fast service too. Vines had led 5–2 in the first set, but in spite of the explosive delivery he could not serve himself out in the eighth game. Looking back to that game from the end, one could see that there the key to victory had first been revealed. At the time, under the impact of Vines's tremendous blasting, it was attributed to a slight carelessness, with the set already well in hand and a lot to spare. What had been noted but not properly understood was that Crawford moved in to take the service, hit down on the rising ball, blocked it back with a little spin, and waited. He won Vines's service and his own before Vines got the set.

Now began that long set of twenty games so vital to Crawford, since if he lost it he would have to win three sets in a row against that withering fire. During its progress I once or twice thought back to that long set I had seen Brookes and McLoughlin play in 1914 when Brookes, that other great Australian, had attempted to deal with the cannonball serve in the same way as Crawford was now doing. I did not really remember this from observation but from reading, but I had seen Cochet and Lacoste stand in to Tilden's service the same way, and Dick Williams could hit anybody's service for a winner at times. People forget that the fine player can take many, though not all, express services, striking down on the rising ball and letting repercussion come to his aid.

Crawford was standing right up to the ball and using the force of the serve itself to send it back fast and deep so that the server could not always get in behind the ball, had to stay back and exchange drives. Only the finest of players, of course, have this ability. It was not at all easy against Vines. Crawford seemed afraid to go to the net, for that was dangerous ground. Even so it was there that Jack finally won the two successive games necessary to win the long service-governed second set. Each time he advanced he hit deep to Vines's backhand corner after fencing awhile from back court and then brought off the volleying coup with certainty.

The Australian thus revealed the weak spot in the American armor, the vulnerable spot which Vines, for all his avalanche of aces, deadly long forehand cannonading, and devastating overhead, could not in the end protect. By searching it out and exploiting it, by steering the ball to this sector in the crises that lay ahead, Crawford made his still arduous task a little easier.

Vines played some of his finest and most resolute tennis in this second set, for he knew its value to Crawford. But Jack had begun with the service and so was always a game ahead when he had won. He could lose his own service and all would not be lost, for he could still get back even by winning Vines's service game. Vines, always a game behind when Crawford won, had never the stimulation of a service game in hand. He served each time after 4–all to save the set, never to win it and, with this hanging over him through a dozen games, he played wonderfully well.

Those who would change the scoring rules to eliminate the deuced set have splendid motives, and most of their arguments are sound. But they never seem aware that they would also eliminate the drama, the excitement of these service battles where two fine players probe long and earnestly, searching to find a way in which the big serve can be overcome. How many fewer great moments there would have been in tennis without this.

Crawford had been probing and waiting since the match began, and now in the twentieth game of the second set that for which he waited arrived. However well Crawford handled the service he could not win it so long as Vines could serve aces when in trouble. Now the big one at last missed the mark. Not one first service came into court and Crawford knew how to deal with the second. Now he could strike those beautifully controlled balls, low and spinning, into the backhand corner and reach the net before they came back. His volleys were decisive and they brought him back even at one set apiece.

Vines seemed discouraged a little in the third set and played below his best for the only time during the match. Crawford's pace of service and drive increased and, significantly, he several times threw up lobs that Vines could not handle effectively. In the fourth set the play returned to a high plane, sometimes to outright brilliance but was somewhat less interesting because Crawford, falling behind early, appeared willing to yield the set since he was leading two sets to one, rather than make a strong and perhaps tiring charge to make up lost ground. He seemed to be resting a little, one thought, not stirring himself beyond trying to make Vines work a little harder for his games, looking toward the crisis of a fifth set and saving his ammunition for that.

Vines was serving altogether too well at this stage to hope for a break before he should win the set after he had once got ahead. And that fearsome service would have to be won twice if Crawford was to win the match in that fourth set. And so after two hours of play they came to the fifth set, dead level, each having won twenty-three games.

The culminating set was remarkable both for the very high quality of the play and the attitude of the crowd that filled every center-court space. It was completely impartial and hardly ever disturbed the progress of the play with either applause or those explosive outbursts that usually accompany a tense match. The whole thing now turned on whether Crawford, confident that he could hold his own service for a little while longer, could get one service game from Vines before he should have to yield one himself, through fatigue and strain.

It certainly did not seem possible the first time Vines served, for he never in his life served better, putting over four balls that either flew past or could be struck only at an angle out of court. But Vines also hit Crawford's service out of court in the third game and we sat forward now, wondering if the strain were telling and seeking signs of it. Had the perfect timing at last gone off? No.

More aces came in the fourth game for 2–all, and then in the fifth Crawford stood within a single point of losing his own service. With

Vines still serving aces, to be 2–3 down probably would have been fatal. And now, alive to the danger, Crawford, with that deceptively easy, almost flat-footed service swing of his, cut the ball wide with spin to Vines's forehand service line and followed it to the net for a winning volley. It was the first time since play began that Jack had gone to the net behind a service.

The game was saved and on they went with both men playing tennis that, in view of the length and strain of the match, was surprisingly good, full of forceful play, each attacking and defending with fine shots. Once more Crawford was a game ahead with his service won, and he came to 5–4 with some beautiful strokes, pulled out on the move, that once again caused the Vines backhand to yield to pressure.

With the first point of the tenth game we all felt that the real crisis might have arrived. Vines sent a blasting service to the forehand corner of the service court. Crawford, stepping in, blocked it back across court with a stroke that began at the shoulder and stopped as it met the ball, the racket canted backward. The shot was not very deep or difficult to handle, and Vines crashed a blistering forehand that barely cleared the net down Crawford's backhand line. It seemed that Jack would not be able to reach it at all, but he had begun moving before the ball was struck, and quickly, without seeming to hurry, he was there as Vines dashed for the net to cut off a possible reply.

And now Crawford, as calmly as though it were only a pregame warmup, threw a lob from corner to corner, exactly calculated as to height so that Vines could not back up and put it away as he had done so often earlier. Seeing that he was trapped, Vines turned and tacked in his forward progress and scrambled back to get behind the ball as it fell no more than an inch inside the base line. He struck at it as it rose from the court but was so off balance that the ball bounced before it reached the net.

It was felt now that Crawford had, with that perfectly controlled lob off one of Vines's hardest thrusts, struck the decisive blow. And so he had. A spinning ball to the backhand corner on the next point and Vines missed it badly, hitting right into the bottom of the net. A little desperate at being behind 0–30 and within two points of defeat, Elly came in behind a serve off which he had taken a little to be sure it would be good and Crawford, with perfect touch after more than two hours of tension-filled play, brought off a beautiful backhand passing shot. Love–40 now against the biggest service known to man, three match points in a row. Only one was needed. Crawford placed the ball on Vines's backhand again to draw the final error from a stroke that had gradually broken down under persistent pressure.

Crawford was Wimbledon champion at last and that delicately struck backhand passing shot, moving slowly across the body of the rushing volleyer and just out of reach, and the lob with which he began the final game still are remembered perfectly, almost visually, so long afterward.

This was an occasion on which Vines, though beaten, justified many of the fine things said and written about him. He did not always play this well and his record, especially the Davis Cup record, is quite spotty. And a player's failures as well as his triumphs must go into the record. In 1932 and 1933 Vines was the acknowledged world champion and even, as we have seen, had been hailed in some quarters as the all-time greatest player after his overwhelming defeat of Austin. But the United States did not win back the Davis Cup until four years after Vines had become a professional.

Directly from that victory over Austin, Vines went to Paris for the Davis Cup play as leader of his country's forces. He was confidently expected to bring the Cup home, but he failed badly. He was beaten 6–4, 6–2, 3–6, 6–4 by the thirty-five-year-old Borotra in the first Challenge Round match and all chance of winning back the Cup went with that defeat. After losing his Wimbledon title to Crawford, but still U.S. champion, Vines crossed to Paris on a second Davis Cup quest as head of the team. This time we met Great Britain in the inter-zone final, were beaten 4–1, and Vines did not win a point. Again in the opening match Vines was beaten in three quick sets by Austin 6–1, 6–1, 6–4, and also was beaten by Perry in the fifth match, which had no bearing. This latter match was the one in which Vines collapsed at match point to Perry, the scores being 1–6, 6–0, 4–6, 7–5, 7–6.

Returning home then to defend his U.S. singles title, Vines was beaten by Bryan Grant and that wound up a short but often exciting and sometimes brilliant amateur career. Vines was top man among the professionals until Don Budge arrived among them, but he has no actual achievement either as amateur or pro that compels that he be rated above several others. Nevertheless, I cheerfully admit that were players to be ranked on their peak performances alone, on the brief flashes of superlative play, Vines would take his place beside Dick Williams, for at times both played tennis on the very highest plane.

CHAPTER NINETEEN

C ONTINUING in the same vein, another match worth studying is the Wimbledon final of 1930 at the end of the so-called Golden Age. This Wimbledon of 1930 brought us to the end of Tilden's reign as the greatest of the kings of the court in a most fitting way, putting the seal on his glittering record. Now in his thirty-eighth year and ten years beyond the winning of his first title there, Tilden came to the final through a victory over Borotra that surely must have been one of his most remarkable achievements.

Here Tilden had to overcome not only a Borotra in brilliant form but a super gamesman who, though rated by some the greatest "sportsman" of his time, actually stepped many times very close to the boundary line of what one considered good sportsmanship. So infuriating were Borotra's tactics on this occasion and so clever his tongue, that Tilden refused to go near him. At each change of courts Bill would wait to see which way Borotra went and then would cross over at the opposite end of the net so as to be out of reach of the Basque's needle.

Borotra always made more of a match than a mere game of tennis. With him it was a fight against odds in which one's sympathies could be on one side only. It is doubtful that Borotra ever played a match anywhere in the world without gaining the sympathy of the crowd, and even in foreign countries he was very often the crowd's favorite against the home player. There was in him this power of dominating his matches as there was in Tilden, and inevitably there was this clashing of temperaments when they met.

But Tilden, always in a sort of cold fury when playing Borotra, nevertheless always did beat the Basque. Borotra never defeated Tilden on an outdoor court. Bill won their matches in a variety of ways and by employing different weapons on different occasions. Before going into court this last time with Borotra, Tilden boasted that he was going to win with the lob. I never had heard Tilden boast and never did again, and I am sure it was his intense dislike of Borotra and his tactics that prompted it.

"He's got the best overhead game in the world, hasn't he?" Tilden asked. "Well, watch me. I will do nothing but lob and I will beat him."

He did lob throughout the long five-set match and he did win, 0–6, 6–4, 4–6, 6–0, 7–5. At the start Borotra, forcing the pace, put the lobs away with untouchable, unreachable smashes, winning every game easily. Tilden served at half speed, rather softly to give himself a chance to throw up lobs in every game. Often he did not even bother to look toward the place where the ball bit into the turf. I thought he was making a serious mistake when Borotra won the first set so easily, without really working for it. But it was I who was mistaken, not Tilden. I failed to note with what care Bill had tossed the lobs. They were all deep and most were thrown toward Borotra's backhand corner so that he had either to run back behind the ball after it bounced or leap and smash with straining muscles. Several times he needed a second smash to win the point, and I was sorry at the end of the match that I had not kept count of the number of lobs Tilden had used when he could have as easily used another stroke.

This continued in the second set with the difference that Tilden now made certain of holding his own service games. And when at 4–all he decided to go for the one enemy service necessary to win the set, suddenly there were no more lobs. Instead there were passing shots, and just enough of them did pass to give Tilden the set in the tenth game.

The third set was a repetition of the first tactically, but now there was a great difference in the effort Borotra had to make to win it by a quite narrow margin. Tilden lobbed and lobbed, but he also introduced the drop shot and Borotra, always a likely winner, was made to run up and back far more often. So often, in fact, that he decided to take a rest in the fourth set. There is no rest period at Wimbledon, and Borotra often used a fourth set for this purpose when leading two sets to one. Against lesser antagonists than Tilden he would bring out the old dying-Gaul act at these times, pretending utter exhaustion, staggering about the court. Knowing Tilden would not be fooled by such antics, the Basque now wagged his head, made gestures toward the stands, and remained on the base line. Tilden, refusing to give him a long rest period, rushed through the set, finishing off every point as quickly as he could.

And then Borotra, taking up the balls to begin service in the fifth, was all fire again, dashing for the net, smashing and volleying with all the old verve and skill. I had seen it before and I knew that, as always, the crowd would respond. So had Tilden seen it and knew perfectly well it would come with the deciding set.

But now Tilden, instead of throwing up lobs at every opportunity, chose more carefully the times for his calculated tosses aloft. Twice in the early games of the set he disguised his intention so well Borotra, caught too close to the net, was forced to jump and not quite reach the ball. The result was two flubbed smashes. Tilden also was twice close to winning Borotra's service when the Basque could not put the volley away at the first try. Borotra still had left some of that extraordinary power of his to leap to the kill, and no break was possible yet. Ten games had to be completed before the Frenchman was ready to yield. Tilden was patient, but he knew when the time had come.

Borotra, who had been foot-faulting atrociously all along with a great show of contrition each time he was called but with not the slightest change in his service action, was just a little slower in the eleventh game in getting to the net behind the service. It was not obvious to the crowd, but Tilden saw that Borotra was hanging back just a little now looking for the lob that never came. For Bill was now holding the lob in reserve and he did not even try to pass Borotra with the reply to the service. He sought only to give a difficult volley that could be picked up. The second shot would make his man stretch a little wider, stoop a little, and strain as the ball dipped after crossing the net. Only the third passing shot would be hit to score.

On three points in a row, after Borotra had gone to 30–love, Tilden made him stretch and stretch until you could almost hear the grunts as the Basque lunged for the ball. Finally, as Borotra moved in behind a well-struck service at 30–40 to Tilden, the lob was thrown.

It fell untouched squarely in the center of the base line, the most perfectly gauged lob thrown in the whole match. Borotra was now too spent to dash back as he had done earlier, and as they changed courts with Tilden leading 6–5 and his own service to come, it should be noted that Borotra acknowledged his master as graciously as anyone could ask. Tilden stopped by the umpire's chair and said something to Borotra. He didn't fear what his old enemy might say now, and I have often speculated on what it might have been he said. Both knew the issue had been decided and both may have wondered if it were not to be the last time they would meet on a tennis court, as in fact it was. In the final game there came the cannonball, which Tilden had still in hand, and Borotra could not take them any more.

Wilmer Allison also came to the final that year by defeating Cochet, the defending champion, 6–4, 6–4, 6–3, in the quarterfinal and John Doeg, who was to be U.S. champion two months later, 6–3, 4–6, 8–6, 3–6, 7–5 in the other semifinal. Allison also had the quality of dominating a match. With him one always felt, even in his easier victories, that here was a dour fighter with his back to the wall. He was a fighter all right. His victory over Cochet, it should be kept in mind, came two years before Vines met the little Frenchman, but the really significant thing about the 1930 Wimbledon is, I think, that in the final Allison, who also was to be U.S. champion, could not win a set from the thirty-seven-year-old Tilden.

Tilden won 6–3, 9–7, 6–4, and when he had done so he was once more the owner of both Wimbledon and U.S. titles at the same time, ten years after he had first won them in 1920. One need not elaborate on this remarkable achievement beyond pointing out that all who had won at Wimbledon and Forest Hills between Tilden's first and last championships already were done as champions even though all were years younger than he.

Still another match recommended to the raters of tennis players occurred in 1939 in the semifinal round of the City of London Championships at the Queens Club, the prelude to Wimbledon. I always thought this one most revealing. Gottfried von Cramm, the German Baron, had been for many months previously in a Nazi concentration camp. He had played a tournament or two after being released, one in Egypt, I think, but it could hardly be said that he was in top tennis form when he arrived at Queens that week.

Cramm's entry had not been accepted at Wimbledon, but he was expecting at that time to come to the United States. He had a notion that if he could win at Forest Hills, a likely thing if he could get back in top form, he might join Budge, Perry, and Vines to form a professional doubles tour that no doubt would have been quite successful financially. Cramm's estates had been confiscated and, although now free, he was without resources. I had been told that Cramm's incarceration had been only partly because of the so-called moral turpitude but more for political reasons, since he was said to have expressed anti-Nazi feelings.

I had had glimpses now and then into the life led by the set in which he and his pretty wife moved from one European resort to another throughout the year, and I knew that for some it had become in the years immediately preceding the war a sort of round, smooth, tasteless monotony. We all knew that a certain amount of experimentation with all sorts of things that could be called degenerate had been going on, and I always felt that Cramm was less guilty of these things than some others in the set, certainly far less than some of his own German tennis associates.

Cramm declined to discuss any of these matters at Queens that summer of 1939, but he did speak of his hope of starting a new life, perhaps in America, although he was a little vague about that. Of course, his application for a visa was turned down and World War II was only weeks away. He did not anticipate being turned down by the United States and of war there was no mention, though I imagine he did anticipate that. Whatever else he was thinking he was determined to demonstrate at Queens, which represented his only chance, that he still was a fine player.

And he did most convincingly in that semifinal match. He simply smothered Bobby Riggs. Riggs lost the first eleven games, won one game, and that was all as the German ran out the match. And yet, two weeks from the day on which this match was played Riggs was Wimbledon champion and he twice won the United States title. In the Wimbledon final Riggs needed five sets to defeat Elwood Cooke, a player who never had been ranked higher than seventh in his own country.

Riggs won at Forest Hills that same year and went on to be rated among the greatest because of postwar victories over a Budge well past his best. Cramm never won a singles title at Wimbledon or Forest Hills, where he also had beaten Riggs in Budge's final year as champion. The only major title the German baron ever did win was the French. He was unfortunate that the best years of both Perry and Budge overlapped his own, else he might well have been world champion more than once. Almost certainly he would have been. This titled aristocrat with a most beautiful game could beat the young Budge while Perry was champion, but by the time Perry had joined the professionals, Budge had advanced just enough to have a very slim edge over Cramm, as witness their five-set final at Forest Hills in 1937 and their memorable Davis Cup meeting that same year.

This latter match has been called the greatest ever played. Walter Pate, the American team captain, has insisted upon it so often since, that many people who did not see it have accepted his judgment, because he is a man loved for his person and respected for his tennis knowledge. I think I was, on the whole, a more objective observer than Walter, and while I can almost agree with him, I cannot quite. I do not deny that he could be right, and I too have love and respect for him and am forever grateful for his kindness and help during these weeks of 1937. But there have been so many "great" matches. I have not seen them all, nor has Walter, but I have seen so many fine ones it is no more possible for me to rate them than to rate players.

On the other hand I saw this particular match under extraordinary circumstances and may not be an altogether competent judge. It may be for this reason that I took more pleasure from watching the Vines-Crawford affair, and am inclined to rate it an even finer match.

A few days before these inter-zone final matches between the United States and Germany were to begin on the Wimbledon center court, I arrived at the New York *Herald Tribune* office in Bush House to find a note from John Tunis and an urgent message to call Miss So-and-So at Broadcasting House. The note said that Tunis had become too ill to broadcast the matches for NBC, was sailing for home immediately, and had told the people at the British Broadcasting Company that I would do it in his place. I was still in a state of mild shock from reading this when Miss So-and-So, who turned out to be a charming British lady, phoned without waiting for me to respond. I was to come at once to Broadcasting House to talk it over and get things settled. The time was short. New York wanted to know at once.

Broadcasting House was up around Piccadilly Circus somewhere, in Regent Street, I think, and I walked all the way, down the Strand and up Haymarket to put off as long as possible the moment when I would have to tell them I couldn't do it. The thought that I would have to sit in a booth and speak into a microphone all during a tennis match, or at any other time, terrified me.

The kind and efficient lady who received me said that was nonsense. "Utter rot" were the actual words she applied to it. Tunis, my friend, had said I could and would do it and that was that. When she told me they would pay $500 each for inter-zone final and Challenge Round, I began to wonder if she might not be right. This was an awful lot of money at that time and I was swayed by greed. I agreed to do it and thereby lost much sleep worrying about how in the world I should ever get away with it.

It did not sound as bad as I had anticipated when I learned that there would be only two fifteen-minute sessions of live description of the play at Wimbledon and then a fifteen-minute roundup in a studio at midnight, which would be only seven o'clock in New York.

The day before the matches were to start, Pate called a press conference and, to the surprise of all those gathered, announced that Bryan Grant, the Atlanta player known to all as Bitsy, had been chosen to play singles with Budge. I knew Walter's tennis judgment to be quite sound and I could not understand this choice. Besides Budge, the team members were Gene Mako, his doubles partner, Frank Parker, Wayne Sabin, and Grant. Whereas Grant had done nothing spectacular at the Wimbledon just ended, Parker had beaten Henner Henkel, the German number two player behind Cramm, and had lost a close semifinal to Budge himself.

I suspected that the choice was not Pate's, but had been dictated in higher U.S.L.T.A. circles in New York. The tennis fathers had been for some time under a good deal of pressure to play Grant, a very popular little man. Southerners, and especially Atlantans, had charged discrimination, pointing out that Grant had beaten nearly everybody ranked above him at one time or another. This was true enough, for Grant was a great little competitor who could always be counted on to beat any man who played badly, although his own game appeared innocuous enough to those who did not note the absolute soundness of his method. The trouble now was, though, that on these big occasions men playing for their country seldom play poorly.

I sat across the table from Pate trying to figure this one out, and I decided that the so-called brass, annoyed by the constant clamor for Grant, decided, with the inter-zone series safely in the bag, as they thought, to throw Bitsy in, get him beaten, and dispose of both him and their critics at one blow. Budge would, of course, win two singles. Had he not just beaten Cramm in straight sets in the Wimbledon final? And Budge and Mako would win the doubles. That would be enough to win the series and qualify for the Challenge Round against England, when the Cup would inevitably be won back after its ten-year residence abroad.

I did not care to put Pate on the spot, so instead of suggesting this explanation immediately, I kept silent while the other American and British reporters asked him to explain his reasoning. He was not quite convincing. He said that Grant was a great fighter and had a good record in American zone matches. Pate thought that Grant would sell his inevitable defeat by Cramm at a much higher price than Parker could exact, since Bitsy was the greatest retriever in the game. He was prepared, the captain thought, to make Cramm play a long, tiring match and that might be a factor in winning the doubles. And, if the doubles were won it would make little difference whether Grant or Parker played the other singles.

This did not sound like Pate and, as a matter of fact, it did make a very great difference which man was to play. It seemed to me to be evading the undeniable fact that Parker had beaten Henkel less than two weeks earlier and seemed entirely capable of doing it again. Furthermore, the draw had not been made at this time and the Grant-Cramm match might just as well be the last of the five instead of the first. But even if it were the first, it would be of small value anyway, because no tennis was played on Sunday in England and Cramm would have a day's rest between the first singles and the doubles.

My respect for Pate made me hesitate to put the question directly to him before that bunch of British writers, some of whom were ever on the scent of a "sensation," even as some of our own. But since there would be no chance to speak privately, I felt I must. I asked if it had been his own decision or had been made in New York. Pate did not even then give a direct answer, and I did not press him. He said that as captain he was in complete authority over the team and could chose any combination he thought right. Grant's choice, he felt, was the correct one. I never did find out about this, although I tried when we all came back home later. Selection committees always turn their backs on strange errors they commit, as if they were children detected in an act of naughtiness. They pretend they haven't been anywhere near.

I did not think it the correct selection, but I do know that all who saw the series can be grateful for the error. Had Parker been chosen he might well have beaten Henkel and there would have been no critical Budge-Cramm match on the third day to be writing about and telling about down through the years. On the first day, a Saturday, Cramm beat Grant 6–3, 6–4, 6–2, and Budge beat Henkel 6–2, 6–1, 6–3. Then Budge and Mako repeated their Wimbledon vicory over Cramm and Henkel in the doubles on Monday 4–6, 7–5, 8–6, 6–4.

So everything was going according to plan, but in the first singles match on Tuesday Grant never had a chance against Henkel. The German won 7–5, 6–2, 3–6, 6–4, beating Grant in the way Grant could be beaten, by superior force continually applied from close quarters. Henkel was not a top-class player by any means, but he could hit hard and volley decisively. Grant played his usual game, very well in fact, but he could not deal with the German's pace. It was some satisfaction to have one's judgment thus confirmed, and with the score now tied at two matches each, I looked forward to the deciding match between Budge and Cramm with confidence of an American victory, which surely would mean capture of the Cup in the Challenge Round a week later. Perry had become a professional, and it was felt that Great Britain could no longer successfully defend against either the United States or Germany without him.

I never was so mistaken about how a tennis match would go. There was a surprisingly large crowd in the center court stands, and the big-match atmosphere of expectancy was there. It was as if the public had sensed what was to come where the experts had missed it. Cramm, who had been a great favorite in England for years now was carrying British hopes. British crowds are loyal to their champions even when like Budge they are foreigners, but they also reckoned that they would have a much better chance of retaining the Cup another year if the Germans should be the challengers. Budge won this match, but before he got through he had lost the first two sets, stood 1–4 down in the fifth, and Cramm had saved three match points before yielding in the fourteenth game. The final scores were 6–8, 5–7, 6–4, 6–2, 8–6.

Throughout the long fight which, with the rest interval, covered nearly three hours, I was cooped up in a tiny booth at one end of the court, talking. I had done my stint on Saturday and Monday without incident and felt mistakenly that I was now an experienced broadcaster ready for anything. I had gone down to Wimbledon early on Saturday in the hope of having a chance to consult with the BBC announcer, a retired Colonel Something, who would broadcast the matches locally. He was a bluff and quite friendly man with a don't-mind-if-I-do personality, who was willing to have me buy him any number of spots and splashes, but he did not communicate much of the technique of describing a tennis match. He had been at it for several years, and I'd hoped to learn something of how he went about it, but the most I could get out of him was "Nothing to it, old boy. You'll do well. Don't worry."

I took a lot of worry into the little booth. It was just large enough for me and had a glass front down to about an inch above the board through which the microphone protruded. The space at the bottom of the glass was so that someone could keep sticking through notes of instruction. I'd no idea how to proceed and made something of a botch of the first fifteen-minute period in the Cramm-Grant match. I soon learned that the action was too fast to keep up with a running description. I could not talk that fast, and after a while I saw that there would be time between points to describe them a little, and then there was the longer interval after the odd games when they changed sides.

At first these intervals seemed great voids that had to be filled with words, but later they got to be much too short to catch up on the play. Because I was so preoccupied with my own troubles and so nervous, I do not remember much about the details of four of these five matches and the accounts I wrote about them later in the evening back at Bush House. They now seem, when I read them, concerned with some strange tennis contests I never saw at all. The big one has been discussed so often that the impression of it remains intense, if not altogether clear.

I had prepared some notes on the styles of the players in case I got stuck, which I thought might well happen. I was arranging these so they would be handy just after the match began, when somebody stuck a piece of paper under the glass with a message reading "Stop rattling those papers. Sounds like thunder over the air."

This threw me off stride entirely. I kept looking toward the notes but didn't dare touch them even to turn a sheet over. I still have those notes, and if I couldn't give them then I can now. Cramm, I was going to say, has a game of clean, wide drives and an offensive service that is mechanically perfect. What he lacks is a certain subtlety, an ability to break up the other fellow's game. This is more than a matter of strokes.

"Though he strikes the ball very quickly, Cramm must have his feet planted and must address the ball, whereas a player such as Budge or Perry can perform miracles on the run. Yet Cramm can hit fine winners against Budge, and few players ever had a stroke to compare with his 'flat' backhand, with which he occasionally blinds the gallery.

"Whereas Cramm is all elegance," I wrote then, "Budge presents an angular figure. It is strange," the notes say, "that so great a player with so fine a game is yet so little graceful compared with the other great ones. But then Budge too is an individual, as Tilden was.

"When in form Budge presents no weakness. His forehand, though not a pretty shot, does not falter, his backhand is the world's best, and only Borotra, with his powerful punch down on the ball has matched that acute-angled backhand return in recent years."

I had written these notes while watching the end of the Henkel-Grant match from the press box. My second fifteen minutes did not come until Budge and Cramm went into court. By now I had learned that the thing sticking out of the board I used for a desk would not snap at me and I was waiting for Grant's defeat for two selfish reasons. First, it would make me look good because of what I had written in advance, and it would make the final match the decisive one and, therefore, more interesting both to speak about and to write about. Before it was over I would have been glad to take that back.

As I left the press box at the end of the Grant-Henkel match to go down under the stands and back up to my little booth, I heard as much German spoken around me as English. An interval of about half an hour was declared, and I was glad of it because I would have to summarize the first match at the beginning of the second and needed to get ahead a little. I wanted to repeat an expression a Frenchman near me had used over and over as Grant made his marvelous "gets." "*Comme il court!*" this man kept saying, and how he did run, but to no avail. In the end Grant wagged his head, tossed his racket into the air, and acknowledged defeat.

People were saying how nice it was that the final match had now become a real one and not a perfunctory affair. It deserved to have significance, for it was a match between the Wimbledon champion, now rated the world's number one, and the finest player of Europe, the handsome owner of the most elegant game of all, whose misfortune had been to be born about the same time as Fred Perry, even as Little Bill Johnston had been a contemporary of Tilden. Now they were meeting to decide which country should advance to the Challenge Round against Great Britain.

Since either was likely to defeat Britain, this one match would probably decide the fate of the Cup. A great occasion, and they both rose to it, producing a wonderful match for tennis history and for me something of an ordeal. The play was absorbing from the start, and it was a great surprise to me when a slip of paper came through the slit reading, "New York says continue for another 15 minutes." I did not realize that the time had gone. After another interval there came another message: "New York says continue."

By now Budge had lost the first set and they were well into the second. Both were playing tennis of such a high quality that we could hardly think it would continue. But it did and that is the principal reason people call this match the "greatest"—that the two finest amateurs in the world should play so superlatively well at the same time, during the same exchanges, over so prolonged a period.

Toward the end of the second set the crowd passed from enthusiasm to something near hysteria. Women would shriek now and then, men would yell, cheer, and groan. I do not know how I managed at all. I just kept on talking. I may have been a little hysterical myself. Although I made a deliberate effort to remain calm, I am sure I must have shouted into the little gadget at times. I saw that I had gone past the second fifteen-minute period and turned to look around at the technician or whatever they call the boss man, but he was behind the booth, reaching around to slip his little note in, and all I could see was his hand unless I opened the door to my left, which I dared not.

Just as Cramm won the second set another note came slipping under the glass. It said, "New York says continue to end. Programs canceled." I had thought that I would surely be through at the end of the set and be able to go outside and watch the rest of it in comfort. Now the thing had really got critical and the thought flashed through my mind that if Cramm won, I would not have to broadcast next week. They'd probably call off that one, calling off also the $500. It seemed almost worth it at the moment.

They took plenty of time after the second set, toweling themselves at the umpire's chair. I could just see across the Royal Box to the contestants' stand, and there sat Henkel in the front row, his very wide mouth wide open in an admiring grin when he caught Cramm's eye as the Baron came toward his end just beneath to receive service.

For two sets now Budge's wonderful backhand had been matched by the German's, and Cramm's forehand had been better at nearly every crisis where it had been put to the test. With these weapons Cramm brought off some of the most daring coups I have ever seen on a tennis court, and when the third set began, the Davis Cup campaign on which the little band of players had set out so hopefully early in the summer was in the gravest danger of failure one step before success. At every one of the recurring crises of the first two sets Cramm had been a little more incisive, a little steadier, and a little more certain in his choice of stroke to meet the particular situation. He had never, I think, played as well as this and probably never would again. The German seemed poised for an even greater effort in the third set, trying to avoid the longer journey, knowing his chances probably would decrease as the match advanced.

The capture of the third set was, of course, a must for Budge. Cramm could lose it and still win the match, and he played scarcely less well in losing it than he had in winning the first two. It was a very close thing. One service break for Budge decided it. Don did not dominate, and the way things went he might easily have lost it. But he served out in the tenth game and there was great relief when they left the court for the rest period, which is the custom in Davis Cup play but is never allowed in the Wimbledon Championships.

The interval was the worst time of all for me. I wanted very badly to have a cigarette by now, but I had to keep on talking while they were away. I think I said that Budge probably would win but I had no such confidence myself. I did not feel confident even when Budge won the fourth set with what I felt, but did not say, was deceptive ease. The German was reacting from the strenuous efforts earlier and, I thought, saving his strength for the vital fifth set, to which he appeared to be looking all through the fourth. Budge served well, hit deeply, and Cramm decided to let the set go after falling behind. This was the only period during the long match when the issue was not really joined and the play of either man dropped from the earlier standard.

The fifth began quietly with both serving well enough to win without strain. When Budge began service in the fourth game 2–all seemed altogether likely and one of those long service-governed sets seemed in prospect. There had been no indication of what was to follow. Budge lost the first point with a weak forehand that led to a missed volley and the second with an even weaker forehand that Cramm hit for a winner. Love–30! And then the break.

Germany was ahead 3–1 with Cramm's service to come. A love game followed and now it was 4–1. Budge's forehand had unaccountably reverted to the old method, and it had let him down. Now he must win Cramm's service twice and never lose his own again, else all hope of winning the Davis Cup this year would be gone. The situation was desperate, almost hopeless. But man's spirit is a worker of miracles. We reserve our greatest admiration for the man who, pushed into a corner from which there seems no escape, escapes death and achieves glory. Never was a tennis player in a tighter corner on so important an occasion as Budge at this stage, for Cramm was again playing magnificently.

It was at this moment as they changed courts that Budge is supposed to have reassured his worried captain, sitting at courtside, with words that have become part of tennis legend: "Don't worry, Cap. I'll make it." That's what we were told afterward he said to Pate, with a little pat on the shoulder. I suppose he did say it, or something like it. Both Pate and Budge were so honest I refrained from asking if it really was this way or thought up afterward, for fear of destroying a good story, and if this be one of those legends that grow after the event, Budge surely did give it credence. Don played a champion's game now. At this critical moment, when even one mistake might bring defeat, his aim was sure, his nerve steady, and he was at his wonderful best.

The faulty forehand became a champion's shot again. Budge won his service at love for 2–4 and, attacking with the same sort of boldness that had won the first two sets for Cramm, he captured the German's service also without the loss of a point. Two love games, eight straight points, against an opponent who had been outplaying him and who was still playing wonderfully well with victory in sight. I think we must count this one of the finest moments this game has known and I have never seen a champion in any sport do a better thing at so critical a moment.

When Budge served himself back even at 4–all, we felt that the tide, running overwhelmingly against him, had turned his way almost at the last possible moment. Cramm had not given up his advantage easily at all. The battle for Budge's service, coming after the two games in which the German had not won a point, was fierce and prolonged. Cramm had twice been within a point of winning it to lead 5–3, so that he would need only to hold service once for victory. At the first of these points the German hit a ball that seemed sure to be decisive. It was hit to the deep forehand, but here Budge pulled out the first of a series of forehand shots that were to take him safely out a little later after a series of exciting adventures. He scored with a ball hit with great speed straight down the enemy's backhand line.

Now at 4–all began the real battle for the match and the Cup. The battle had run for more than two hours, and I think they are correct who call it great during its final stages. I doubt that any two other players ever performed so brilliantly after being in court so long in such a tense and critical situation with so much at stake. Playing for one's country is not the same as playing for an individual title. It carries a much heavier burden of responsibility and we were not to know until afterward what this match really meant to Cramm, on whom the pressure to produce a Nazi triumph was enormous. We may imagine what it would have meant to the Third Reich at this moment of 1937 with its philosophy of the Master Race, to have the Davis Cup, the famous emblem of world superiority, on display in Berlin. We ought to keep this in mind when we remember this match and how Cramm played it.

There came now two long deuced games in which winners were hit off balls that themselves appeared to be certain winners. Almost nothing was given away on either side. Cramm served and led 5–4, the last point a service ace. Only one game to win and Germany would be in the Challenge Round. Budge pulled back to 5–all.

Cramm, serving as magnificently as at any time in the match, went to 6–5 with another love game, and was again within one game of victory. Once more Budge faced the crisis calmly. Neither did he lose a point in coming back to 6–all.

Even more calmly Budge brought off winners when Cramm, forcing still to the formerly shaky forehand, came to the net after preparing the way with that long, hard spinning shot dead into the corner of the court. Budge hit again straight down the line a ball at which Cramm lunged futilely as it passed him. The man with the world's finest backhand was now winning with shots as fine from the weaker forehand under extreme pressure. Cramm forced again to this sector and again was beaten, and Budge, sensing the moment, hit everything with all the force he had left. The German was serving as well as ever, it seemed, but Budge now brought his own game to its highest peak and Cramm could win only one point in this thirteenth game. For the first time since play began hours earlier, Budge was ahead 7–6 in the fifth set. Now the time had come. The occasion had arrived for Budge, his team, and his country.

But the great effort to take Cramm's service, and finally to take the lead, had cost Budge. Fatigue also had arrived, slipping in unnoticed as tension continued over so long a period. Both men moved quite slowly to their places for the fourteenth game after pausing overly long at the chair. Budge took up the balls to serve, seemed about to do so, and then relaxed before striking the first ball.

There were to be no service aces this time. Instead we had a long, anxious, and excruciatingly tense game of tennis. The score went six times to deuce, and three times Budge was within a single point of victory. Each time Cramm played perfectly. The German would not yield. It seemed Budge could not get that final point, and twice Cramm himself was within a point of winning the game, one point away from 7–all and a chance to fight on. A little unlucky too, it seemed, not to win one of those points.

And then, finally, after the sixth deuce point Budge won the advantage and stood for the fourth time one point away from victory. Three times Cramm had saved match point and seemed certain to save a fourth when Budge served weakly this time, giving the German a chance to step in and pound the ball to the forehand corner once more. Since Don could not come across court off such a ball, Cramm dashed in and crowded the other side. And Budge hit now the finest shot of the match, a truly gorgeous forehand as straight as could be down the line, swift, low, and certain. I can see the picture yet. The bending of the knees for the crouch—with Budge it was an ungainly squat—the lifting of the low spinning ball with all the weight going into the swing as the knees straightened and locked. Cramm lunged to his left, hiding the ball from me as it flew on its way to pitch just beyond the service court, where a little puff of white marked the spot as it fell. Cramm had fallen to the court in his futile effort to intercept. He rose quickly and, without looking back, came around the net to congratulate Budge. No need to look back. He knew and we all knew the moment the ball was struck that it was a winner and the wonderful match was over.

It is difficult to say here which of these men played the better, for they were about as level as two players can be in the scoring and in resolution and fortitude. Cramm showed that great flat forehand down the line and across court at its best. It was superior to Budge's version both in pace and execution. The backhands were about equal, and both could attack from this wing as few have been able to do. On the volley there was little, nothing really, to choose, for they both brought off many difficult shots brilliantly under pressure. Budge had a slight edge in service, although he did not serve actually at his very best. We took Budge's victory to be expected beforehand, and we could have only admiration in addition to surprise at Cramm's resistance. When shall we see another such wonderful tennis fight? I think we have not seen one since, and I think those who cannot resist the temptation to rank players in lists should keep in mind that Riggs, a champion at home and abroad and placed among the elect by many authorities, could win only one game from a Cramm, playing certainly not nearly as well as on this splendid occasion.

The Challenge Round of 1937, played a week after, was an anticlimax. Parker, replacing Grant, defeated Charles Hare 6–2, 6–4, 6–2, but lost to Austin 6–8, 6–3, 4–6, 3–6. Budge beat both with the loss of one set to Austin and with the victory of Budge and Mako in the doubles over C. R. D. Tuckey and Frank Wilde 6–3, 7–5, 7–9, 12–10, the United States won the series 4–1 and brought the Cup home ten years after the French had taken it across the ocean in 1927.

I was more or less an old hand at broadcasting by that time and had trouble only with the first set of the Budge-Hare match, which

Budge won 15–13. I kept trying to remember the score of the Mc-Loughlin-Brookes match of 1914 so I could mention it if this were longer. I couldn't recall, but there was little resemblance anyhow. The left-handed Hare, reaching the greatest moment of his career, served very well to keep the set alive, but Budge just waited calmly and ran out the match with the loss of only three more games, 15–13, 6–1, 6–2.

CHAPTER TWENTY

F INALLY, there is one match between professionals that I'd include in my list of the memorable. Such key matches among the pros are hard to find because for so many years they have preferred exhibitions to real tournaments. This match, with Jack Kramer playing Don Budge, was in the semifinal round of a tournament in 1948, the only professional tournament that I remember at all well. It was at Forest Hills, where the West Side Tennis Club ran the tournament with a draw of thirty-two of the world's best players. Both of these conditions, proper management, and a large field contributed to the artistic and financial success of the event.

There were a number of good and exciting matches during the week—Kramer vs. Welby Van Horn; Budge vs. Dinny Pails, the Australian; Bobby Riggs vs. Frank Kovacs; Kramer vs. Riggs—but Kramer's victory over Budge by 6–4, 8–10, 3–6, 6–4, 6–0 is the match which, I feel, tells us most.

At this time Kramer was the world's finest player by common consent. All were agreed on that and some rated him the "all-time greatest." One poll of sports editors across the country a year later named Kramer the finest tennis player of the first half-century. Whatever one may think of such a rating, Kramer was the acknowledged number one in the world at that time.

Budge, by the late 1940s, was at least five or six years past his best days. I think myself that he had not been anywhere near that best since suffering some sort of shoulder trouble at the beginning of his war service. His forehand, which he had corrected so well after it had given him much trouble early in his career because of faulty footwork, or basic incorrect body positioning, was by now once more an insecure stroke, improperly made, and unreliable under pressure.

Budge also had lost some the priceless assets of youth, and the formerly keen eyesight that had permitted him to see a little quicker than others was so weakened that he had to wear glasses on the court, further reducing the exactness of his timing. He could no longer overcome the forehand defect by an extraordinary physical effort, for he could do this only so long as he retained the perfect co-ordination of youth.

These things did not prevent Budge from disposing of lesser play-ers, since the other parts of his game—service, volley, and that extra-ordinary backhand—still were the strokes of a champion. But he was no longer the superb player of the 1930s, and waiting for him when he reached the semifinal was Kramer, the current all-time greatest.

This meeting was for me one of the most interesting of tennis encounters. It involved one I knew in my own judgment to have been one of the greatest of players, with another about whom I had not been able to decide. I looked to this match to help me decide, but I don't feel completely able to do so because, other than in the final the next day when he defeated Riggs, I never again saw Kramer play anything but exhibition matches. He told me once that he felt he never had played better than in the Budge match, but I am not sure I ought to trust his judgment any more than my own.

For these reasons I watched the play closely, but since I did not write down my impressions at the time, I am indebted to Levan Richards, that practically perfect tennis umpire, who sat in the chair, for corroborative detail and opinion. We are agreed, Lev and I, that, up to a point it was the finest match between professionals we ever saw. We also are of the opinion that Budge probably would have beaten Kramer if Don had not been attacked by severe leg cramps when leading by two sets to one, 4–3 in the fourth and about to serve for a 5–3 lead.

When, having won Kramer's service in the seventh game, Budge prepared to deliver his own powerful service, I had no doubt that he would win the two service games necessary to give him the set 6–4 and the match. In spite of missing a lot, Don was definitely on top. He had been dominating the play in this seemingly decisive fourth set. As Allison Danzig, that most competent of critics, wrote in his report of the match for the New York *Times:* "The California red-head laid about him with such destruction from his mighty back-hand, his service, and volley as to keep the gathering roaring in delir-ious joy." This was no great exaggeration. People were delighted with the old champion.

Kramer had played really well too, but there had been, it seemed to me, an inflexible pattern to his moves. He served and hit most of his forehand shots to Budge's backhand. It seemed that his game, a very forceful attacking game, was based largely, if not altogether, on service and ground shots directed always, or as often as could be, to the enemy backhand. Kramer owned one of the finest forehands I have ever seen. It was a stroke comparable in quality to Budge's backhand. Jack also was one of the finest servers, and the volley, for which the other strokes were the preparation, seemed bound to be effective against most players because the preparation was so good.

In this match it puzzled me that Kramer hit so many of his forcing shots to Budge's backhand. Every chance he had to hit off the ground the ball went to Don's stronger side. Kramer followed every serve to the net and went up behind every booming forehand. The pattern always was the same. He seemed incapable of improvisation and departed from his plan only when forced to.

It is a pattern that net rushers have employed more or less through the years and when Kramer perfected it after World War II, it began to be called "power tennis." You make certain of holding your own service by following every one to the net, and you direct all preparatory shots to the other man's backhand because the "percentage" is greater there. Hit everything hard, never willingly hit a forehand across court or a backhand down the line. Employing this power-percentage system to hold your own service, you wait until there comes a poorly served game by the other fellow, when you make an all-out attack to win it. Then, having got it, you merely serve yourself out. It is a rather unimaginative, conventional style of play based on the theory that Kramer would always be the attacker, never the defender. There was little or no surprise in it.

Kramer thought that too many means spoiled the end. "It is better to have one good shot and use it repeatedly," he advised young players, "than to have two or three or half a dozen." And he told them that "the less you think, the better off you are."

It seemed to me that Kramer was hipped on this power game-percentage theory and possibly deceived by the fact that he became a wealthy man by playing it and promoting tennis exhibitions with amateur champions turned professional. I remember a night when Ken Rosewall, the clever and beautiful little Australian stroke maker, performed in his professional debut against Richard Gonzales for Kramer at Madison Square Garden. Jack came to sit beside me in the mezzanine press box. I spoke with some enthusiasm of the fact that now he had at last the perfect act for his tour that the people would love. The big, rather surly man with the bludgeon whom one could dislike mildly, against the tiny artist with the rapier. Big Pancho storming the net and little Ken trying to foil him from back court.

Kramer looked at me as if I had confessed to an insurmountable love of heroin. Pityingly for my lack of judgment. "They pay to see the big game," he said, putting the term in quotation marks as usual. It was at this point that I began to wonder if the pros ever would make a go of competitive tennis.

Jack was playing this big game of his against Budge that day, and there were some wonderfully satisfying exchanges. It was not all big-game tennis. The first two sets really were excitingly and well played, and by the end of the second Budge, largely I thought, because Kramer neglected to exploit the forehand weakness, had revealed something about Kramer's own backhand that had been suspected but not previously seen. This was not the stroke of a great player, as was the forehand. Against all other opponents Kramer had been able to conceal this shortcoming because of his highly developed attacking ability. These others always were too busy defending to test Jack's own defenses thoroughly.

Now, pinned down repeatedly in that backhand corner because of the way he was playing Budge, this was revealed as a weakness. He played Budge as he played everyone else apparently, depending on service, volley and smash to carry the day, putting the ball whenever possible in the backhand corner. Even against a Budge no longer at his best, this was fatal, or nearly so.

The Kramer backhand was heavily cut and had no real pace even when he brought it off. The grip used prevented the effective handling of spinning balls that came low off the turf, and as the match progressed, Budge could count on winning the point any time he had a chance to direct his own backhand to that sector. Since Kramer hit so many of his fine forehands to Budge's backhand, there were many chances.

And so, with only a part of his long artillery in proper working order, with poor eyesight but with some of the strokes and all of the personal elements of greatness still there, Budge came, years after his championship days were done, within sight of victory against the acknowledged current number one player of the world. He was never to make it. Before he reached the serving position in that eighth game of the fourth set, having won Kramer's service for the vital match-winning break, the first cramp hit him. He never recovered from it, and soon after the other leg was hit also.

Budge never won another game. He was suddenly helpless as Kramer ran nine straight games for the match. In the final 6–0 set Budge won only one point when Kramer netted a backhand. I remember that they played a recording of the National Anthem before the players left the court, why just at that stage I don't know, but Budge standing at attention with the others, swayed as if he would fall, and probably would have if someone, Kramer, I think, had not put out a hand to steady him.

The willingness of the public and the less thinking part of the tennis world to accept the current top player as the best ever has led to a continuing series of "greatest" players. There seems to have grown up a belief, or a supposition, that the game has been steadily developing through the decades as champion succeeded champion. Given this belief it follows that the current great player is necessarily the all-time greatest. However unrealistic it may be, there always have been those who accept the view that once you name a player great at any period, he must be greater than all who preceded him, and to have carried the game to new heights.

There is some doubt, however, that the game of tennis is fundamentally different today from what it was in the old horse-and-buggy days. So far as I can see, there is nothing in the tennis of the 1960s that would have startled the world in the year the *Titanic* met the iceberg, with Dick Williams aboard, and there is evidence that you could go back a decade or so earlier and make the statement.

Certain champions have influenced the game by their strokes and their personalities. A study of the men who have placed their names on the championship rolls of this country and Great Britain in the first half of the twentieth century, however, seems to indicate that the changes that have come, aside from the steady improvement in materials and implements of the game, and the consequent speeding up, have been a matter of individuals rather than of methods. The champions seem to have been individuals who chose in every case the methods best suited to themselves.

Sometimes these seemed to have been a step forward to something new, but closely examined they turn out to be a reversion to and refinement of methods used by a predecessor who passed from the scene earlier. Vines used the controlled speed of Tilden, which had been the game of the Doherty brothers at the turn of the century, although both the later champions hit much harder. Budge did the same thing even better than Vines, and Riggs was a direct throwback all the way to the Dohertys, although a lesser champion. Cochet, with his insolent half-volleys, wore the mantle of Williams, but we may read in contemporary accounts that Oliver Campbell, the United States champion of 1890, was "taking the ball on the rise as he advanced to the net," even as they. And Perry did it perhaps even better in 1935.

McLoughlin, the redheaded young Californian of enormous appeal, helped greatly to make the game popular with his dashing play, and his sudden appearance had the effect of something new injected into international tennis. But men had used this exact style before, and there were men present when the Comet came storming out of the West who knew what to do about it. His game could not prevail for long, because the means of thwarting it, learned through experience, already were there.

Norman Brookes and Anthony Wilding were the ruling champions at Wimbledon when McLoughlin arrived. They saw immediately that the young American's ground strokes were not first class and that if the big service could be returned into play and the server with inferior equipment forced to conduct extended exchanges, their own superior, if less forceful, strokes would prevail. They had seen it done before. Therefore, they concentrated on taking the service early, blocking it back in a way that it could not be easily volleyed or smashed for an outright point, and then themselves sought the volleying position after having prepared the way properly.

Are we not told that the Dohertys used these methods against the net rushers of an early generation, and have we not seen Cochet and Lacoste stand up to Tilden's cannonball in the same way more than a decade later? Remember how Crawford stood to Vines in the 1930s? Both Brookes and Wilding defeated the "big game" of McLoughlin in the Challenge Round of 1909—Brookes in three sets, Wilding in four—and Brookes repeated his victory in the series of 1911, when Brookes was thirty-five. Wilding did not play in that one.

McLoughlin won the U.S. title in 1912 and 1913, but it is significant that he could never win the bigger title at Wimbledon even when at his best in 1913. He was beaten in the final by Wilding. He never did beat either Wilding or Brookes until the 1914 Challenge Round at Forest Hills, when Brookes was nearly thirty-eight. Of that 1913 final at Wimbledon a contemporary account said of Wilding that "his return of service was faultless. . . . he found the weakness on McLoughlin's backhand and never left it . . . he was superb in every department. Though threatened and pressed he never gave ground." By the mid-1920s the pace of the game had become ever faster, but the forty-eight-year-old Brookes was still able, at the 1924 Wimbledon, to break up the game of Frank Hunter, which depended on speed of stroke for its effectiveness.

Jack Kramer, as noted, is given credit by those with short memories or insufficient background with inventing what he and they began to call the "big game" and passing it on to a group of players who, like Kramer, were former amateur champions. Then, when aging legs and bulging bank account induced him to retire, Kramer, as promoter, sent the troupe barnstorming about the world to spread the gospel of "power tennis." I do not know if Kramer, a shrewd and highly personable businessman who could wheedle reams of publicity from uninformed newspaper columnists, really subscribed to this fiction. He used the term freely and, so far as I know, never questioned or denied that it was he who introduced the "big game."

He certainly did not appear to know that this very term was being used in the 1920s to describe a very different game, the all court game that Tilden and Johnston played about the time Kramer was born. It seems unlikely that he ever realized that his own game was identical with the game McLoughlin played a decade before Tilden was champion, and even then was by no means new.

As in all games, tennis champions rise, rule for a while, and are overthrown. Their mastery of this or that manifestation of style or skill forces upon their contemporaries the adoption of methods calculated to thwart them. Until belief in the "big game," as the only true method took hold in post-World War II tennis, it happened that the new champion now and then was an exponent of a type of game different from the champion he succeeded. This is what gave rise to the belief that the game moved forward until it reached its ultimate development in the "big game."

But I am wondering as I write if any new strokes have come into the game since Holcombe Ward, the champion of 1904, and Dwight Davis worked out the "twist" service as undergraduates at Harvard in the Mauve Decade and introduced it sensationally into the second Davis Cup series in 1902. Every first-class player since has used this service, although it is not considered essential to the "big game." Some players—Rodney Laver, the Australian left-hander, for instance—probably make it better than Ward or Davis ever could, but it is the same stroke. Tilden reintroduced the drop shot to Wimbledon and was booed for using it, but the stroke was known when Tilden was a babe.

F. R. Burrow, whose career as player and tennis official covered the sixty years from 1877 to 1937, wrote his reminiscences after retiring in the latter year following eighteen years as referee of the All-England Championships at Wimbledon. In his book, *The Centre Court and Others* (Eyre and Spottiswoode, 1937), Burrow speaks of the Renshaw twins, Willie and Ernest, Wimbledon champions as early as 1880 and as late as 1890, as follows: "They made the volley their chief attacking weapon." And he added of their smashing: "Sheer hard, almost vertical smacks that sent the ball straight into the stands from its first bound were the order of the day with the Renshaws."

Surveying the whole tennis scene from 1937 back almost to the start, Burrow wrote of the Renshaws that "few, if any of their successors have won more points by the smash than they did."

In the book of another famous set of tennis twins, written just after the turn of the century, *H. L. and R. F. Doherty on Tennis* (Lawn Tennis and Badminton, London), we find in their descriptions of various ways of playing the game the following as the second method: "To run in on your service and to volley everything. Campbell started this game in America and Americans in general adopt it."

The reference is to the aforementioned Oliver Campbell, U.S. champion of 1890 through 1892, of whom it also is recorded that "he would take the ball on the rise as he dashed into forecourt."

Of their American contemporaries, the Dohertys had the following to say:

Malcolm Whitman (U.S. champion 1898 through 1900): "He gets up to the net on every possible occasion and when at the net is very hard to pass."

William A. Larned (seven times U.S. champion 1901–1911): "He is quick at reaching the net. Among his strongest points are his forehand volley and his service, which is a capital one of the ordinary straight kind and which he, as a rule, follows to the net."

Beals Wright (champion 1905): "He has a good service which he follows to the net. . . . He is the best in America at the low volley and is very good overhead."

William Clothier (champion of 1906): "Service much the same as Whitman's and he *always* follows it up to the net. . . . Volleys well and is especially severe overhead."

Dwight Davis: "He kills a lob harder than anyone else who ever played the game. His volley is altogether very severe."

The Dohertys' book was written twenty years before Jack Kramer was born, and they included the following statement, which has an especially familiar sound in the 1960s:

"The Americans themselves say that the excessive running in on the service rather spoils the game and that the server has too great an advantage."

He had no great advantage over Hugh Doherty, though. Doherty came to this country in 1903 and won our title without much difficulty, with all those net rushers in the field. He defeated Clothier in the final and won five straight Wimbledon titles from 1902 through 1906 against the same quality of opposition. Neither did the net rushers enjoy any great advantage over Tilden, and the thing to remember here is that Tilden played the all court game of the Dohertys and that this game, given sufficient talent in him who plays it, will always overcome the specialist, serve he ever so many aces.

And yet, I was sitting on the porch at the Longwood Cricket Club one evening during the National Doubles Championship of 1949, talking tennis with a former champion and current Davis Cup player. Following a small silence after I had been speaking of other days, he turned to me belligerently and exclaimed, "Oh, Tilden, my foot! You're always talking Tilden, Tilden. I've seen him play, and

I'm telling you the way we serve and volley and smash today he wouldn't have a Chinaman's chance."

So! My young companion was twenty-seven years old, and Tilden, then exactly thirty years older at fifty-seven, had been world champion two years before my champion was born. It was in this same year that the national poll proclaimed Kramer the greatest tennis player of the first half-century, with hardly any other player making a real showing in the vote. If the poll had been taken ten years later, there is little doubt that Richard Gonzales would have got the top spot and Kramer might have got only a few scattered votes.

Let us try to keep the perspective, as the drawing teacher used to say. It is perfectly possible and permissible to argue that Kramer played the "big game" better than anyone before or since, but to say that he invented it is absurd. Without doubt he played it better than anyone of his period, for he defeated Gonzales regularly in the year or so following the Budge match described earlier. But Gonzales, to whom Kramer bequeathed the "big game," so to speak, then succeeded to the all-time-greatest title after Kramer retired. Pancho played the big game too, but he added nothing to what had been used by some outstanding player at every age apparently, back to the early days of the game.

He played it, that is, until time inevitably began to take its toll of the extraordinary powers of possibly the finest physical specimen ever to play this game. It was only then that we saw how truly fine a tennis player Gonzales was, and we could in his declining years make a striking comparison with that other remarkable performer, Tilden. They were about as different in their persons as two men could well be, and their tennis careers are seemingly so widely different as to make comparisons impossible. But the parallels are there, and they can tell us something about where Gonzales may belong on those fascinating lists that other people make.

We may start with the presumption that Gonzales does belong among the greats of the game. But where? Finding a proper place for him is made much more difficult by the fact that his tennis life has been so different, so unlike any other of his fellow greats. He had barely three full seasons on the amateur circuit, he played in only one Davis Cup series—the Challenge Round of 1949—and he did not win a major title other than his own National Championship.

Pancho never won at Wimbledon, in France, or in Australia. No other player among the admittedly great has so few items after his name in the record book. In assessing other great ones we can recall things they did and pull down the book to bolster our contentions. And the record does speak rather eloquently at times. A great writer or painter may be known by his works to those who come after. An athlete leaves only statistics and memories.

With Gonzales, how many matches may we call to our aid? Only one, really, the final of the 1949 Championship at Forest Hills. In that one Pancho, after forty-two games, was two-sets-to-love down to Ted Schroeder, the 1942 champion, and then won the title in twenty-five more games 16–18, 2–6, 6–1, 6–2, 6–4. This match is well remembered because it was a wonderful tennis occasion. But it is the only one for Gonzales, and the history of tennis is made up of such occasions.

Gonzales turned professional soon after that, toured with Kramer, was beaten in a majority of their city-to-city matches, and then was forced to sit on the sidelines while Kramer, as promoter, milked the touring exhibition business. But those long months of barnstorming, followed by long hours of practice while waiting to be called, developed Pancho's game to its full potential. Whenever he was given a chance in the one tournament the pros called their Championship, in Cleveland, he beat them all.

Finally, when Kramer retired to promotion alone, they needed Pancho to give the tour business a shot in the arm. So they allowed him back in, and thereafter he ate up all the pros and amateur champions who were served up to him—Tony Trabert, Frank Sedgman, Francisco Segura, Mal Anderson, Ashley Cooper, Ken Rosewall, Lewis Hoad, and even after decline had set in, the one some say is the best of all, Rodney Laver.

After that day of the Forest Hills final, Gonzales played hundreds, perhaps thousands, of matches against the little group of pros, fine players all, but he never did play in a real tournament, properly speaking. However decisive his victories over them, none came on a really big tennis occasion in the sense of that final amateur appearance. On all but a few occasions they were little more than exhibitions, and that is Pancho's misfortune and our difficulty.

In a proper tournament the champion must play a different man in each of five, six, or seven rounds. He must discipline his mind as well as his body. He must school himself for a series of tests against possibly a variety of styles of play and be prepared for a greater effort each day as the field narrows. When you are beaten in a championship tournament you can go home, for you are through until next year. There is no chance to recoup tomorrow night in New Haven, Peoria, or Canal Dover, Ohio. No chance to play another day and pile up points in a round robin.

Of all the professionals of the postwar era only Gonzales himself seemed to be aware of this situation. When the favorable vote for an open appeared so near in 1960, he alone expressed doubts about entering it. How did he know, he said, that he could win round after round for two weeks. How did he know he wouldn't be beaten early and thus lose some of his money-making ability as a pro. Only Pancho saw the big difference between losing a two-set exhibition one night with another chance against a long-familiar opponent the next, and playing a five-set match against a new and unfamiliar opponent every day through a final round. Pancho knew that his long absence from tournament play had not prepared him for such a test.

Gonzales played stuff the like of which some of us never had seen before, but the records of his feats are not there. And, since the winning or losing did not really "mean" anything to us, his victories do not remain either vivid or significant. But figures, after all, can be untrustworthy, and figures that upset our fondest beliefs are the most untrustworthy of all. Gonzales, like Vines, has no actual achievement that demands that he be placed above all others, but we all know that he does belong high on the list, for we have seen him play. The trouble is that we have not seen him come through enough critical matches in which our emotions were terribly involved.

It was unfortunate for him that only when he was passing from the picture did the professionals get around to playing a few tournaments that might mean something. Their biggest success came in 1965 at Madison Square Garden in New York, when Kramer, having at last understood the necessity for real competition instead of mere exhibitions, got the whole troupe into this national showcase. And it was the thirty-eight-year-old Gonzales who stole the show away from them. They beat him before the final but not one of them was anywhere near his stature and the crowds knew it.

And this brings us finally to the comparison with Tilden, on whom more people agree as the all-time great than any other. The difficulty in making the comparison is in the fact that Tilden exposed himself through a full decade and more in tournaments around the world and in Davis Cup matches every year, and then played with the pros for another ten. The comparison is striking enough, though.

Tilden undoubtedly was the most complete player of all. He had command of every stroke and with some of them he was better even than the specialist in that particular stroke. Since he could nearly always control the game from the back of the court because of his marvelous repertoire of shots, seldom advancing to the net, there grew up a belief that he could not volley. But Tilden won five national doubles titles with three different partners, one of them a schoolboy of fifteen, Richards, and in one year, 1927, was both Wimbledon and U.S. doubles champion. Those who cannot volley do not win big doubles titles. There was no stroke that Tilden did not have in his storehouse, and he was able to call on any one of them in time of need. Actually, he had such a variety of strokes at his command he was able to face with confidence every kind of attack that might be brought against him.

Well, Gonzales had them too in greater variety than any other player since Tilden. Many of Pancho's admirers were not aware of this because he accepted the "big game" and, until advancing years put something of a strain on his physical powers, needed no other to defeat all his rivals. In the Garden tournament many tennis fans were surprised to see Gonzales playing from the back of the court, controlling the play, substituting guile for power, making every shot called for. He was beaten by physical limitations, not because his weapons had dulled.

On the unusually slow surface he could no longer control things with service, volley, and smash. He served neither to kill nor to wound as in the past, but to prevent attacking reply, knowing that in deep court exchanges he might have an advantage over all, even the two top men, Laver and Rosewall. They could outmaneuver him only because age had brought reduced mobility. He no longer sought, as in the past and as was still the custom among the "big game" advocates, to strike the decisive blow immediately. Pancho, like Tilden, could wait a more favorable moment. He now had more enterprise and elasticity and was a more rewarding player.

Seeing him play thus, one could easily imagine that Gonzales could have won just as well in this way in earlier years. Tilden called forth what strokes he needed with conscious effort to upset an opponent. Gonzales, when the "big game" could no longer serve him, seemed able to make whatever shot he desired without giving a thought to it, almost casually. As Pancho declined physically we saw shots from him we had not seen before and those who thought he was not the complete player, in the Tilden sense, seem to have been mistaken because of lack of opportunity to observe.

The forty-year-old Gonzales showed us what at thirty he had kept concealed because there had been no need of it. But, having seen, it was easy to believe he could, if he chose, make any stroke any player before him used. And wherever he appeared he always stole the show from men who could now challenge or beat him. Therein lies the other parallel. This is exactly what the forty-year-old Tilden did in the 1930s. Vines and Budge and Perry and the other professionals could beat him, but they could never hope to be his equal. They had to take him along on their tours when repetition had taken the bloom from their show, for it was Big Bill still who drew the crowds. And, thirty years later, if the tourists did not have Gonzales, their show was a mild one. It was Big Pancho, no longer top man, who brought excitement and, incidentally, brought the crowds.

Gonzales became a fascinating player when his power-tennis days were done because, like the declining Tilden, he developed stratagems. To see him deny an opponent the favorite shots and angles sought was a revelation. A surly, uncompromising man who looked as if he would as soon knock your head off with a racket as hit the ball past you, he pulled in the people just as the waning but still arrogant Tilden did thirty years earlier.

Gonzales has shown more people throughout the world what tennis on the highest level can be than any player who preceded him. If we cannot actually place him on top of the all-time heap, we may acknowledge him as the finest natural tennis player of all, for that is what he was. No one may truthfully say that he taught Pancho. Perhaps he may not even say he taught himself. Let us hope that the champions who saw him beaten in his declining years will not make the mistake my champion made about Tilden that day at Longwood in 1949 and try to downgrade this truly wonderful performer.

CHAPTER TWENTY-ONE

As this book draws toward its close, the thought occurs to me that younger readers especially may have a complaint because of what they see as an imbalance. The past seems heavily favored over the present. It is true that I have seen, covered, and written about as much tennis in recent years as in more distant days, and that increased knowledge of the present might increase understanding of the past just as much as the other way round. But this is, after all, a book of memories and in such a work an author's right of control over his material may hardly be denied. The things spoken about here are not prehistoric, but it's true that I haven't written as fully about very recent years as I have about the era just before. There may be a sound reason for this apparent imbalance, and here is my explanation.

With few exceptions all the greatest players of the last decade and more have joined the professional parade started by Suzanne Lenglen, Vincent Richards, and Mary Browne in 1926. In the forty years following, the list of champions and near champions who deserted the amateur ranks for the pro gold is impressive indeed—Tilden, Cochet, Vines, George Lott, Lester Stoefen, Fred Perry, Don Budge, Bobby Riggs, Frank Kovacs, Frank Parker, Yvon Petra, Jack Kramer, Richard Gonzales, Tony Trabert, Frank Sedgman, Ken McGregor, Rex Hartwig, Alex Olmedo, Mal Anderson, Ashley Cooper, Ken Rosewall, Lewis Hoad, Andres Gimeno, Rodney Laver, Fred Stolle, Dennis Ralston. Add to this list the names of fine players who never competed as amateurs, such as Karel Kozeluh, Hans Nusslein, Martin Plaa, Robert Ramillon, Albert Burke.

All these men, some among the greatest the game has known, took part in thousands of matches on hundreds of professional tours from 1930 on. Except for the war years there never has been a time when the tours of the pros did not flourish. But if you search the records of these matches, or search your memory of them, since pro records are spotty, you will have the greatest difficulty finding another one to place alongside the Budge-Kramer match and the wonderful amateur matches we have been considering here.

Such matches are so hard to find as to be almost nonexistent, and the one we did find, let us remember, was from the one proper tournament the pros have played, to my knowledge, in all these years. And this fact points to another fundamental weakness of professional tennis, their unwillingness or inability to manage and play real tournaments.

I think I have seen about as many of these professional encounters as anyone not directly connected with them, and I have covered and written about dozens. But it is next to impossible to remember anything significant about them, and, with one or two notable exceptions, I cannot find enough detail to describe one of them, as the amateur tournaments and team matches have been recalled. There may be other reasons for this, but I submit that the principal reason is that not one of these matches had any real meaning in the sense of the big Davis Cup and amateur Championship meetings. They were good as tennis shows, some of them outstanding in this way, and the occasion is remembered for that reason, but they did not "mean" anything.

The professional tennis occasions we remember best, all seem to have occurred in Madison Square Garden in New York. They are remembered easily enough as "occasions," but do we really remember them as tennis contests? Did Kramer beat Riggs on the night of the big blizzard, when an incredible 16,000-plus managed to make it to the Garden through the storm that stopped surface traffic? I'm not sure he did. Or did he? Did Tilden spoil Vines's debut in 1934 by beating Elly? No, certainly not. Big Bill already was forty-one years old that night. But Tilden did win, and in straight sets. One of his rewards was a big hug and kiss from Tallulah Bankhead, the Alabama blushing violet, who surprisingly was present, although she must surely have known there would be photographers. Was Perry playing Budge the night the Englishman tripped on the canvas and injured his back so severely it just about finished his top competitive days? Or was it Riggs? Were Hoad and Rosewall eaten alive by the ferocious Pancho Gonzales, or did the kids stand up to the great man?

Rosewall and Laver have been the finest players, amateur or pro,

257

of the decade of the 1960s. They became the successors, each in his turn, to Gonzales. Hoad, who might also be rated here, nearly always ailed from muscular strain, and he banked his earnings early and called it a career, except for odd appearances. I have no quarrel with those who would rate these Australian stars among the great. I cannot, however, remember Laver's professional debut at all, and I recall Rosewall's only because of the little clash, previously mentioned, with Kramer in the Garden press box. But I can never forget the first glimpse of Rosewall as a boy of sixteen or seventeen on his first visit to the United States as the baby of the Australian team. And there were other amateur occasions which Rosewall made memorable, especially a quarterfinal round match at Forest Hills with Richard Savitt in 1956, the year Ken became our champion with a rather easy victory over Hoad in the final.

These were memories to cherish and the first was one of the nicest tennis experiences of all, the "discovery" of Rosewall, because it was shared with René Lacoste, the old Musketeer. It was at the Orange Lawn Tennis Club, in New Jersey, on a day during the Eastern Grass Court Championships in the early 1950s. Lacoste, a wealthy businessman with international connections, had come to this country partly in their pursuit, but also to enroll his son in Princeton. Having seen François settled and having a free afternoon, he drove over to renew acquaintances and to see some tennis.

There were precious few acquaintances to renew, it turned out. Only one or two of the crowd of perhaps three thousand that wandered about the place showed any sign of recognition, and players, brought up one by one to be presented, did not even appear familiar with the name. Even tournament officials didn't seem to make a real connection with Lacoste.

It was a stifling day. The heat rose from the grass in waves that could be seen enveloping players and even watchers in the shaded boxes on the high ground behind the two show courts. A thunderstorm lurked among the nearby hills and would bring relief later, but now it was all but unbearable.

I found Lacoste seated in a corner box reserved for important guests, under hanging branches where a faint breeze stirred. He had a woolen scarf about his throat, its ends tucked into a woolen jacket, and I remembered that weak lungs had forced his retirement before his unusual tennis powers had begun to wane. The Melancholy Gaul, we had called him in the old days, and the reason for it still was apparent. A rather sad, modest, almost humble man, extremely cultured, a combination rare enough among human beings, not to mention famous athletes.

As we sat through the long hot afternoon, Lacoste followed the play with much interest, but he also looked past it to other days, the days of his greatness, remembering, seeing it all again. There was much to speak about and many matches to recall. Tilden's name kept coming back into the conversation ever and again. Finally, with my back to the court, I saw Lacoste's face light up as though a switch had been turned on. He was looking over my shoulder at the court, where two players had come to warm up for a match. I turned around and there was Rosewall hitting balls back and forth with Dick Savitt. René sat up straight and I moved my chair out of his line of vision.

I had supposed it was the chance to see Savitt that interested him. Dick, who had been Wimbledon champion, was a big, dark, and handsome man whose game was based on solid driving from the deep court, and a wickedly severe service. He was not a beautiful player at all, sometimes seeming positively awkward, but all his shots had a heaviness and pace that made them difficult to handle.

When I spoke of Savitt, however, referring to him as probably the best amateur in the world at the moment, Lacoste said, "No, it is the little one. A beautiful player. And so young!"

By then they were well into the match, which Savitt won in spite of being often put in trouble by the spinning deep-court drives of this new little stroke maker. Each time Rosewall pulled one of his spinning backhands into a corner to beat his heavier-footed opponent, Lacoste would smile his shy, rather plaintive smile. Near the end of the match, with Savitt now obviously the winner, René said, "I think he could perhaps beat the other one even now, if he only knew how good he is. Never mind. He will find out. He is like Henri, is he not?"

More, I said, like the young René, and Lacoste, smiling brightly, replied, "Maybe better than both."

No, not quite that, but little Ken was to become one of the most delightful players of a long span of observing. In the bang-bang-power-game era he was an artist, and it continues to be a joy to see him operate. An altogether appealing little figure as he grew in tennis stature year by year, a perfect foil for and a striking contrast in every way to Hoad, who was an outstanding and exciting exponent of power tennis. Hoad, a picture of young Vulcan, the village blacksmith, could blind you and awe you with his power, and there were days as a pro when even the great Pancho had to take a back seat. He was not, however, a creature of mere brawn. Hoad had a nimble craftsmanship, certainly, but artist in the Rosewall sense he was not.

Laver plays the "big game" too, but more subtly and with a better use of the court's angles. Rod knew how to use spin better than most players of the 1960s, and he is one of the few players I have seen who could make a twist service break either right or left. It seems incredible, but Neale Fraser, fellow Australian, could do that too and, come to think of it, he also was a left-hander.

After so many years of attending tennis tournaments you begin to look ever for the artist in each young player seen for the first time, and it always is exciting when, as here with Rosewall at Orange, you find him. He was so appealing a figure that, if he had remained an amateur and played the tournaments, I am sure I would have developed for him something of the same feeling I had for Little Bill Johnston in my own youth. Moreover, I think we all would. As it is I can call up a most joyous feeling in contemplating Rosewall. The mere thought of the little guy with the delightfully half-embarrassed air he had of apologizing for being so very good, gives the sort of pure pleasure one got from a Perry, a Cochet, or a Williams. And with those exquisite strokes no "big-game" player ever did succeed in keeping Ken quiet for long. To beat him, even Gonzales had to work from the very first, harder than he liked, and keep strictly to business all the time.

But now, what matches of Rosewall would you choose to retell? I search my memory of the dozens played here and there on the tour, and finally am forced back on the two that took place before he ever became a pro. That 1956 meeting of Rosewall and Savitt certainly will be remembered by those who were there, because it presented one of the rare and lovely sights of the postwar tennis era, two men thoroughly well equipped with ground strokes, each playing at something near his best for long periods. It was not surprising that Rosewall had, in fact, learned how good he was, as Lacoste had said; but that Savitt should play such tennis as he did as late as 1956 was a revelation. Following their Orange match several years earlier, Savitt had gone into business and into at least semi-tennis retirement.

Because of this inactivity, the scales were weighted heavily against Savitt, and in the end he had to yield rather mildly in a fifth set 6–1. But before that we had some long sessions of glorious hitting off the ground, and this arena had seen nothing quite its equal since Budge had played Cramm nearly twenty years before. Savitt lost the first two sets 4–6, 5–7, after leading in each, won the next two 6–4, 10–8 by great effort and careful play, and then was done physically.

The point of this encounter is that its first four sets brought back to championship tennis a style of play that seemed to have disappeared from the game. Because of the great interest of the crowd in Savitt's fine battle to become a champion again after a lapse of years, the match became memorable in a way that none of Rosewall's professional appearances could. Ken's professional debut with Gonzales in Madison Square Garden was not far off, and although he was to get better and still better during the next ten years—he was just short of twenty-one that day—he was never in that time to take part in a match that could have the impact of this one.

And so it has been with the professionals. All their splendid openings at the Garden were followed by runs of seemingly endless one-night stands about the world, all now lost in the mists of time. Only the first one, in what amounts to a national showcase, had any wide interest, and it was interesting mostly because it stirred a certain curiosity by bringing the leading amateur of the day against the leading professional, a meeting forbidden all these years by the stuffy rules of amateur governing bodies.

I well remember going to see Gonzales and Kramer play in Jamaica, Queens, on their return to Metropolitan New York months after their Garden debut, but I remember it only because of a remark Gonzales made. They played one of those long service-governed sets, which Kramer won narrowly, and then a second, which Kramer won quickly. Questioned in the dressing room afterward about how he had let the match go after losing the first set, Pancho shrugged wearily and said, "What the hell! Tomorrow night New Haven."

For many years, from 1930 well into the 1960s, this pattern held for the pros. Players came and went, some of them perhaps the equal or superior of any who lived before, but the group of the game's finest always was small and always they preferred exhibitions to tournaments, where the money would have had to be split more ways. It was to the financial advantage of the few, and to the promoter, to go on barnstorming so long as the amateur game continued to provide worthwhile opposition for such dynamic figures as Gonzales. They did shop around from time to time for a promoter willing to take a chance on a tournament, but when they found one they spoiled it for him by restricting the entry to the same handful of current touring exhibitionists who had been meeting one another endlessly. By now they had let technique, which they had developed to a high point within its limits, displace imagination and natural instinct for the game.

There was one instance of which I knew personally when they ruined their finest prospect. The town of Southport, a coastal resort city north of Liverpool, England, put on a tournament for them as a tourist attraction. The leading pros of the time, the 1930s, not only kept the entry to a few players but insisted on spliting up the money before a ball was struck. I had the details of this split at the time from the records of the promoting organization, something like our Chambers of Commerce. The venture was a very big success the first year and a complete flop the second. People caught on quickly and stayed away.

In general the professional tournaments all through these years of the 1930s, 40s, and 50s were only slightly expanded versions of their road shows. They were acceptable as tennis shows and as demonstrations of the game at its best, but as competition they failed and were largely shunned by the public, which continued to support amateur tennis well. The pros never at any time during these years seemed interested in tennis as such, but only in collecting the exhibition dollars.

They have persistently refused to form or join any organization that could either handle their affairs or control their conduct. The fact that there has existed no organization that could speak for them has made it wholly impossible all these years for the amateur governing bodies to deal with the playing pros. These men are, strictly speaking, individuals and an amateur body would have had to deal with each individually if it was to deal at all. This is a situation quite unacceptable to the authorities who operate the game, and the thought that they might deal with a promoter who had these men under contract is so unacceptable as to be absurd. On the other hand, the U.S.L.T.A. can and does deal amicably with the Professional Tennis Association, a solid organization to which most of the club professionals of the country belong.

This, I believe, is one of the reasons, perhaps the one real reason, that the open tournament so many seemed to want, was impossible for so long. There always have been within the official amateur tennis organizations of the world, men who favored trying an open, and actually it was a fairly close thing as far back as 1933, about the time the professional ranks began to be filled with glamorous names.

Early in that year the U.S.L.T.A. voted to hold an open in the autumn and petitioned the International Lawn Tennis Federation for permission. That was the beginning of the move toward open tennis.

In covering the meeting of the I.L.T.F. in Paris that June, I felt that the request was not granted because the U.S.L.T.A. had sent no delegate to present the petition. They left it to the Second Secretary of the United States Embassy in Paris, John McVeagh, who simply presented the case and sat down. Since there was no great feeling against open tennis at that time and it had hardly been discussed at all, I thought that a forceful presentation probably would have brought it to a favorable vote for at least an experimental, or trial open, which was what the petition asked. And what a tournament it would have been!

From the professionals it would have drawn Tilden, Vines, Richards, Hunter, Kozeluh, Nusslein, Cochet, Ramillon, Burke, the Kinseys, and Stoefen. From the amateurs could have come Crawford, von Cramm, Perry, Allison, Van Ryn, Borotra, Sidney Wood, Clifford Sutter, George Lott, Johnny Doeg, Bunny Austin, Roderick Menzel, Jiro Satoh, H. L. de Morpurgo, Bryan Grant, Gregory Mangin, the young Budge, Frank Parker, and Frank Shields.

If that one had been played it might have been so successful as to establish the open championship as the top event in tennis, as it is in golf. In the following years other attempts at a favorable vote were made, but a strong and prejudiced opposition developed in this country and on the continent of Europe. The campaign for open tennis had heavy going at times but never died and, in 1960 it seemed at last very near, although the atmosphere was not nearly so favorable as it had been in 1933. The request for so-called home rule in the matter of open tennis failed by only five votes at the I.L.T.F. meeting, an infinitesimal margin. It was said at the time that some of the smaller nations became frightened and shifted their votes at the last minute.

It was a straw in the wind, though. As the opponents, a little frightened at this close shave, strengthened their position in the international organization, rumors of revolt began to be heard, especially in England, the real home of the game. The British Association gave plenty of notice to the tennis world of its intention as the 1960s advanced, so that the decision to make the 1968 Wimbledon an open tournament without advance approval by the I.L.T.F., actually seemed a little belated.

But they had chosen the time carefully. The announcement came after one of the best years in the long history of the world's most important tournament. The Wimbledon of 1967 was enormously successful financially and competitively. Obviously, it had no need of the professionals for its continued success, and it is significant that the British Association decided to defy the international body at that particular time.

The opening of the gates to the professionals could do nothing for Wimbledon financially and, because of the prize money offered, probably would even reduce the profit. But artistically the pros could contribute much. Wimbledon sought to make its tournament in fact, as well as name, the world's premier tennis event, and to have the title of world champion it would bestow on the winner, mean exactly that. The move was, in that sense, for the good of the game.

If the touring professionals can follow this move, which can benefit them greatly, with their own move toward getting together among themselves or joining the professional association already in existence, tennis might in time achieve the sort of solid organization that golf enjoys.

It was Vincent Richards who made the first and probably the only real move toward inducing his fellow professionals to join together in an organization that would include and control all of them. This was near the end of the first highly successful decade of the exhibition tour business, which he had helped start on its way. To form an organization such as the Professional Golfers Association, which would include all the big-name playing pros and all the club or teaching professionals and would conduct tournaments, was Richards' dream.

By this time Vinnie was an employee of Dunlop Tire and Rubber Corporation, which supplied rackets and balls to tennis, and he would soon become a vice president of that firm. He was one of the leading professionals, if not the leader of them, and he was convinced that the first step on the way toward organization was to play a real championship tournament that would be open to all classes of tennis pros, as the P.G.A. championship is open to any of the thousands of members who can qualify.

To this end Richards canvassed the other sporting goods manufacturers and found them more than willing to put up the money for such an event, which he convinced them could help sales of tennis goods, languishing a bit in the Depression years. I was in close touch with Richards in this venture, and though I do not recall the exact total of the purse he got up for them to play for, it was big enough to cause even golf pros to be envious in that day of modest prize money.

It was Vinnie's notion, and I believed it sound, that there are dozens, even scores of club pros all over the country who play quite well, better perhaps than the majority of the amateurs beaten in the early rounds at Forest Hills. The spectators at amateur tournaments come not only to see this or that player win a match but, more happily just to see people playing very good tennis. As with those who go to an art gallery to see pictures, they wander in the early days, sparing admiration for lesser players without whom there would be no champions. It is these players beaten in the early rounds who "make" a tournament, a fact which the pros have ignored. Without them it cannot really be successful.

It was the Richards plan that every pro who entered the tournament would get expenses, or at least a substantial part of them. Then for every match won the prize money would increase, with the winner taking the big cut. Taking also the right to call himself national professional champion, a title still meaningless or nonexistent toward the end of the 1960s.

The professional championship would have been the best tennis tournament in the world, so good and so appealing that it would have overshadowed the amateur tournament and led in time to an open. It would have had all the top pros such as Tilden, Vines, Budge, Perry, Cochet, Kozeluh, a whole flock of very good but lesser pros, and all the very good teaching pros. Richards worked very hard on this, and the prospect was alluring. With the money ready to hand and the already existing Professional Tennis Association vitally interested, the project had got to the point of approaching the U.S.L.T.A. and the West Side Tennis Club for use of the courts and facilities at Forest Hills. So what happened? Why did it not come off? Because the leading professionals themselves killed it dead. They wanted no part of it as a championship they had to play through to win money.

This one would come in only if guaranteed what amounted to first prize money. That one could not play unless he got ridiculous expense money to come from far away. Tilden must have first doubles money guaranteed him no matter who his partner. All were willing to play, in fact were eager to, but they wanted to split the money beforehand in the same way that had killed the Southport tournament only a couple of years before. Or, failing this, they would be glad to play for the money without guarantees if the field were restricted to no more than eight players so that those beaten in the first round still would profit very well. This would, of course, have defeated the whole purpose of the tournament. Of the whole lot of them I think only Budge, with whom Richards and I conferred over the project, was willing just to go out and play without making conditions.

Richards remained a little bitter over this failure for some time. "They don't give a damn about tennis," he said, and I suspect he was close to the truth. I think myself that if the pros had been willing to go through with this early plan to organize for their own benefit instead of going along as individuals, each on his own, that we might have had the open tournament long since. It was too much to hope for then and may still be for a long time.

Richards saw that a fundamental weakness of the pro game was and is that its season, its year, has no climax. It works up to nothing. Even late in the 1960s, by which time the tour had been expanded to include more players and more four-day tournaments, the pro season still was just a long series of little events, one like another, the same at Binghamton this week as at Longwood last, with about the same results.

The pros themselves, without proper organization, are incapable of putting on tournaments for themselves and so look to some amateur organization to bring them to town. Those among them who have tried to stage tournaments have gone for a packet, as the saying used to be. Kramer himself tried it three times at Forest Hills and registered nothing but dismal failures, both artistic and financial. They have never been able, never have attempted even, to find that synthesis between tennis as a spectacle and tennis as a meaningful contest, a game of that swift, agreeable, and exciting action that is the essence of an amateur meeting.

Knowledge, organization, and willingness to work are required to run a tennis tournament, and the playing pros never have had these things. On the few occasions when pro tournaments have been successful amateurs have run them. And after thirty years and more the question of whether the amateurs are going to take the pros back into the fold in open tournaments is still a matter of debate, even though some beginnings are being made.

Meanwhile, they go on playing their tournaments restricted to, at the most, quarterfinalists instead of joining and coming to terms with the existing Professional Tennis Association, a solid country-wide organization of teaching or club pros, which they could help and which might help them enormously. Such a merging of interests could lead directly to a national professional championship which means something. It has been clearly demonstrated over and again that you cannot start a tennis tournament with the quarterfinal round and have anyone care much, especially if these quarterfinalists have been playing one another every week for months on end. Under these conditions the champions rise, turn pro, pick up what money is to be had before their legs go, and then fade one by one from the picture, public interest in them declining after their debut.

And this brings us to another misconception that ought to be cleared up. Because Australia won the Davis Cup so often in the twenty-odd years following World War II, there grew up the belief, subscribed to by practically everyone, that American tennis, formerly so dominant, had declined greatly. There is a certain truth in this obviously, but it is only a half-truth at best, and in tennis we always seem to take the partial truth for the whole. It comes from placing so much importance, so much overemphasis on winning the Davis Cup, for which, of course, no professional may play.

Up to the period of the great financial success of professional tourism, the history of the Davis Cup, and therefore of tennis, had shown recurring cycles of one-nation supremacy. With the one exception noted earlier, that of Vines, the nation which owned the champion player owned the Cup. With the rise of the tour business this changed, but it is an illusion to suppose that the United States, because it could not win and hold the Cup, was reduced to a second- or third-class tennis nation.

Let us imagine that there never had been any professional tennis in the exhibition tour sense, that all players the world around had remained amateur throughout their careers, as was once the case and as amateur officials would love to have it again. If we can imagine this, then it is entirely possible to state that Australia would not have won the Davis Cup at all between 1919 and the early 1960s, which latter time we may take as the beginning of the decline of Richard Gonzales.

Australia lost the Cup to the U.S. at the end of 1919 and did not win it again for twenty years, or until 1939, the first year that Don Budge, by then a pro, was not available to defend it. They won it by the margin of one match, 3–2, from lesser players. Could they have won it with Budge on the team? Hardly. The Aussies held the Cup through the war interval but lost it to Kramer and Ted Schroeder, when play was resumed in 1946, without winning a point. They won it again in 1950 after both Kramer and Gonzales had become professionals, and held it until 1954, when Tony Trabert and Victor Seixas, both Wimbledon and U.S. champions, brought it back for one year before Trabert also joined the pros. With no champion to call upon, the United States nevertheless won the Cup again in 1958 and 1963.

Now, what would have been the result if Kramer, Gonzales, and Trabert had remained available with Seixas, Hamilton Richardson, Chuck McKinley, Schroeder, and other members of the team? Since no Australian had much chance of beating Gonzales until well into the 1960s, it is reasonable to suppose that the famous trophy would have remained in this country throughout the postwar period. American tennis in that case would have been said to be supreme, which was actually the case, since the champion player was an American.

It is perfectly true that American tennis did not produce during the later years of this period any outstanding new personalities. There is no doubt much wrong with the administration of the game and much reform needed, but it is no good blaming the people who run things for lack of talent at the top. You cannot hatch out a Gonzales, a Budge, or a Kramer in an incubator, but you can search them out and help them if they exist. Development programs can do a lot, as Australia has shown, to produce more good players, but it is a fact that the great ones—a Gonzales, a Perry, a Tilden—have always found their way to the top, even unaided.

Certainly there does not appear to be anything much wrong with the game of tennis itself, although proposals for changing it always are with us. There has been little change since the rules were settled upon and possibly improvement could be had by changing some rules, but a game so stylized as tennis should be treated with great restraint. One of the things wrong may be that so many people keep trying to alter it to suit other people who do not really play it.

Everyone who followed the fortunes of the professionals since World War II noted that the new player supplied to the troupe by the amateur game has in every case improved rapidly. This seemed to have surprised many observers who supposed the newcomer would be overwhelmed by the old pro. They need not have been surprised. The lesser players of the game always have improved by competing against the top men, often surpassing them in time. The difference is that formerly they did it in amateur tournaments.

The changes brought to the structure of tournament tennis, both amateur and professional, by jet air travel have been great, and their significance has been slow to impress itself on tennis authorities. Air travel has made an enormous difference.

In 1920 Tilden and Johnston were five weeks reaching Auckland, New Zealand, by boat to play the Challenge Round, and they did not arrive back with the Davis Cup, won in December, until well into February. In 1967 Roy Emerson, the leading Australian player, could win one tournament in Brisbane on Sunday and another in the Caribbean the following Sunday, only seven days later. In 1966 Jan Erik Lundquist played and won the final-round match of a tournament in his native Sweden on Sunday and then played a first-round match in the United States Indoor Championship in Salisbury, Maryland, the very next day. And Lundquist, who had won our indoor title in 1965 and so was defending champion, was beaten in that first-round match.

By the late 1960s this had become the accepted thing. Men were winding up tournaments one day and starting play in others halfway around the world the next. No one gave it a second thought. Especially tennis officialdom gave it too little thought, since it was changing the whole pattern of world tennis.

Formerly all the world's best players, the champions as well as the lesser men and women, came together in big international tournaments. Many top players also played together in sectional and other tournaments that were important to their rankings. The schedule was not so crowded and no one attempted to play a tournament every week. Young, developing players could meet the top players reasonably often and there was the time to relax, to practice, and to develop more slowly and more soundly.

With the coming of fast air travel all this changed. The various gradations of tennis talent came together only once a year at Wimbledon, and to a lesser degree at Forest Hills. Some players of world class have said that they cannot afford to play at Forest Hills, meaning they can get more expense money for playing elsewhere far away during that time. Tennis no longer is suspended elsewhere during big tournaments, as once was the case.

The call of international tournament play became incessant and all but irresistible throughout the year. There no longer was any such thing as a tennis season. During the American grass court tournament circuit, which once drew a good portion of the world class players, there appeared daily reports in the papers of European tournaments in which such men and women were playing. The grass court circuit—Merion, Orange, Southampton, Nassau, Newport, Longwood—once the proving ground for rising talent, was reduced to a series of minor invitation events. These could not compete for the best players with European resort tournaments on the same dates, and the home circuit seldom got all the best of the home players either.

The overall standard of play certainly had risen, in the sense that there were many more good players in the world than ever before. Their number had multiplied and multiplied again but the standard of play at the top had declined. An idea of this drop in class may be arrived at by comparing the semifinalists of the 1967 Wimbledon with the champion of 1947, who was Kramer, and of 1937, who was Budge. I do not think any of these four men could have remained alive in the same court with Kramer or Budge.

And the strain of a never-ending, non-stop round of international tournament play was a contributing cause. The call of the fat expense account for play in glamorous places is hard to resist, but the cost is great. Players were being yanked back and forth through time zones at the speed of sound, and consistency had gone from the game that once was thought to be the most formful of all. The number of tournaments in which it was profitable and desirable for amateurs to appear had increased with the ease with which distant places could be reached in a hurry. And, as the bidding for top players went up, the pressure of tournament play became so great that no player could be consistent in the old way. The "upset" became the order of the day as defending champions were beaten in first-round matches as two unseeded players, as likely as not, contested final rounds. They play so much their records are bound to be tarnished and all the talented young players of many nations could join this non-stop parade. Once they did there would be no time for the practice that perfects skill. In the year 1967, before her nineteenth birthday had arrived, Rosemary Casals, one of the most promising young girls in a decade, had played in South America, Australia, Paris, Sweden, England, South Africa, and New Zealand before the end of August, and, after several tournaments at home, had hit the trail again before the end of October, beginning in Buenos Aires.

Something comparable also happened in professional tennis. Where the tour promoter once was principally interested only in the amateur champion, the tour became able, as the 1960s advanced, to offer a sound financial future to players well below the top. Such men as Andres Gimeno of Spain, Pierre Barthes of France, Mike Davies of Great Britain, and Earl Buchholz of the U.S., none of whom ever won an important title, did very well as playing professionals, and the troupe grew larger for that reason.

The rewards became more widely distributed and the attraction for players below the top of the amateur ranking list was greater. So the game's finest players were split between amateurs and professionals who could not meet, and the remaining amateurs, heeding the insistent call of many international tournaments, also were split, coming together rarely. This does not appear to have hurt the amateur game, other than artistically, as the professionals continue to skim off the cream, and the tennis governing bodies of the world appear to be sensitive only to finances.

Prejudice rather than common sense continued to rule, but international tennis seems to flourish in spite of it. The game obviously could not attain the highest standard of play until it was once more open to all. Both the general standard of play around the world, which has risen, and the standard at the top, which has declined sharply, can soon find a proper level when all the fine players in the world are brought together in tournaments open to all, as is done in golf.

I hestitate to mention golf, because those who advocate open tennis most strongly are forever pointing to the other game as an example of what could be done in tennis. It sounds logical, but there is a serious flaw in the logic and we must not continue to make the mistake of comparing the two games. The differences are great, so great that they have little in common.

First of all tennis at the top level is a very much more difficult game to play. It requires a great deal more actual skill at games-playing and much more hard work to attain a reasonably high proficiency. A simple consideration will show this quickly.

In the New York City area there are about three hundred private golf clubs affiliated with the Metropolitan Golf Association, besides many semiprivate and public courses. Taking a conservative average guess we may safely assume that at each one of these clubs there is at least one golfer who plays at scratch, meaning that he is likely as not to turn in a par score any time he plays. That is to say, he is a golfer who on many occasions has the ability to play his game as well as the tennis players ranked in the country's first ten play theirs. A scratch golfer has attained the top ranking of his game, for he plays without handicap. And there are perhaps three hundred of them in the Met district alone without even considering the membership of the eight or nine thousand other golf clubs in the country.

If there is exaggeration here, it is slight and it is justified in emphasizing the point. There is no question of preferring one game over the other, but theoretically at least it should be possible to take a bucket of golf balls out and keep hitting them until the proficiency to become expert is acquired. No such thing is possible in tennis for the obvious reason that you are always hitting a ball previously hit by your opponent.

In the National Open Golf Championship, the game's premier event, a field of 150 is chosen by qualification tests from the 2,500 or so applicants to start the four-day tournament. Theoretically, it is possible to say that every one of them is competent enough at the game to win the title, and it is a fact that most of them actually can play golf well enough to become champion. And elsewhere in the world at the moment the championship is being played are hundreds more of close-to-the-best who are not involved at all.

Of course, we all know that more, much more, than merely striking the ball well goes into becoming a golf champion, and no stroke in tennis can be harder than the three-foot putt you've got to sink for money. But from the point of view of proficiency of execution, the statement is true.

At Wimbledon, the most important tennis meeting, there is an entry of 128 in the men's singles. Here it would be absurd to say that all are capable of winning. In all the world there are only a little handful of tennis players good enough to win Wimbledon, no more than a dozen at a liberal estimate, and there have been years in which you could cut that in half.

There is one other difference that is so important that it does away forever with superficial similarities. Everyone familiar with tennis knows perfectly well that if amateurs were not supported by liberal expense accounts—paid to play as some maintain—there could be no tournament tennis as we know it. There simply would not be any tournaments played anywhere except informal ones with only those involved who could afford to take the time and pay their own way.

But there still are people who do not know this. A few years ago when the Nassau Country Club in Glen Cove, Long Island, decided to revive the Nassau Bowl, its famous tennis tournament that had been allowed to lapse, it selected the same week in which the Metropolitan Golf Association had scheduled its amateur championship at the club. The sixty-four golfers, who had been culled by qualifying tournaments from the hundreds of applicants at member clubs in Westchester, Long Island, northern New Jersey, and southern Connecticut, mingled with the international field of tennis players, both using the club's facilities.

I was sitting one day at a table in the grill room with a group of golf competitors, when John Humm, of Rockville Links, one of the district's finest amateurs, and for that matter one of the country's best, noticed a tennis player at a nearby table signing a luncheon check. Humm, who was to be finalist to Bob Gardner, the champion, on Sunday and come within a stroke of being champion himself, looked up and asked: "Is that fellow getting a free lunch?"

I shall never forget John's astonishment when told what else the fellow was getting besides a free lunch. He was incredulous.

"You mean to say they get everything free, get put up, and get expense money and rackets besides?" he asked unbelievingly. "My God! If I accepted a drink from a golf manufacturer I'd be a pro before nightfall."

Well, it is almost literally true, what he said, and there are eight or nine million golfers in the United States in the same boat with John, who played better golf that week than the best tennis player at Nassau played tennis. Amateur golfers may accept nothing from anybody and remain amateur. Amateur tennis players may accept anything they can jimmy out of tournament officials, and the better they are the better the jimmying.

AFTERWORD

I N THE LATE summer of 1957 Maurice McLoughlin, then sixty-seven, was called from his home in California to Newport to be enshrined in the Lawn Tennis Hall of Fame. As I drove through the pleasant New England countryside toward the Jamestown Ferry that would take me to a meeting with my old hero, I was thinking of the eager schoolboy of 1914 and of the long trail that lay between then and now. I tried to find this eager youth in the still-eager but aging tennis reporter, and I thought that what had been begun forty-odd years earlier was now approaching a certain resolution.

In all the years that had run away like sand in the glass I never had encountered McLoughlin and had seen him play only once again, in that first postwar championship of 1919. Now I was going to meet him, perhaps speak with him, and after all these years I was surprised to find a little of the old awe of him rising in me. When I drove off the ferry at the foot of the hill that rises to Belleville Avenue, as I had done for so many summers gone, I almost wished I might avoid the meeting and keep intact the youthful picture I had held so long.

For it is not at all the curse of familiarity that it breeds contempt, but that it removes the magic cloak and reveals the mortal. It is essential to true hero worship of the kind we practiced in our youth that the object be a little clothed in mystery. As I drove up the hill I had the feeling that I would like to drive on and not arrive at the meeting.

Of course, it was not possible. James H. Van Alen, director of the Hall of Fame and of the Newport tournament, and rescuer of the famous old Casino where both McLoughlin's national titles had been won, had arranged a pre-induction luncheon at his home along the shore beyond Bailey's Beach. Luncheon was served at small tables set in the garden overlooking the sea, and when I arrived a little late, the entire luncheon party had assembled.

When I was presented to McLoughlin I found before me a kind-looking, rather stout gray-haired gentleman with a smile in his eyes. I was getting on a bit myself, and I was again surprised to find I was quite shy in his presence. I couldn't think of a thing to say to him and when he said he used to read my stuff from Wimbledon thirty years ago, I was thrown into confusion. I have never been so embarrassed in the presence of the eminent. I felt an absolute sap, a schoolboy again.

"I think we are sitting together," McLoughlin said, no doubt to help me over the obvious hump, and we walked to a table where we sat side by side. Now I began to feel a little ashamed of myself for my "betrayal" of him by having admitted, even to myself, that there had been greater men than he. I found I wanted to explain to him how that judgment, forced upon me by experience, had not really made any difference, since I could still call up the feelings of that preposterously hot August of 1914. I was pondering, under the influence of a couple of glasses of Van Alen's excellent Barsac, just how to open up the topic, when the old Comet turned and asked my opinion as an "expert" on some tennis matter.

I nearly fell off the chair. I must have shown my confusion, for he asked, with a charming smile, if he had made some sort of social error. Whereupon I told him the whole story of schoolboy worship and betrayal and with, I am sure, a good deal of schoolboy gush and embarrassment. At this my hero permitted himself a hearty laugh. I could see that the idea really did give him enjoyment.

"Its really absurd," he said, "but its worth coming all the way across the continent just to hear."

We talked on then until it was time to go to the Casino, where McLoughlin would be made officially the tennis immortal he had been for half a century in my own personal shrine. For me this conversation was a little sad, a sort of bittersweet experience as we sat, sipped our wine together, and looked across the sea. The magic cloak was gone when the old Comet, whose flaming youthful figure still was faintly visible through the haze of the years, said with a good deal of amusement that it was ridiculous for me to keep on calling him Mr. McLoughlin.

"You have seen much more first-class tennis than I have," he said, "and you are better able to judge. You probably are right about my position among champions, but I really am delighted to learn that I used to be a hero to small boys."

The dingy old pavilion of the Casino was nearly filled when the Comet walked out for the ceremony onto the turf where he and other great ones of the past had played. Many of Newport's grandest ladies and gentlemen were there and some of the ladies, grandly caparisoned, seemed to deny the passage of time. It was easy to think of them as having been there unchanged when McLoughlin became champion in 1912 and 1913, and for that matter when the first ball was struck more than thirty years before that.

Tennis at Newport encourages nostalgia. It is one of our most hallowed sports centers. Both tournament and Hall of Fame are enclosed by the famous old Casino, built in a fit of pique, they say, by Commodore James Gordon Bennett across Belleville Avenue from his own mansion at the head of that strand along which the fabulous habitations of the fabulously rich still stretch back toward the Victorian Age.

Here on this turf the first National Championship was held in 1881 and continued for thirty-four years, a period encompassing much of Newport's glory. McLoughlin himself had hit the last ball of the last championship there in 1915 and had hit it into the net to make Williams champion. The old Commodore's house is gone, and in its place is a huge supermarket. Hundreds of cars park daily where his front lawn was and another supermarket encroaches on the grass courts from the other side beyond the pavilion. Many of the mansions of the wealthy along the shore that swings past Bailey's Beach toward Narragansett Bay were dark of nights by 1957. Some of these incredible dwelling places were open to inspection by the public on payment of a fee, and some were being torn down. Few of the younger members of the old Newport dynasties were any longer willing or able to live in such grandeur.

But the Commodore's Casino still stood, and the tournament, rescued by Van Alen from death by strangulation as the real estate developments made their encircling movements, carries on. So when McLoughlin walked through the dingy rotunda from Belleville Avenue late on this summer afternoon, he turned his back on supermarkets and progress. He entered for the first time in forty-two years on a scene that told eloquently of how things were in his own day.

277

He found things much as he had known them in 1912, when he first became champion, and very nearly as planned and built by the Commodore forty years before that.

There is a life-sized white marble bust of Bennett sitting under the eaves against the ivy-clad wall of the inner courtyard. The Commodore also has turned his back on the offensive supermarket across the way, so the sightless eyes may look out to where the band used to play of an evening in the open gallery, and beyond that to where the building that once housed the indoor courts and the theater still stands.

It is an excellent likeness of Bennett, but there were only a few present on this day of the belated enshrinement of the Comet who had known the Commodore in the flesh in his flamboyant Newport days. Tennis players hurry past his likeness, arms filled with rackets, without giving him a glance or knowing he ever existed at all. But the Commodore's Casino remains as the noblest and no doubt the very last of his many remarkable works. Apparently safe now from destruction by human hands, it will be there to bring joy to new generations of tennis players and to remind young and old of the days that were.

As I stood with McLoughlin at the end of play in the tournament that day, the shadows began to move across the scene of his triumphs, even as the twilight approached nearer our own lives. I felt that life had reached a certain goal toward which it had been moving for nearly half a century.

Used to be a hero, the Comet had said. It still was a little true that day, although it has been much easier since to call up the picture of the kindly, intelligent man with whom I had sat and talked in the garden above the sea, than the flaming, godlike figure from so far away and so long ago. Far away and long ago, perhaps the most haunting words in the language.

Before another summer came around, McLoughlin had died, and although it was not the end of the tennis trail for me, there in the old Casino with the soft voice of the old Comet in my ear, is perhaps a good place to end this chronicle, recalling the sad valediction on the flyleaf of Housman's *Last Poems*:

> *The year draws in the day*
> *And soon will evening shut*

INDEX